Public Policy in Latin America

D1365425

PITT SERIES IN POLICY AND INSTITUTIONAL STUDIES

PITT LATIN AMERICAN SERIES

John W. Sloan

Public Policy in Latin America

A Comparative Survey

University of Pittsburgh Press

Published by the University of Pittsburgh Press, Pittsburgh, Pa. 15260
Copyright © 1984, University of Pittsburgh Press
Feffer and Simons, Inc., London
Manufactured in the United States of America

Library of Congress Cataloging in Publication Data

Sloan, John W.
  Public Policy in Latin America.

  (Pitt Latin American series)
  Includes bibliographical references and index.
    1. Latin America—Economic policy.   2. Political planning—Latin America.
  3. Latin America—Politics and government—1948–   I. Title.   II. Series.
  HC125.S58 1984   338.98   84-40093
  ISBN 0-8229-3810-3
  ISBN 0-8229-4800-1 (pbk.)

Figure 1, "Population Age Profiles, Mexico and the United States, 1979," is taken from
the *New York Times* of November 5, 1979. Copyright © 1979, by The New York Times
Company. Reprinted by permission. Figure 3, "The Changing Structure of Society and
Power in Iberian and Latin American Development Patterns," is reprinted by permis-
sion from *The Continuing Struggle for Democracy in Latin America,* edited by Howard J.
Wiarda. Copyright © 1980 by Westview Press, Boulder, Colorado.

To Patty

Contents

Tables

Figures

Public Policy in Latin America

Introduction

Students of Latin American politics labor in a difficult field. Most are in general agreement that there is an entity called Latin America, composed of twenty countries,[1] and that the United States plays an important role in the political economy of these countries. There is also a consensus that, although the countries of Latin America shared a similar colonial experience under Spain and Portugal, today the twenty nations are characterized by great diversity in terms of economic and political development. Beyond these simple generalizations, the field is racked by acrimonious debates over such issues as the consequences of U.S. influence in Latin America, the existence of social classes, the political orientation of the middle classes, the viability of reform efforts within the present political systems, whether the military plays a modernizing or predatory role in development, and even whether there is any significant change taking place in the region at all. This last issue is particularly intriguing because it illustrates the power of ideology in the intrepretation of what occurs in Latin America. Under the influence of what might be called "cold war liberalism," the books written about Latin America during the late 1950s and early 1960s tended to have titles that stressed volatile change under crisis conditons: *Political Change in Latin America; Evolution or Chaos; Latin America: Evolution or Explosion;* and *Reaction or Revolution in Latin America.*[2] The dominant metaphor of the period was that it was "one minute to midnight in Latin America," suggesting that, unless the nations engaged in democratic reforms immediately, they would succumb to Castroite revolutions.

By the late 1960s, the combination of the U.S. intervention in Vietnam and the Dominican Republic, the rise of multinational corporations, the increasing number of military coups, and the failure of guerrilla movements caused new interpretations of Latin American realities to arise and challenge the older views. Since the mid-1960s, book titles have reflected an entirely different perception: *Obstacles to Change in*

Latin America; The Politics of Conformity in Latin America; The Un-revolutionary Society; The Politics of Immobility; Authoritarianism and Corporatism in Latin America; and *The New Authoritarianism in Latin America.*[3] The new interpretations stress that there are few, if any, "fundamental changes" (a phrase frequently used by these scholars) occuring in Latin America. With the exception of Castro's Cuba, most regimes are trying to develop in a "capitalist" manner, but this simply will not work because such a strategy would benefit only the upper middle class, the large commercial farmers, and the multinational corporations instead of the bulk of the population. Whereas the scholars of the 1950s had viewed development and democracy as being compatible, the scholars of the 1960s and 1970s believed that Western-style development and democracy were blocked by dependence nurtured by the capitalist economic order and/or by the cultural constraints of corporatism.

The above serves to illustrate that the study of Latin American politics is an ideological battleground. Although such debate has sometimes provided important insights, more frequently it has served to distort understandings of Latin American realities. To claim that only a socialist revolution would bring about fundamental change is to define as ideologically trivial a myriad of other changes, such as the altered attitudes and behavior of the military in several countries, the increasing competence of many of the bureaucracies, the rising level of literacy, and the diversification of exports.

The problem for ideologically controlled students of South American politics is that events often do not conform to ideologically determined predictions. Only those who wear ideological blinders that screen out facts that do not fit their theories can see their particular perspectives being unambiguously supported by recent history. For those who deny the existence of U.S. imperialism, there is the Dominican Republic intervention in 1965 and the revelations about CIA and ITT activities in Allende's Chile. For those who deny that a socialist can win an election, there is the example of Allende winning the 1970 presidential contest in Chile and assuming power. For those who deny the possibility of a progressive role for the military, there is the behavior of the Peruvian military from 1968 to 1975. For those who believe that the Latin American middle class is not nationalistic, there is the behavior of the Venezuelan middle-class political party leaders in nationalizing U.S. oil, gas, and mineral investments and raising the price of oil. The point is obvious: the diversity of political events in Latin America defies simplistic ideological conclusions.

The Need for a Policy Approach

What is needed is a new approach, one that avoids ideological distortions and is capable of handling the diversity of behavior in the twenty nations of the region. Such an approach tries to answer the question: What are the Latin American governments doing? I believe it is more important to know what government does than to know who is doing it. What government does is called *public policy* and is determined by each nation's political process. Public policy is purposeful behavior by governmental actors designed to maintain or change some existing circumstance or mode of conduct. Public policies reveal the intentions of policymakers; they are usually contained in executive and administrative decisions, budgets, public expenditures, legislative laws, and judicial decisions. One can also argue that policies (as intentions) can be exposed by non–decision making; that is, when state activity is not mobilized to attack racism, anti-Semitism, unequal land distribution, or bureaucratic corruption, then policymakers are at least tacitly accepting such phenomena.

In the study of comparative public policy, *policy output* may be defined in terms of what governments do to achieve their intentions— for example, how much they spend on primary education. A *policy impact* or outcome may be defined in terms of the consequences of governmental activity—that is, the short-term and long-term results, the intended and unintended outcomes. For Howard Leichter, "Public policy is the end product of a process involving many factors, including the ideological and cultural traditions of a nation, the needs and resources of the society, and the very way in which the policy process operates. And in the final analysis, policy is made by people—men and women with unique personalities, political biases, and intellectual capacities."[4] The elites who make policy in the present are conditioned by policies of the past and are trying to alter those of the future.

Our approach to Latin American policymaking is predicated upon the assumption that governments have limited resources and thus cannot accomplish all—or even a major part—of what they are requested to do. Under these circumstances, public policymaking is a matter of choice-taking, and each choice involves tradeoffs and opportunity costs. Policymakers must select among competing goals *and* among competing means of achieving those objectives. The art of policymaking is to reconcile conflicting economic and political interests in order to create workable solutions. While it is true that policymaking is often an imitative art, since policymakers borrow from each other a limited number of programs, the process remains an applied art because each nation has unique cultural, economic, and political realities. Hence, public policies applied successfully in one polity (such as social security) are likely to be emulated by many nations through the process of diffusion, but they undoubtedly will have varied impacts in different nations. This means that "policy formation is apt to be an activity of guesswork, of high risk, in which the capacity to anticipate consequences of proposed actions . . . is most restricted."[5]

The policy choices we are most concerned with are those involved with promoting development. Latin Americans are painfully aware that they exist on the periphery rather than at the center of the international economic order. To make it to the center, they must modernize. Modernization means that a nation must develop; it must increase its political and economic capabilities. Not all nations are making progress toward modernization. For those that are, it means that the political system is increasing the nation's capability to adapt to changing conditions, to define the public interest, and to mobilize the resources necessary to achieve national goals. In Latin America, modernization is expected to be a product of public policy. However, once modernization is begun, most political systems have great difficulty directing the process of development and adapting to changing social conditions. The process of development is made complicated and risky by the divisiveness of the issues that have to be resolved in order to achieve it, and most political systems find they are overwhelmed by the increased demands coming from a more urbanized, literate, and industrialized society. Developmental policy in Latin America is disruptive because it sometimes produces changes that challenge and reduce the power of domestic and foreign entrenched interests. In brief, while the aspiration to achieve modernization in Latin America is widespread, the process of development often disrupts the established order and introduces new conflicts and problems.

As "late developers," Latin American governments play a greater role in promoting economic development than was true in the United States at an earlier period. Latin Americans not only desire development, as conventionally measured, but also, because of their historical experience as victims of economic and political exploitation and their intense nationalism, they demand "autonomy" as an integral component of authentic national development. There is not a reform or revolutionary movement in Latin America that does not aspire to increase its nation's independence from the United States. In general terms, the standards of adequate developmental performance for a Latin American nation can be outlined as follows:

a. increasing the availability of investment capital;
b. increasing the rate of industrial and agricultural growth;
c. reducing the rate of inflation;
d. promoting full employment;
e. eliminating balance of payments difficulties;
f. providing a more equitable distribution of income;
g. diversifying exports;
h. reducing dependence on the United States.

The legitimacy of most Latin American regimes is now contingent upon adequate progress in all of these areas. Promoting development has therefore become a national security concern in many Latin countries because it affects the ability of a particular government to survive. However, there is no consensus over which policy choices are necessary to achieve these goals. Debates rage over whether there should be an emphasis on distributive justice or capital investment; on centralization or decentralization of political power; on military or civilian governments; on public, private, or foreign investment; on agriculture or industry; on population control or no population control; on cooperation with the United States or autonomy. These are not sterile debates; the variety of developmental experiences in Latin America suggests that no ironclad historical or cultural determinism is at work. Alternatives are available. Marshall Wolfe is correct when he writes, "All national societies at all points of time and at all levels of poverty or prosperity confront a certain range of accessible alternatives with different combinations of advantages and disadvantages. The capacity of their dominant forces to choose specific alternatives depends not only on objective conditions but also on their subjective appreciation of these conditions and on the momentum of what has already been done. Choices or failures to choose are continually closing doors and opening different ones."[6]

The set of choices we will use as a means of comparing public policies in Latin America is a revised version of Egil Fossum's classification of political strategies of change.[7] Fossum claims that most political scientists, dominated by the thinking of Gabriel Almond, G. Bingham Powell, and Samuel Huntington, usually emphasize the following dimensions of political development: differentiation, mobilization, capability, stability, and institutionalization. Fossum proposes to substitute a more politically relevant set of critical developmental policy choices for study. These include two sets of variables: accumulation/distribution and bureaucracy/mobilization. The first set of variables—accumulation and distribution—are essentially concepts designed to assess the economic performance of a political system. A government choosing accumulation will give priority to pursuing economic growth, measured in terms of the gross national product (GNP), and will be less concerned with how the accumulated wealth is distributed. One basic goal of poor countries is the accumulation of wealth through modernizing—that is, making the agrarian and industrial sectors of the economy more efficient and productive. When priority is given to the accumulation of wealth instead of its distribution, the result will be increasingly beneficial for select privileged social groups and cities. Large landowners, industrialists, and top-level policymakers are likely to get richer, and the gap between the rich and poor wider. Moreover, there are likely to be growing disparities between the developing and the stagnating cities and regions of the nation. The paradox of economic growth is that both its absence and presence can promote instability. A regime that does not promote growth will find itself confronting more social conflict with less legitimacy. A regime that succeeds in aiding growth will find itself faced with intensified imbalances and inequalities that will inevitably nurture political pressures to correct some of these problems.

Of increasing concern is the question of how this accumulated wealth is to be distributed. Both of these dimensions—accumulation of wealth and its distribution—are equally necessary for national development; the critical choice for policymakers is the relative priority to be given to each in pursuing these goals. A government choosing distribution will give priority to the distribution of income, property, and services (such as education, health services). We can measure distributive performance by comparing such subjects as agrarian reform policies, income distribution profiles, proportion of school-age children in school, and infant mortality rates. In the past, because of the experience of the capitalist development of most Western nations, the belief was that a nation (especially its bourgeoisie) accumulated wealth first; later its policymakers would aim for a more equitable distribution of this wealth through such government policies as allowing the working class to unionize, legislating progressive taxes, and instigating welfare reforms. Thus, in the older Western countries, the social concern and the policy attempts to achieve a more just distributive system came *after* considerable wealth had been accumulated through a process of economic modernization. In the contemporary world, however, after the experience of Russia's rapid development and Mao's revolution in China, policymakers must confront a situation where plausible economic and powerful ideological arguments are offered to support both of the two competing strategies of development: (1) accumulation first, distribution second; or (2) distribution first, accumulation second. Nevertheless, the example of the Communist revolutions and the present emphasis on social justice in the Western democracies mean that Latin American policymakers are subject to earlier and more severe distributive demands than were other policymakers in the West during earlier periods of modernization.

The second set of variables—bureaucracy and mobilization—are fundamental political concepts that help us to understand how a society is to be organized. Policymakers who choose developing the public bureaucracy over social mobilization believe that the creation of an efficient bureaucracy is necessary for an orderly process of modernization. The proponents of bureaucratic government, including many military officers, wish to construct paternalistic and technocratic states that will modernize their nations by subjecting an increasing number of policy areas to bureaucratic authority and rationality. They wish to restrict political turmoil and reduce unpredictability by limiting autonomous political mobilization. In their view, uncontrolled political mobilization of the masses would result in anarchy, insatiable consumption demands, soaring inflation, political instability, and the nation's inability to accumulate the wealth necessary to finance modernization. Given the political culture in Latin America and the elites' concern for controlling mobilization, many of the policymakers are attracted to variant forms of corporatism.

On the other hand, there are those who advocate that social mobilization should precede or be independent of bureaucratic development. Such advocates may be radicals or dissident members of the elite (a Juan Perón, for example). This choice refers to public policies concerning who is (and who is not) allowed to mobilize and articulate demands vis-à-vis the state. This is an increasingly important issue because Latin American societies are undergoing social changes that are positively correlated with increasing rates of political participation. Citizens of Latin nations are becoming more urbanized, more literate, more educated, more subject to mass media influences, and more aware that the state makes decisions that affect their welfare. Hence, as a society modernizes, citizens depend upon the state for protection and other social services, and increasingly demand them, while the state, in its interaction with society, increasingly needs the compliance and support of the people, as well as the information necessary to the provision of those services.

While the proponents of bureaucratic development believe that development should be constructed on top of the present society, many radicals assert that the old social system must first be destroyed by the mobilized lower classes before authentic development (usually some variant of socialism) can take place. The radicals believe that bureaucracies will be more concerned with maintaining order than with the changes associated with development and that the latter can occur only if the peasants and workers are mobilized. They claim that traditional elites will only allow large landowners, the business elite, and foreign investors to mobilize in pursuit of their respective interests, resulting in societies where the bulk of the population will continue to be condemned to the lifelong poverty that they have endured since colonial times. The one limitation the radicals insist upon is that both the workers and peasants be subject to the political control of leaders who possess an authentic revolutionary consciousness—namely, themselves. The mass mobilization of the population will allow the revolutionary elite to destroy the existing social order by a redistribution of wealth and property. After this distribution takes place—as exemplified by the first five years of the Castro revolution in Cuba—then the second stage of accumulating wealth in a socially just manner may proceed. The radicals have faith that a continuously mobilized population can avoid both the socially unjust concentration of wealth that is endemic to capitalist development, and the conservatism of bureaucracy that is likely both under a capitalist and a Russian communist style of development.

The differences among Third World nations in the kind of modernization process found in each one stem from the relative priority each government gives to accumulation versus distribution and bureaucracy versus mobilization. In Fossum's words, "It matters which factor or dimension one gives first priority or places first in a time series. . . . Every choice tends to narrow possibilities for the range of choices at a later point of time, especially when what happens is intimately related to power and its distribution."[8] For example, who is allowed to mobilize will certainly affect both the process of accumulation and distribution.

Finally, we should note that these two sets of choices are sufficiently abstract to cover a wide range of cases and also sufficiently real to be familiar to actual policymakers. These two sets of choices also help us to understand that the agenda of policymakers is crowded. Case studies that portray policymakers concentrating on a single issue for a long period of time distort political reality. To understand the political reality, we have to examine the context in which public policy is made.

The Context of Latin American Public Policymaking

Each nation's policymakers make their choices in a policy environment influenced by a unique constellation of geographical, cultural, situational, economic, and political factors. Nevertheless, we can make some generalizations about the Latin American policy environment. For the most part, policy is made in an environment characterized by a rising population, increasing urbanization, spreading unemployment, uneven income distributions, continuing or widening disparities between internal regions, chronic inflation, a negative balance of payments, rising consumer expectations, and political instability. Latin American policymaking occurs in an atmosphere dominated by insecurity. In countries that are dependent upon primary goods, policymakers are insecure about fluctuating prices, market variations, weather changes, ocean currents (a change in the Humboldt Current reduced the availability of anchovies for Peruvian fishermen), earthquakes, and depressions in the developed countries. In industrializing countries, policymakers are insecure about recessions, balance of payments difficulties, inflation, unemployment, and protectionism in the more developed countries. Policymakers in politically unstable nations are insecure about future job opportunities, coups, and terrorism.

Uncontrolled population growth contributes to the insecurity of many Latin American policymakers. In 1900 the United States had a population of about 76 million while Latin America had about 30 million. By 1979 the population of the United States had grown to 225 million while the Latin American population had soared to an estimated 333 million (see table 1). In the year 2000 the Latin American population will likely skyrocket to 600 million. This population growth is caused by a significant drop in mortality rates, particularly infant mortality rates. For example, the average life expectancy at birth for a person born in Latin America in 1930 was less than forty years; by 1960 it had risen to between fifty and sixty. Terry McCoy's study

TABLE 1
Total Population and Growth Rates in Latin America, 1960–79
(in thousands)

	1960	1975	1976	1977	1978	1979	Average Annual Growth Rate 1970–79 (%)
Argentina	20,611	25,383	25,719	26,056	26,389	26,729	1.30
Bolivia	3,313	4,890	5,019	5,151	5,286	5,425	2.60
Brazil	70,758	107,145	110,123	113,208	116,393	119,656	2.80
Chile	7,701	10,253	10,428	10,656	10,857	10,917	1.70
Colombia	16,233	23,476	23,935	24,420	24,922	25,523	2.10
Costa Rica	1,320	1,952	2,003	2,056	2,110	2,166	2.60
Dominican Republic	3,036	4,725	4,846	4,978	5,125	5,275	3.00
Ecuador	4,336	6,746	6,972	7,212	7,461	7,689	3.30
El Salvador	2,433	4,108	4,224	4,255	4,397	4,436	2.90
Guatemala	3,965	6,079	6,255	6,436	6,622	6,813	2.90
Haiti	3,574	4,584	4,668	4,749	4,833	4,919	1.70
Honduras	1,895	3,093	3,202	3,318	3,439	3,564	3.40
Mexico	34,923	60,145	62,239	64,594	66,944	69,408	3.60
Nicaragua	1,420	2,162	2,218	2,325	2,393	2,463	3.10
Panama	1,062	1,668	1,719	1,771	1,825	1,881	3.10
Paraguay	1,710	2,647	2,739	2,813	2,888	2,973	3.30
Peru	10,022	15,470	15,908	16,358	16,836	17,328	2.90
Uruguay	2,483	2,764	2,782	2,846	2,852	2,886	3.20
Venezuela	7,352	11,993	12,361	12,737	13,155	13,587	3.20
Total	198,147	299,283	307,360	315,939	324,727	333,638	2.65

Source: Inter-American Development Bank, Economic and Social Progress In Latin America, 1979 Report (Washington, D.C.: IADB, 1979), p. 399.

indicates that "decline in Latin American death rates began in the more advanced countries in about 1910 and spread to the less developed countries where the rate of decline accelerated after 1930. . . . Recently declining mortality is due largely to the importation of advanced medical and sanitary practices through international public health programs. Because it occurs independently of local socioeconomic modernization, death control has thus arrived in varying degrees in all Latin American countries, even the most backward."[9]

Declining mortality rates represent the first stage in the "demographic transition." The second is a decline in the birth or fertility rates which, in the West, is associated with social modernization. With the exception of Argentina, Cuba, and Uruguay, the nations of Latin America have yet to begin the second phase of the demographic transition, which is characterized by fertility rates of below 30 births per thousand population. With the exception of Chile, which is approach-

FIGURE 1
Population Age Profiles, Mexico and the United States, 1979

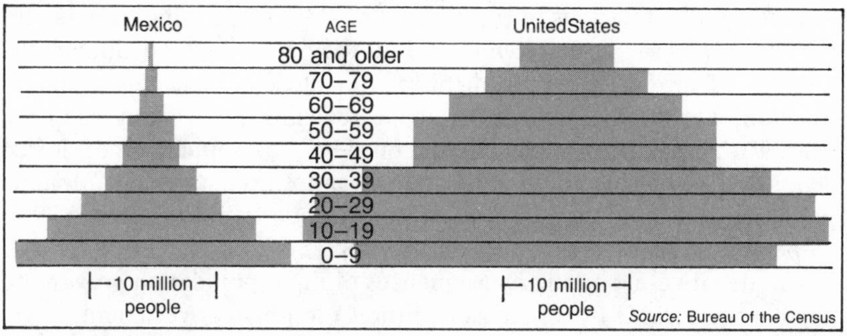

Mexico	AGE	UnitedStates
	80 and older	
	70–79	
	60–69	
	50–59	
	40–49	
	30–39	
	20–29	
	10–19	
	0–9	

⊢10 million⊣ people　　⊢10 million⊣ people　*Source:* Bureau of the Census

Source: *New York Times,* 5 Nov. 1979.

ing the 30 mark, most of the countries have fertility rates of above 40 per thousand. The result of this fertility-mortality imbalance is a rising population in most of the countries, although this growth is slowed in Honduras, the Dominican Republic, Haiti, and Bolivia by continuing high death rates. In the 1970s the population growth rate for Latin America averaged about 2.7 percent, with the proportion of the population under fifteen years of age (and thus economically inactive) a little over 40 percent. Figure 1 graphically portrays the population age profiles of Mexico and the United States.

In the past many Latin American statesmen saw the lack of population in their countries as an impediment to national development. In nineteenth-century Argentina, for example, Juan Bautista Alberdi proclaimed that "to govern is to populate" and Domingo F. Sarmiento dreamed of a nation with vast multitudes. Today most Latin American governments have discarded their pronatalist policies because the negative aspects of uncontrolled population growth have become obvious. A nation cannot accelerate the growth of its per capita income while it has the high birth rate of a less developed country and at the same time approaches having the low death rate of a developed nation. In McCoy's words, "A country with an annual population growth rate of 3 percent and economic growth rate of 4 percent will double in population in only 24 years while per capita income will take 140 years."[10]

The negative effect of population growth on the unemployment rate is a major source of concern. Because of Latin America's population increase, the nations of the region encounter an unprecedented demand for jobs, a trend that will continue. The fear is that mass unemployment is likely to lead to mass violence, repression, and political instability. Most nations of the region are already suffering from unemployment and underemployment, but they will have to double the number of jobs by the end of this century to eliminate this problem. To eliminate unemployment for those reaching job-seeking age each year, Brazil has to provide 1.3 million new jobs annually and Mexico 800,000. A 1970 International Labor Organization study in Colombia predicted that a continuation of present trends would result in a 30 to 35 percent level of unemployment by 1985.

The negative economic consequences of rapid population growth are nicely summarized by an advisor to the Colombian government:

A compound rate of growth in population of, say, 3 percent per annum means an unfavorable relation of workers to dependents, with over half the population being under 18 years of age. It also means that most of the saving and investment must be devoted to supplying the needs of the additional people rather than to raising the standards of the original number; it means resorting to less favorable and less accessible land; it means the assignment of large sums to the infrastructure of transport and services rather than to a more immediate raising of the standard of living of the poor; it means the depletion of natural resources of lumber, fish and game, top soils, and the stepped-up consumption of irreplaceable resources of energy. Finally, it means the continuance of woefully inadequate educational opportunities.[11]

Although there is great variation in the population control policies of the twenty Latin American countries, there is an emerging understanding that a nation cannot simply wait for the second stage of the demographic transition to automatically reduce fertility rates. That is, the state can and must promote family-planning practices to significantly reduce the birth rate. Beginning in the mid-1960s, Colombia did this and dropped the population growth rate from 3.4 percent to less than 2 percent. In Mexico, the 1972 decision to initiate a family-planning campaign has already succeeded in reducing the birth rate from 42 births per thousand in 1975 to about 35 births per thousand in 1979.[12]

The Latin American policy environment is influenced not only by a population explosion, by also by a population implosion in the form of rapid urban growth. Since colonial times Latin American societies have always been more urbanized than one would expect, judging from the low levels of national development. Today their cities are expanding much more rapidly than population is growing in rural areas. Fertility rates are higher in the countryside, but many rural people are "pushed" off the land by the lack of jobs in the countryside and "pulled" to the cities by the lure of jobs and better social services such as education and health. In the past quarter-century, over 40 million peasants have migrated to the cities. With an annual urban growth rate of 4.4 percent, Latin America will be more urbanized than Europe by the end of this century. At the beginning of the twenty-first century, Latin America will have some 475 million city and town dwellers, compared with approximately 220 million in 1979.[13] Perhaps 40 percent of this urban growth is incorporated in the slum settlements that surround many cities with names such as *barracas, poblaciones callampas, tugurios, callejones,* and *villas miserias.* Urban growth problems are particularly severe in Mexico and Brazil. Mexico City's present population of 11 million is expected to grow to over 30 million by 2000, while it is predicted that São Paulo in Brazil will expand from its present 11 million to 25 million. We should stress that even the small countries have large urban populations. For example, Havana in Cuba has a population of over 1.6 million; Santo Domingo in the Dominican Republic has 671,000; Guatemala City has about 1,000,000; and Montevideo in Uruguay has over 1,000,000. Only in Paraguay, Honduras, Haiti, and Bolivia—which combined account for 7 percent of the region's population—are fewer than four in ten citizens now city dwellers (see table 2).

Probably nothing tests the administrative capabilities of a political system more than attempting to provide adequate services to growing numbers of people concentrated in a city. The rise in urban population brings about demands for increasing investment in water lines, sewerage, utilities, transportation, housing, and education. Beyond a certain point, responses to these demands become increasingly expensive. Water must be pumped in over longer distances, sewage must be treated, and transportation becomes more costly.

A third factor that contributes to the insecurity of policymakers is inflation. Most of the nations of the region have suffered from inflation, and it is generally considered to be a chronic problem in Latin America. Since World War II inflationary problems have been most severe in Brazil, Chile, Argentina, and Uruguay. Inflation creates insecurity among policymakers because they do not know what causes it,

TABLE 2
Urban and Rural Population in Latin America, 1960 and 1979
(in thousands)

	1960			1979			Urban
	Urban	Rural	Urban (%)	Urban	Rural	Urban (%)	Growth Rate (%)
Argentina	15,172	5,439	73.6	22,724	4,005	85.0	2.1
Bolivia	887	2,426	26.8	1,755	3,670	32.4	3.7
Brazil	32,598	38,160	46.1	75,546	44,110	63.1	4.5
Chile	5,222	2,479	67.8	8,815	2,102	80.7	2.8
Colombia	8,256	7,977	50.9	19,091	6,432	74.8	4.5
Costa Rica	432	888	32.7	979	1,187	45.2	4.4
Dominican Republic	914	2,122	30.1	2,745	2,530	52.0	6.0
Ecuador	1,515	2,821	34.9	3,309	4,380	43.0	4.2
El Salvador	935	1,498	38.4	1,783	2,653	40.2	3.5
Guatemala	1,347	2,618	34.0	2,003	4,810	29.4	2.1
Haiti	568	3,186	15.9	1,181	3,738	24.0	3.9
Honduras	438	1,457	23.1	1,250	2,314	35.1	5.7
Mexico	17,705	17,218	50.7	44,574	24,834	64.2	5.0
Nicaragua	545	875	38.4	1,394	1,069	56.6	5.1
Panama	441	621	41.5	999	882	53.1	4.4
Paraguay	605	1,105	35.4	1,083	1,890	36.4	3.1
Peru	4,630	5,392	46.2	11,967	5,361	69.1	5.1
Uruguay	2,006	477	80.8	2,347	539	81.3	0.8
Venezuela	4,901	2,451	66.7	10,470	3,117	77.1	4.1
Total	98,937	99,210	49.9	214,015	119,623	64.1	4.2

Source: Inter-American Development Bank, *Economic and Social Progress In Latin America, 1979 Report* (Washington, D.C.: IADB, 1979), p. 399.

how to stop it in a politically acceptable manner, or how to prevent inflation while still promoting economic growth. A social environment characterized by inflation creates uncertainties about future income distribution, encourages speculation in nondevelopmental investments, discourages savings and long-term investments, and threatens those on fixed incomes. Inflation is both a symptom of—and a spur to—social, economic, and political disintegration. A high inflation rate increases social tensions as each group grapples to maintain or increase its share of real income. In addition, each group will argue that some other group should bear the sacrifice of adjusting to inflation, that its own efforts are not greedy attempts to get ahead, but justifiable attempts to catch up.

Latin American policymakers are concerned what effect their decisions will have on the inflation rate because the latter influences political instability. Political systems under inflationary pressure are in serious trouble because it is so difficult to mobilize support to combat inflation. To slow down inflation, a government usually engages in a number of unpopular policies such as tightening credit for business-people and farmers and holding down real wage rates for workers. Such behavior is likely to erode public support and provide dissident leaders an issue that is tailor-made to mobilize opposition. Latin American policymakers have learned what the United States has only begun to understand—namely, that the known cures for inflation are often more painful than the disease. However, while inflation may cost a U.S. president an election, in Latin America its consequences are much more harmful to the political process. Skidmore's study concludes, "Since 1945 not a single major Latin American nation has been able to preserve a competitive political system and, at the same time, achieve sustained control of inflation once the latter has exceeded 10 percent per year for three years or more. Indeed, the social tensions exacerbated by inflation have contributed significantly to authoritarian coups in Brazil (1964), Argentina (1966), and Chile (1973)."[14] In short, high levels of inflation in Latin America are associated with political instability and repression.

Finally, the factor that probably most affects policymakers is political instability itself, which causes most governments to be primarily concerned with "regime survival." Whether pursued by civilian or military regimes, the politics of achieving development in Latin America is burdened and distorted by the politics of regime survival. The political systems of the region are not blessed with the respect commanded by legitimacy. Indeed, Irving Horowitz claims that the norm in Latin America is illegitimacy; that is, virtually every regime is considered alien and inappropriate by varying but significant portions of its citizens.[15] The persistence of illegitimacy is demonstrated by the fact that since the end of World War II all Latin American governments, with the exception of Mexico (and even in Mexico there were rumors of a coup in 1976), have undergone at least one "illegal" change of government. Barry Ames reports that between 1945 and 1972 governments in seventeen Latin American countries (that is, all but Bolivia, Cuba, and Haiti) ended their terms with elections in sixty-five cases and military coups in forty instances.[16] Bolivia is undoubtedly the most unstable country in Latin America, having endured about 200 coups since 1825 (but only one authentic revolution—in 1952).

Trying to create a legitimate political system in Latin America is analogous to constructing a large dam over several geological fault lines. The shifting fault lines are personal, group, generational, sectorial, regional, ideological, and class cleavages. Despite their shared colonial heritage of language, religion, and culture, the nations of Latin America have evolved in a variety of directions. There are democracies and dictatorships; no-party, one-party, and multiparty systems; unitary and federal systems; corporatist and noncorporatist systems; military and civilian regimes; traditional caudillo, patrimonial, bureaucratic-authoritarian, and socialist caudillo governments. This variety suggests that no regime is "natural" to Latin America. The region has a fragmented political culture; within most of the nations multiple and incompatible political traditions compete with one another, sometimes peacefully, sometimes violently. No ideological blueprints seem adequate to construct the political system that would appear legitimate to the bulk of the population. There have been political experiences that seemed compatible with national situations but which proved incapable of adapting to changing conditions: the Porfirio Díaz regime in Mexico, the *Estado Novo* in Brazil, Perón's government in Argentina, Goulart's populism in Brazil, Christian Democracy in Chile, Allende's socialism in Chile, Onganía's military dictatorship in Argentina, and Peru's left-wing military dictatorship. Howard Wiarda notes that in Latin America "patterns of fragmented political culture have been increasingly prevalent, contributing to nonconsensual political styles and making for periodic crises and occasional breakdowns. Of course, the Latin American political culture has always been 'individualistic' and 'atomistic,' but in the present context the differences have become both more intense and they reach further down into society. As politics has tended to become more class, interest, and issue oriented, the possibility for society-wide disintegration and collapse has also increased."[17]

There are qualitative differences between policy choices made in stable and unstable political systems. In the former, if one makes a policy choice that produces the "wrong" outcome, one may be defeated in the next election or be removed from a government job—moving over to industry, academia, or a think-tank; in the latter it may result in a significant reduction in one's income, imprisonment, exile, or death. In the United States, for example, government policies may be subject to partisan attack, but everyone understands that the president's administration has the right to survive to the end of its term, and no one doubts that legitimate power will be peacefully transferred after the next election. In most Latin American countries, however, legitimate power has not yet been established, so it can hardly be transferred. Without such legitimacy, the government's right and ability to survive are constantly questioned. Anderson stresses that "in Latin America, where few leaders can count on a guaranteed tenure in office to work out a strategy of governance, the weighing of potential effects of policy choices on political survival becomes a constant, day-to-day concern."[18] The factor of political instability makes personal government almost inevitable because chief executives must be constantly concerned about the personal loyalty of their collaborators in order to protect themselves from possibile conspiracies. An important tax-policy advisor to the Colombian government asserts, "It is clear . . . that the needs of economic policy are always going to be subordinated to those of political stability."[19] One of Allende's ministers puts it this way: "In the absence of consolidated political power, economic policy has to be conducted within a framework of permanent political struggle; the economic situation itself, economic tendencies, and the management of economic policy become weapons in the political struggle."[20] In brief, political instability in Latin America forces policymakers to spend scarce resources to attain legitimacy or at least survival rather than developmental objectives. There are pressures to follow policies that will have visible, short-term payoffs—what is facetiously referred to as the "edifice complex"—even though the eventual effects may be negative for development. Under conditions of political instability, crisis-management decision making is likely to overwhelm developmental decision making.

The lack of political stability, like the absence of Dostoyevsky's God, helps to create the illusion, the fear, and the possibility, that all things (choices) are possible. Clearly, a political environment in which all choices appear possible, from Castro's Cuba to Pinochet's Chile, is a very insecure and competitive one. The list of phenomena that "could not happen in Latin America" but did happen would include: the Mexican Revolution in 1910; the Bolivian Revolution in 1952; the Cuban Revolution in 1958; the survival of an anti-U.S. government in Cuba for several decades; the nationalization of U.S. foreign investment in Mexico, Cuba, Chile, and Venezuela; the election and assumption of power in 1970 by a Marxist government headed by Salvador Allende in Chile; Bolivia's selection of a female president in 1979; the prolabor policies of Juan Perón; the left-wing military dictatorship in Peru; and the success of the Sandinistas in overthrowing the Somoza dictatorship in Nicaragua in 1979.

Within an insecure and competitive environment, policymakers are confronted with an extraordinary array of policy choices derived from a variety of ideologies. The wide variety of choice insures that many will be disappointed in whatever is decided. This disappointment frequently manifests itself in popular opposition and/or lack of cooperation with government policies, which may result in a lack of immediate success and thus contribute to the lack of legitimacy of the whole process. Albert Hirschman suggests that the Latin American policy-making style is to attempt to resolve public problems that are not yet understood. Latin American policymakers frequently "import" policy solutions (central banking legislation, economic planning agencies, common market organizations) designed to fit the conditions of other, more developed countries, but which frequently do not work as well in their own. The result is often the failure of a policy to accomplish its intended outcome. Policy failure has created an ideological climate which nurtures an overdose of proposed solutions and results in rising frustration. In Albert O. Hirschman's words, "In recent decades Latin American societies have been subjected to an increasing and unprecedented barrage of proposed structural reforms. It is as though the inflation of the price level has produced in the ideological realm an inflation in the generation of 'fundamental remedies.' When the policies that are thus proposed are considerably beyond the capabilities of a society, a pervasive feeling of frustration is easily generated. . . . Indeed it would almost seem that the less satisfactorily a previous task has been grappled with, the bigger was the jump in difficulty of the next task and the sooner was it introduced."[21] Thus Latin Americans continually rewrite their constitutions; demand rapid growth and distributive justice simultaneously; and call for regional integration, help from Washington in achieving greater autonomy from the United States, and the creation of a new international economic order that will be more compatible with their developmental aspirations.

Conclusion

This introductory chapter has argued that the complexities of Latin American politics require a new approach, one that both avoids ideological distortions and handles the diversity of behavior of the nation-state in the region. Such an approach is provided by Egil Fossum's two sets of strategic policy choices—accumulation/distribution and bureaucracy/mobilization. I believe that these accurately describe the parameters of political debate and behavior in Latin America and will therefore allow us to understand post–World War II developments. Developmental policy is essentially an attempt to encourage economic growth, to provide distributive justice, and to strike a balance between the necessities of bureaucratization and the aspirations for meaningful political participation.

I have emphasized that formulating public policy in Latin America is choice-taking in a situation usually characterized by multiple and conflicting goals, scarce resources, escalating demands, limited information, and uncertain outcomes. Insecurity is the result of such factors as rapid population growth, increasing urbanization, spreading unemployment, chronic inflation, and political instability. Consequently, scarce resources are frequently used to promote the survival of a regime rather than developmental goals. Shifting political coalitions, a changing international economy, oscillating ideological currents, escalating utopian solutions to policy problems—all make it terribly difficult to create legitimate political systems and to pursue a consistent developmental strategy. Hopes, fears, and frustrations are all amplified among different sectors of the population because so many choices appear possible but so few promises are fulfilled.

In the coming chapters we shall explore the various dimensions of Latin American development policy. Chapter 2 discusses economic growth policies; chapter 3 analyzes a variety of distributive policies including the subjects of agrarian reform, education, social security, and health; chapter 4 examines the bureaucratic development of Latin American governments; chapter 5 deals with how Latin American governments have responded to the demands of increasing political participation; chapter 6 compares the public policies of Cuba and Brazil, two countries that have chosen opposing models of development, in an attempt to assess their disparate policy models as well as to reveal the inevitable accession to aspects of the opposite model that each government must make in its endeavor to modernize. Finally, chapter 7 summarizes and integrates our conclusions concerning the four components of development policy—namely, accumulation, distribution, bureaucracy, and mobilization.

The Politics of Accumulation: Economic Growth Policies

Although most Latin American nations are more developed than other nations in the Third World, they feel poor in comparison to Western Europe and the United States. A major motivation of Latin American policymakers is to guide their nations to an economic status comparable to that of the United States, Great Britain, France, and West Germany. To achieve this, policymakers recognize that there are two prerequisites: a much more efficient agrarian sector that will provide a sufficient supply of food for feeding the population and as a source of exports, and an industrial base that can satisfy domestic needs, compete in international markets, and make profits for the owners of industries (private and public). In Max Weber's terms, they want to rationalize their economy by finally overcoming the mercantilistic legacy of 300 years of Spanish and Portuguese colonial rule. The aim is to use the factors of production—land, capital, and labor—more efficiently so that rapid and self-sustaining economic growth will take place.

A regime that gives priority to policies designed to promote economic growth as measured by such indicators as the gross national product (GNP) and per capita GNP is engaged in what I shall call "the politics of accumulation." Political scientists have generally avoided this subject and, especially since the 1960s, have been far more interested in studying the politics of how accumulated wealth has been distributed. Until the 1960s, with the exception of radical economic theorists, the opposite has been true of economists; they have been more concerned with the accumulation of wealth than its distribution. This has been an unfortunate division of labor.

It is likely that political scientists have avoided studying "the politics of accumulation" because they believe that such inquiries suggest a conservative predisposition. They have also reacted to the rising tide of criticism against economic growth models that ignore the distributive aspects of economic systems so essential for human welfare. However, this study views the politics of accumulation as being equally as important as the politics of distribution. The economy is assumed to be composed of "engines of growth" and "engines of distribution," and both engines are influenced—and sometimes are determined—by public policies. This chapter will analyze public policies that have been designed to promote economic growth. Its analyses will deal with capital formation and economic development, Latin American development policies, and the consequences of ISI policies.

Capital Formation and Economic Development

A useful distinction is frequently made between economic growth and economic development. The former refers to increases in physical output; the latter involves the more efficient use of natural and human resources. In Farley's words, "Growth can take place . . . without development, but there can be no development without growth, and capital formation is a key determinant of the rate of growth in the economy."[1] Development depends upon large-scale capital investment, which is necessary to increase the future capacity for production of goods and services. For most nations, the accumulation of capital must come mainly from domestic resources, which can be mobilized by the state, and/or from private entrepreneurs. An economically developed nation is distinguished from a less developed one largely through its use of inanimate energy and advanced technology in the productive process for enormous increases in the product per work hour.

The process of economic development in either capitalist, mixed, or socialist societies requires an increasing rate of capital formation. Capital formation equals the proportion of national income that is invested instead of consumed. An economy can grow only when it produces more than it consumes at the same time. All Third World nations must confront the dilemmas posed by the vicious circle of underdevelopment diagramed in figure 2. To convert this circle of causality to one of development, a nation must hold down overall consumption and rationalize its economic structures so that there is a greater efficiency or output per simple unit of input. The industrialized nations tend to underestimate the revolutionary changes in thinking and behavior necessary to overcome the vicious circle of underdevelopment; they are as profound as the changes necessary to promote distributive justice.

From a developmental point of view, the purpose of capital investment is to increase the capacity to produce goods and services for

FIGURE 2
Vicious Circle of Poverty

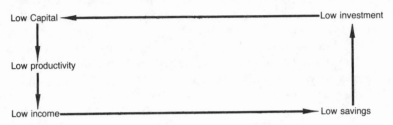

future consumption. The political problem associated with postponing the present consumption of people who, because of advertising and the mass media have already become aware of and attracted to a wide variety of consumer goods, is that it requires painful abstinence on the part of the lower class and frustrating austerity for the middle sectors. To promote economic development in either capitalist or socialist societies, a considerable proportion of the national income must be saved and invested. Simon Kuznets points out, "If for underdeveloped countries we assume that a gross capital formation of about 7 percent is needed to replace capital consumed and that enough capital must be provided to permit GNP to grow 1 percent per year while the reproducible capital-output ratio remains 3 to 1, the minimum proportion is 10 percent, compared with 24 percent in the developed countries in a period of generally high capital formation proportions."[2] For Latin American economies to grow at about 6 percent a year, the capital formation would have to be between 20 and 22 percent. It has generally failed to reach that amount, although investments have increased in the last decade. The percentage of the gross domestic product that has been invested by Latin American countries between the years 1960 and 1979 is given in table 3.

The second political problem for policymakers trying to accumulate capital to accelerate economic growth is summarized by Latin America's most influential economist, Raúl Prebisch:

The accumulation must be more strenuous in the periphery [Latin America] than in the centres [the industrialized nations]. In the latter, technological development takes the form of an increasingly high density of capital per person employed, in close interdependence with the growth of the income and the capacity

TABLE 3
Latin America: Gross Domestic Investment, 1960–79
(percentage of gross domestic product)

	1960–64	1965–69	1970–74	1978	1979
Argentina	20.0	18.8	20.8	n.a.	n.a.
Bolivia	14.8	16.2	15.2	23.0	24.0
Brazil	22.0	19.1	23.1	22.0	21.5
Chile	17.1	16.1	14.2	n.a.	n.a.
Colombia	19.2	19.6	20.4	23.0	n.a.
Costa Rica	18.1	19.2	23.4	23.5	24.5
Dominican Republic	12.6	13.9	20.5	24.1	23.7
Ecuador	14.2	18.0	24.1	26.3	26.8
El Salvador	14.1	14.2	16.1	23.7	18.6
Guatemala	10.3	12.7	14.3	21.6	18.8
Haiti	7.8	6.2	9.2	14.9	14.2
Honduras	14.3	17.6	19.6	27.7	28.4
Mexico	16.4	18.8	20.2	25.1	28.0
Nicaragua	16.8	20.3	20.8	13.1	−1.3
Panama	18.3	21.3	28.5	28.9	26.6
Paraguay	12.1	15.9	16.9	27.2	28.6
Peru	21.2	17.1	15.3	13.7	14.0
Uruguay	15.0	11.5	12.0	15.9	18.5
Venezuela	21.9	25.7	26.4	42.6	34.1

Source: Inter-American Development Bank, *Economic and Social Progress in Latin America, 1976 Report*, p. 61; and *Economic and Social Progress in Latin America, 1980–81 Report*, p. 65.
Note: Table is based on figures in national currencies, using current prices; n.a. = not available.

for accumulation. This correspondence obviously does not occur when the same technology penetrates to the periphery where the incomes and the capacity to accumulate capital are relatively low. Thus a greater proportion of total income is needed to absorb the same amount of manpower in the periphery, where, moreover, the labour force grows at a higher rate, so that the accumulation effort has to be stepped up more vigorously still.[3]

A third political problem for nations relying upon private investment is that policies designed to win the battle of production—that is, to encourage a few rich individuals to channel their savings into capital investments—often mean that a society will lose the equally important battle over distribution. Today, while virtually everyone must pay at least lip service to egalitarianism, policies that produce economic growth and greater income disparity also create the potential for class warfare. Economically, many of these policies are not "conservative" because they call for major changes in how goods are produced in Latin America. These policies are frequently socially conservative, however, in that they rely upon a small, wealthy segment of the population to channel their savings into lucrative investments that the state will protect and nurture. As a result of the extension of privileges to the already privileged, many of the elitist characteristics of Latin American societies do not change even though the nation may be undergoing a fundamental alteration from an agrarian to an industrialized society. Roger Hansen captures the dilemma accurately: "The problem is that policies designed to fuel the savings-engine investment of growth—if they are successful—have a decided impact upon the distribution of welfare within a society. During periods of rapid industrialization the incomes of certain rather small groups tend to rise rapidly, while earnings of the rest, including all those near the bottom of the income scale, increase slowly or not at all or actually decline. Thus the bill for rapid growth is generally paid through foregone consumption on the part of those segments of society who can least afford it."[4]

Latin American Development Policies:
Import-Substitution Industrialization

The twentieth century, with its wars, depressions, technological changes, revolutions, and energy crises, has proven to Latin American policymakers that industrialization is vitally important to national security. The very legitimacy of a regime is greatly influenced by such factors as how fast the economy is growing, the balance of payments situation, and the rate of inflation. As Farley writes,

> The demand for industrialization has come to be fed by a nationalism which requires industrialization as an escape route from the inertia and feudal constraints of the agricultural sector and a cushion against the adverse effects of war and depression. The push for industrialization came to symbolize a revolt against colonial status, with primary production and external economic dependence as its symbols. The demand for industrialization expresses the Latin American determination to bridge the gap between underdevelopment and the economic status of a developed nation, in fact, nothing less than national equality with the developed nations. With the emotional drive behind industrialization,

the tension springing from any frustration of this effort is likely to
be of more than ordinary significance.[5]

The policy chosen by most Latin American countries to achieve
economic development is called import-substitution industrialization
(ISI). An import-substitution policy may be defined as a program to
begin manufacturing goods domestically that were previously imported. It starts with the establishment of simple industries producing
consumer goods, such as textiles and processed foodstuffs, and pro-
gresses to the creation of complex industries, such as the manufacture
of iron and steel and machinery.[6] The ISI strategy assumed that the
previous period of relative free trade had created a domestic demand
for consumer goods serviced by imports that would now be catered to
by domestic industries. In contrast to the Soviet Union, which initially
emphasized heavy industry, most Latin American nations decided to
stress light industry first. Latin American policymakers believed that
light industry would attract private investment because it uses relatively small amounts of capital per worker and yields rapid returns on
investment since it does not take long to become operative.

However, if ISI is not to stagnate at the level of light industry,
nations pursuing this strategy must constantly increase their *capacity to
import* the capital goods necessary to develop more complex industries
and economic growth. According to the Argentine economist, Aldo
Ferrer, if the capacity to import "is not sufficient to bring into the
country all the commodities needed to fully utilize the installed capacity of light industry and to purchase the machinery and equipment
needed for domestic investment, part of the industry's capacity will be
wasted, and capital formation will be impeded. Therefore, the development not only of industry but of the whole economy (insofar as it
depends on the expansion of capital assets and the assimilation of
technology) is conditioned by the capacity to import or, more precisely, . . . by the level of imports."[7] That is, the level of exports is
expected to provide the foreign exchange necessary to maintain the
capacity to import.

ISI policies were as much "forced" upon Latin American policymakers by circumstances as they were selected. That is, the two world
wars, the Depression, and chronic balance of payments probems cut
Latin American nations off from the exports of the industrialized nations; Latin American nations were compelled to produce for themselves what they formerly imported. Countries that had previously

exported primary goods—coffee, sugar, wheat, meat, oil, copper, tin, and so forth—to earn the foreign exchange necessary to import consumer goods now were determined to produce those manufactured goods domestically. Throughout the hemisphere ISI policies were implemented by the use of higher tariffs, quotas, import licensing, preimport deposits, and multiple exchange rates. In brief, the most "open" of nations during the latter half of the nineteenth century and the early part of the twentieth, have become the most "closed." In a manner that Alexander Hamilton and Friedrich Liszt explained to their fellow citizens, Latin Americans hoped that protection from the more efficient foreign producers would create and stimulate infant industries.

What had begun as ad hoc responses to wars, depressions, and balance of payments difficulties became rationalized into a coherent policy of industrialization by the Economic Commission for Latin America (ECLA) after World War II. ECLA, a regional association of the United Nations predominantly staffed by Latin American economists under the intellectual leadership of Argentina's Raúl Prebisch, championed the idea of Latin American industrialization. Prebisch, while executive director of ECLA in 1949, formulated a doctrine that had enormous appeal to the growing nationalism of Latin Americans. The ECLA doctrine was based on the following propositions:

1. The gains from trade are not equally divided between the center (the industrialized countries) and the periphery (Latin America); the terms of trade are constantly moving against the primary producing countries. That is, over time a periphery nation has to sell more and more of a primary product (say, bags of coffee) to buy manufactured goods (say, a tractor) from the center nations.
2. As incomes rise in the center, the percentage expenditure on imports from the periphery declines. As incomes rise in the periphery, however, the percentage of income that goes for imports from the center increases. This discrepancy is held to cause the recurrent tending toward balance-of-payments difficulties and, therefore, once more toward a deterioration of the terms of trade for Latin America.

The ECLA economists stressed that industrialization in Latin America would not occur spontaneously; because of the colonial heritage, the lack of innovative entrepreneurs, and the growing gap between the developed and underdeveloped nations, this goal would require vigorous state activity well beyond mere protectionism. The new state-centered style of development was reflected in Brazil when Getúlio Vargas set up export price maintenance schemes for coffee during the 1930s and established the National Steel Company which built the Volta Redonda plant in 1940. In Chile, the popular front government created the Corporation for the Development of Production (CORFO) in 1939 which established steel, oil, sugar, and other industries during the 1940s. In Colombia, the Institute for Industrial Development was founded in 1941, and Mexico founded the National Finance Corporation in 1939. According to an Inter-American Development Bank report, between 1950 and 1974 the total number of public, mixed, and private development banks rose from 46 to 262.[8] Under ISI policies these development banks are supposed to channel public investments into bottleneck-breaking activities in such areas as electric power, transportation, communication, and irrigation. The Chilean economist Osvaldo Sunkel summarizes the strategy of ISI: "The essence of the logic of these development policies was that fast economic growth could be achieved on the basis of the protection and stimulation of industry, which eventually with the aid of appropriate government action would induce the modernization and advance of other sectors of the economy and improve the social conditions of the population, more or less following the pattern of the Industrial Revolution in Western Europe and North America."[9] What really took place is the subject of the next section.

Consequences of ISI Policies

The conventional wisdom in Latin America is that ISI policies failed in their attempts to modernize their economies. However, although ISI policies were unsatisfactory in their total impact, when they are evaluated in terms of promoting economic growth, a more qualified judgment should be made. Before condemning ISI policies, one should recognize that they were attempts to overcome enormous obstacles to the economic modernization of the region. Many of these obstacles may be traced to the colonial legacy of Spain and Portugal, which left Latin America with inefficient agriculture dominated by latifundia, governments stifled by corrupt bureaucracies, and a value system that cherished a disdain for manual labor; others include political instability, an almost total dependence on imported technology, a rapidly expanding population—especially in the cities—a bourgeoisie with very limited entrepreneurial skills, and a highly skewed income distri-

TABLE 4
Gross Domestic Product, Total and per Capita, in Latin America, 1960–80
(in 1980 U.S. dollars)

	Total (in millions)				Per Capita			
	1960	1970	1975	1980[a]	1960	1970	1975	1980[a]
Argentina	27,896.6	42,549.0	48,871.9	53,637.3	1,371.2	1,791.7	1,904.8	1,935.0
Bolivia	1,260.0	2,049.3	2,708.2	3,173.3	382.5	477.1	552.2	566.7
Brazil	47,759.7	86,088.6	144,026.3	200,176.7	669.9	929.6	1,364.6	1,664.2
Chile	8,558.4	13,241.8	12,434.2	17,660.4	1,082.7	1,413.4	1,219.0	1,590.5
Colombia	8,240.2	13,712.7	18,432.0	24,068.0	477.6	646.8	784.2	921.6
Costa Rica	1,106.3	1,970.1	2,641.4	3,395.2	838.1	1,150.1	1,353.2	1,527.3
Dominican Republic	1,781.6	2,923.0	4,503.9	5,704.8	513.0	673.0	927.3	1,050.4
Ecuador	1,841.9	3,148.4	4,788.7	6,310.8	415.9	529.1	694.2	789.2
El Salvador	1,409.3	2,439.7	3,183.0	3,277.2	529.4	681.7	766.8	680.9
Guatemala	2,855.2	4,878.5	6,402.4	8,453.0	728.2	927.6	1,051.3	1,198.5
Haiti	899.3	920.2	1,095.5	1,339.2	251.6	217.5	239.0	267.4
Honduras	933.3	1,545.7	1,709.6	2,358.4	469.2	570.6	540.7	639.0
Mexico	31,520.0	62,114.0	81,736.6	107,263.0	878.6	1,240.3	1,381.5	1,534.5
Nicaragua	930.1	1,813.2	2,376.2	2,172.0	618.8	950.3	1,105.2	896.8
Panama	1,088.5	2,341.7	2,977.1	3,522.6	892.2	1,564.3	1,795.6	1,917.6
Paraguay	1,029.6	1,588.7	2,199.4	3,583.5	525.6	637.8	783.0	1,131.2
Peru	9,454.7	15,450.8	19,327.8	20,925.5	910.3	1,142.0	1,251.7	1,137.3
Uruguay	3,963.3	4,621.8	4,938.8	6,320.6	1,513.8	1,671.5	1,738.1	2,163.9
Venezuela	13,605.9	24,633.6	31,248.6	37,011.7	1,779.5	2,295.6	2,485.0	2,437.5

Source: Inter-American Development Bank, *Economic and Social Progress in Latin America, 1980–81 Report,* p. 400.
Note: n.a. = not available.
a. Preliminary estimate.

bution which means that significant portions of the population are not part of the money economy.

Given these circumstances, the figures revealed in tables 4 and 5 are better than one might expect. The evidence suggests that although there were no economic miracles in Latin America, most countries experienced reasonable economic growth between 1950 and 1980; however, many countries had short periods of growth followed by years of slow growth (the famous stop-go pattern), and several countries suffered from almost no growth at all. According to the Inter-American Development Bank's 1980–81 report, the least successful countries in terms of their average rate of annual growth in per capita income between 1960 and 1980 were Argentina (1.7 percent); Bolivia (2.0 percent); Chile (1.9 percent); El Salvador (1.3 percent); Haiti (0.3 percent); Honduras (1.6 percent); Nicaragua (1.9 percent); Peru (1.3

TABLE 5
Latin America: Annual Variations in Gross Domestic Product, 1961–80
(in percent)

	1961–65	1966–70	1971–75	1976–80	1979	1980[a]
Argentina	4.5	4.3	2.8	1.6	6.8	1.1
Bolivia	3.9	6.3	5.7	3.2	2.0	0.8
Brazil	4.5	7.5	10.9	6.8	6.4	8.0
Chile	5.0	3.9	−0.9	7.3	8.2	6.5
Colombia	4.7	5.8	6.1	5.5	5.1	4.0
Costa Rica	4.6	7.4	6.1	5.2	3.3	1.9
Dominican Republic	3.1	7.7	9.1	4.9	4.8	5.6
Ecuador	5.3	5.7	8.9	5.7	5.3	4.6
El Salvador	6.9	4.5	5.5	3.7	−1.6	−8.7
Guatemala	5.3	5.8	5.6	5.7	4.5	4.0
Haiti	0.7	1.0	3.7	4.1	1.8	3.8
Honduras	5.0	3.2	2.1	6.6	6.7	2.4
Mexico	7.2	6.9	5.7	5.6	8.0	7.4
Nicaragua	10.1	4.0	5.6	−1.3	−17.4	10.4
Panama	8.2	7.7	5.0	3.4	4.9	5.5
Paraguay	4.8	4.2	6.7	10.3	3.4	3.4
Peru	6.7	4.4	4.6	1.6	3.0	3.5
Uruguay	0.9	2.3	1.4	5.1	8.6	4.5
Venezuela	7.3	4.6	4.9	3.5	0.7	−1.6

Source: Inter-American Development Bank, *Economic and Social Progress in Latin America, 1980–81 Report,* p. 7.

Note: Table is based on constant market prices, with reference to the base year used by each country.

a. Preliminary estimates.

percent); Uruguay (1.8 percent); and Venezuela (1.6 percent). Cuban growth figures, which were poor, will be given in chapter 6. If one accepts the Alliance for Progress goal of an average yearly increase in per capita income of 2.5 percent as the mark of success, then the following nations achieved this goal between 1960 and 1980: Brazil (4.6 percent); Colombia (3.3 percent); Costa Rica (3.0 percent); the Dominican Republic (3.6 percent); Ecuador (3.2 percent); Guatemala (2.5 percent); Mexico (2.8 percent); Panama (3.9 percent); and Paraguay (3.9 percent). As we will examine in greater detail in chapter 6, the politics of accumulation were played most successfully by Brazil. Using the 1980 U.S. dollar, Brazil's gross domestic product expanded from $48 billion in 1960 to $200 billion in 1980. Mexico's growth totals were also impressive; its economy grew from $32 billion in 1960 to $107 billion in 1980. But Mexico's soaring birthrate meant that an excellent 6.3 percent annual growth rate of the GDP between 1960 and 1980 was diluted to a moderately successful growth rate of the per capita GDP of about 2.8 percent. By 1983, however, the growth policies of both Brazil and Mexico were severely constrained by enormous foreign debts.

Moreover, despite the fact that a number of Latin American nations experienced better economic growth than the United States, few Latin Americans were pleased with the impact of ISI policies because, by the end of the 1950s, certain problems connected with this strategy of development had become painfully evident. First, the ISI strategy neglected agriculture and the slow growth of farm production became an increasingly serious bottleneck in the hemisphere's development. A growing agricultural sector can aid economic development by providing food for the expanding urban population and by generating export revenue to finance industrial development and ease balance of payments difficulties. Instead, table 6 indicates that, in per capita terms, agricultural

TABLE 6
Latin American Indexes of per Capita Agricultural and Livestock Production, 1971–75 (base period 1961–65 = 100)

	1971	1972	1973	1974	1975
Argentina	95	93	96	100	100
Barbados	91	76	81	77	74
Bolivia	110	114	120	121	123
Brazil	105	109	105	110	107
Chile	102	95	81	94	92
Colombia	100	97	96	98	99
Costa Rica	131	133	132	131	137
Dominican Republic	101	104	102	101	98
Ecuador	98	93	93	101	98
El Salvador	96	92	95	103	99
Guatemala	110	114	115	118	125
Guyana	99	90	81	97	91
Haiti	100	101	101	101	101
Honduras	117	119	112	104	106
Jamaica	98	94	89	91	93
Mexico	102	98	94	94	89
Nicaragua	107	106	107	115	112
Panama	122	119	116	116	117
Paraguay	102	100	102	102	107
Peru	96	92	95	90	91
Trinidad and Tobago	106	102	93	91	85
Uruguay	88	80	81	86	83
Venezuela	118	116	119	121	129
Total	99	97	96	99	97

Source: Inter-American Development Bank, *Economic and Social Progress in Latin America, 1976 Report,* p. 14.

production since 1961 has remained the same or has declined in Argentina, Chile, Colombia, the Dominican Republic, Ecuador, Mexico, Peru, and Uruguay. Latin American agricultural production in 1975 was only 34 percent higher than it was in the early 1960s. From 1970 to 1980, agricultural output increased by only 3.4 percent and between 1977 and 1980 the growth rate decelerated to 2.6 percent.[10] Instead of aiding economic development, the sluggishness of the agricultural sector has meant that governments have had to use scarce funds to subsidize food prices to placate politically the growing urban population and to import food; this has become a contributing factor exacerbating Latin America's chronic balance of payments problems.

Despite the vast redistribution of land that took place as a result of the 1910 revolution, the agrarian problem remains severe in Mexico. In the Mexican system of land tenure, predominantly poor communal farms known as *ejidos* exist along with thriving modern, privately owned estates of up to 250 acres. The peasants within the *ejidos* have received land from the Mexican government, but not the credit, seeds, fertilizer, machinery, and infrastructural support (roads, dams, irrigation) necessary to make them more efficient and productive. Consequently, 80 percent of the 28,000 *ejidos* cannot support themselves. The private farmers do receive this kind of state aid, and they produce the bulk of the marketable surplus which is sold in the cities and exported. The magnitude of this unsolved problem is revealed in the facts that there are still 4 million impoverished peasants agitating for their "revolutionary right to land," and that Mexico spent US$600 million to import food in 1977. In December 1977, President López Portillo endorsed an accumulation preference over distribution by stating, "The solution is not to divide up the land but to multipy production. To bring justice to the peasant is not to give him land nor to divide it up, but rather to create new units of production, to increase efficiency and to generate wealth."[11] In March 1980, President López Portillo created the Mexican Food System (SAM) to promote national self-sufficiency and adequate food supplies for the poorest segments of the population through a series of consumption and production subsidies. But in 1982, partly because of droughts, Mexico had to import over 10 million tons of basic grains from the United States.

Nowhere is the irrationality of agrarian policy better revealed than in Argentina. Argentina has plenty of fertile land, a good climate, and an educated population (91 percent literacy); it does not suffer from problems found elsewhere in the region: a population explosion, protein deficiency, or a peasant sector agitating for land. After World War I, Argentina was one of the six or seven richest nations in the world in per capita income; it was one of the largest wheat, meat, and corn exporters. However, ISI policies in Argentina were financed to a great extent by taxes on both imports and farm exports. Politically this policy was acceptable because the new urban elites considered the large landowners to be too wealthy and to be responsible for Argentina's lack of industrialization. The result was that Argentine farmers had to sell their farm products to state agencies at prices *below* international market levels while they had to pay prices *above* international levels for heavily protected domestic manufactured goods. Argentine agriculture has suffered from two sources of price instability: the price fluctuations of the internal market and the price fluctuations due to internal politics as succeeding governments have constantly shifted agrarian policies, taxes, and exchange rates. Consequently, Argentine production has not modernized itself, production has stagnated, and the economy has suffered from inflation and balance of payments miseries.[12]

The second reason why Latin American policymakers have become dissatisfied with the impact of ISI policies is that the strategy did not produce the modern, efficient, well-integrated economy its proponents had predicted. Instead, ISI policies both produced and maintained an economy characterized by horizontal specialization, an excess of protectionism, a self-indulgent consumerism for a privileged minority, high rates of unemployment and underemployment, and a pathological concentration of wealth among certain groups in certain cities. No wonder that scholars (ideologues have no problem) find it so difficult to describe Latin American economy in terms of what it is and are forced to describe it in terms of what it is not. Victor Alba pictures the Latin American economy thus:

> It is not strictly feudal, since along with latifundism and serfdom there are modern industries, labor unions, and technological progress, and along with an antiquated banking system there are very modern methods of marketing. Neither is it a typically capitalistic economy, since private and public investment coexist in it, as do private initiative and free enterprise, government planning and intervention. . . . It is not an agrarian economy, for industrialization and urbanization are rapidly increasing, but neither is it an industrial economy, since there is not a significant rural market, nor is the bulk of the income derived from industry. It is not

strictly a market economy, because in the majority of countries the mass of the people are not consumers of industrial products; but it is not strictly a subsistence economy, since the same mass of people performs an economic activity linked to the market.[13]

According to William Glade, since 1930 the rising middle class has succeeded in "the grafting on of a species of state sponsored industrial capitalism to the trunk of an agrarian anachronism which had previously been modified only enough to permit the export sector to sprout."[14] The result is a unique form of capitalism based on state-encouraged monopoly rather than laissez-faire competition. It is not only hard to describe the post-ISI Latin American economy, but also difficult to analyze and explain its failures.

The ISI strategy has been less effective than expected because it has been implemented in an ad hoc and indiscriminate manner. The combination of crisis situations, lack of expertise, and political considerations has meant that no Latin American nation designed and carried out a systematic body of measures to develop industries rationally selected to achieve economic growth. This irrational policy process took place in many nations. Carlos Díaz-Alejandro summarizes it for Argentina: "The policy of import substitution for some industrial products was not an integrated and thought-out plan. Rather, it proceeded from one improvisation to another, reacting to short-run economic and political pressures. Toward the end of the war and during the early postwar years, the main preoccupation was defending industries that had arisen and expanded during the war regardless of their efficiency."[15] Under Juan Perón, Argentina squandered the huge reserves of credit it had earned during World War II without modernizing the potential of its agricultural and industrial economy. The inevitable strains of dealing with an economy that has a vast potential for growth but is distorted by insecurity and irrationality is reflected in the fact that between 1952 and 1970 Argentina had eighteen ministers of economy.[16]

The record of Argentina and those of the other Latin American countries suggest that the ISI strategy of development channeled these countries' economies in a manner that emphasized *horizontal* rather than *vertical* specialization. In vertical specialization, a group of industries is integrated in one activity—that is, making cars or watches—from start to finish so as to produce final goods, intermediate goods, and especially the capital goods necessary to make these products. No nation can afford to vertically specialize in all, or even most, industries. A reasonable strategy is to specialize vertically in a selected number of industries where the possibilities of exporting manufactured products are good. The nation can import other goods from the most efficient producer. However, the ISI strategy has resulted in *horizontal* specialization in which there has been an emphasis on producing an even greater variety of consumer goods. This excessive diversification inhibits the growth of a more dynamic economy. Most of the capital goods and technology necessary to produce these consumer goods have to be imported.

The fact that Latin American nations do not provide their own technology, but import it, and frequently do not even adapt foreign technology to their own needs, is a crucial distinction between Latin America and the more developed countries in which industrial development began long ago on a simpler scale. "Even when the early industrializers were predominantly in the light consumer goods stage (from the point of view of labor force or valued added), they were already producing *their own* capital goods, if only by artisan methods," writes Albert Hirschman; "ISI brings in complex technology, but without the sustained technological experimentation and concomitant training in innovation which are characteristic of the pioneer industrial countries."[17] By copying what is created in developed countries, Latin American nations preclude the possibility of developing more dynamic and more autonomous economies of their own.

The impact of ISI policies has been disappointing for another reason, namely, that policymakers have overprotected their economies. What was originally conceived as temporary protection to encourage infant industries to grow has become ossified into permanent protection. The proponents of ISI did not foresee that this strategy would develop its own constituency: industrialists, politicians, and privileged unions who would succumb to the self-indulgent notion that if some protection is good, then more is better. This overprotection has resulted in a price structure that is too high, thus preventing many Latin American industries from being competitive in international markets.[18] Bela Balassa points out that "the sheltering of these industries was generally conducive to a 'live and let live' attitude and provided little incentive for product improvement and technical change. With continuing protection assured to them, the high costs observed in many of the firms may then be considered a result rather than the cause of protection."[19] Table 7 contrasts the average effective rates of protec-

TABLE 7
Average Effective Rates of Protection in Several Latin American Developed Nations, about 1965 (in percent)

	All Manufacturing	Consumer Goods	Intermediate Goods	Capital Goods
Argentina	246.0	220.0	315.0	194.0
Brazil	118.0	160.0	89.0	100.0
Mexico	32.6	34.0	27.6	34.7
Japan	29.5	50.5	29.2	22.0
United Kingdom	27.8	40.4	28.7	23.0
United States	20.0	25.9	23.1	13.9
European Economic Community	18.6	30.9	20.0	15.0
Sweden	12.5	23.9	13.0	12.1

Source: Rawle Farley, *The Economics of Latin America: Development Problems in Perspective* (New York: Harper and Row, 1972), p. 224.

tion (in percentages) in several Latin American and developed nations during the mid-1960s.

Protected from internal and external competition by controls of the nation-states, Latin American capitalism is characterized by poor management techniques, poor quality control, and high production costs. By the early 1960s, ISI policies had brought about a situation where the nations of the hemisphere produced about 86 percent of their manufactured goods for domestic consumption, but the duplicative nature of this development in each nation, the high cost of production, and the high levels of protection in each of these countries meant that only 7 percent of Latin America's exports were manufactured goods.[20]

The problem for policymakers is that they have not yet overcome the Latin American entrepreneur's traditional fear of risk and competition. After interviewing a number of Latin American businessmen, Albert Lauterbach reported, "The interviewee typically did not think of either business or expansion in terms of risk. The latter is something to be avoided; when there is a risk there will be no new investment. Risk might be all right for companies in wealthy countries, but in the poorer areas nobody could afford it."[21] In these same interviews, businessmen stressed the need for tariff protection and claimed that without it no industry could develop or survive in their country. As for competition, at best it was considered a luxury that poor countries could ill afford; at worst it was considered a form of aggression. Similarly, interviews with Chilean businessmen by Stanley Davis during the late 1960s revealed that they were burdened by considerable uncertainty and fear of socialists and communists coming to power: "The most important frequent response to questions about how organizations modernize and develop was, 'How can I worry about development when I'm trying to survive?' "[22]

In brief, ISI policies have encouraged Latin American businessmen "to be monopolists, operating on license and privilege in preference to innovation and risk."[23] Too often the source of profit is protection, not efficiency. These profits frequently represent a transference of income from the consumer to the protected producer. And if that producer is a foreign corporation that has set up plants within the protective barrier, much of these profits will be transferred abroad, thus adding to the already chronic balance of payments problem.

The efficiency of the ISI strategy was further retarded because of the dominance of consumerism. Since colonial times Latin America has been burdened by an upper class that emulated the consumption habits of the well-to-do in the more developed nations. ISI policies have not changed this pattern; indeed, the pattern now includes the middle class. The emphasis on responding to the consumption demands of the privileged minority at the expense of the poverty stricken majority has reduced the accumulation of capital and increased the need for social repression. Many leftists contend that the Latin American bourgeoisie's propensity to accumulate consumer goods is preventing them from performing their "historical function" of accumulating capital. In brief, Latin America has modernized its consumption habits far faster than it has modernized the economy.

The problem is that ISI policies were applied in societies with drastically uneven distributions of income since colonial times (see the section on income distribution in chapter 3). The ISI strategy did not cause the unequal distribution of income, but it did not overcome this condition, and, indeed, helped to perpetuate it. By adapting to the skewed income distribution of the different nations in Latin America, ISI has been socially conservative and economically limited in its impact. By initiating a strategy of industrialization geared to consumer demand, policymakers have selected a method that does not alter the marginality of the majority of the people in Latin America. ECLA estimates that 80 percent of the demand for manufactures other than foodstuffs in Latin America comes from persons whose income is higher than an annual per capita income of more than US$500, but half of the population of the region earns less than $500. The ISI strategy ignores the fact that low per capita income, combined with its unequal distribution, means that a large proportion of the population is unable to translate its needs into effective demand. In 1974 ECLA estimated that the proportion of the population with an annual income of less than $500, and who are therefore effectively excluded from the market, is 30 percent in Argentina, 40 percent in Venezuela, 50 percent in Chile, 60 percent in Mexico, 80 percent in Colombia, and 90 percent in Honduras.[24] Even a country the size of Mexico can only generate the consumer demand of a small developed nation such as the Netherlands. Given the income distribution in Latin America, conspicuous consumption can only be minutely democratized. For most Latin American nations, the rationale of the consumer society is not congruent with the interests of society as a whole.

Under the ISI strategy, the structure of income distribution has determined the structure of industrial production. The production of consumer goods has been emphasized over that of capital and intermediate goods. The income distribution of the Latin American nations has meant that the production of consumer goods has repeatedly gone through a depressing two-phase cycle: rapid growth during which there is too much reliance on the preexisting demands of the high-income groups, and a much more difficult expansion period during which attempts are made to maintain demand by extending purchasing power to new groups. New industries grow rapidly until the middle and upper income levels have satisfied their demand for their products and then the industries stagnate. Under these circumstances, Latin American economic growth has had a sporadic stop-go quality; planners' aspirations for continuous growth at a rate of between 5 and 8 percent a year have not been achieved. Such growth can be attained only if larger proportions of the lower classes increase their income and/or there is a dramatic increase in exports.

Both of these strategies are thwarted by a kind of consumerism that prevents most Latin American nations from achieving the higher rates of capital formation necessary to rationalize their economies. A nation in which half the population is underemployed and undernourished should not be wasting its savings potential so that a small proportion of its population can have access to consumer credit facilities in order to buy a car, a stereo, or a trip to Disney World (two million Latin Americans visited Florida in 1976). Thus the chief criticism of the ISI strategy is that it has not had a favorable impact on the 180 million marginal peoples—that is, the Indians, peasants, slum dwellers, and subproletarian army of the unemployed and underemployed. To the horror of conventional economists and policymakers, the kind of economic growth inspired by the ISI has not reduced the unemployment rate. However, it must be understood that economic stagnation increases unemployment even more rapidly.

A major part of this problem, as we have seen, is the high rate of population growth in most Latin American countries, which means that the region must achieve an economic growth rate of over 7 percent annually just to prevent additional unemployment and to provide employment for the new workers entering the job market. This problem is most severe in Mexico, a nation whose leaders have been successful in promoting an average annual economic growth rate of about 6 percent since 1940. However, Mexico's high birthrate means that 800,000 new jobs must be created each year to match the number of youths pouring into the labor market. Since Mexico cannot do this, the nation's already high unemployment and underemployment rates, estimated to represent about a third of the 16 million work force, will continue to rise. In other countries the unemployment rate is estimated at between 5 and 18 percent—rising to 25 percent if the underemployed are included.[25]

The problem is that employment in manufacturing for Latin Americans has increased at a rate of only 2 percent per year, which is less than the population increase *and* considerably less than the growth of most cities. The proponents of ISI have been disappointed that less than 15 percent of the increment to the region's labor force between 1950 and 1969 has been absorbed by manufacturing.[26] Policymakers had believed that, given Latin America's stage of development, employment would increase in the manufacturing sector more rapidly than in services. However, industrialization is taking a unique path in Latin America by not following the Western pattern in which the economy is first dominated by the primary sector (a plurality of the work force), then the secondary sector (industrial workers), and finally the tertiary sector (service workers). Between 1925 and 1950, about 30 percent of the net increase in employment was in services; this rose to about 40 percent during 1950–55 and 47 percent during 1955–62. In short, employment in the service sector has grown much more rapidly than in the industrial sector.[27] The expanding numbers of Latin Americans in the service sector who eke out their existence selling trinkets, newspapers, food, sex, and so on, are a concrete symbol of the failure of ISI to provide productive employment.

One major source of the unemployment problem is the kind of technology used in Latin America. As was noted earlier, Latin America produces very little of its own technology and is therefore forced to import most of it from the more advanced nations. The imported technology is usually capital-intensive and reflects the needs of, say, General Motors more than the needs of a labor-surplus, capital-scarce nation in Latin America. This dependence continues today, despite the fact that most Latin American economists fully understand that the indiscriminate importation of labor-saving, capital-intensive technology from industrialized countries—in which labor is relatively scarce, workers are relatively well educated, and capital is relatively available—into nations in which the opposite conditions prevail guarantees the continued "marginalization" of a significant portion of the population. It seems that many countries would prefer to produce lawyers who can give speeches in the United Nations condemning this condition rather than altering their educational systems so as to produce more technicians who could invent technologies more in line with the economic and social needs of their own particular countries, or at least could adapt foreign technologies to their own use. (See the section on education in chapter 3.)

The dilemma for Latin America is that the capital goods used by industry are much more labor-saving than those used in the industrialized countries at the end of the nineteenth century. Whereas it took 370,000 British workers in 1870 to produce the first annual million tons of steel, today it takes only about 8,000 workers in Argentina, Brazil, or Mexico to produce a million tons of steel.[28] By copying the production styles of the more advanced nations, policymakers are not confronting the unemployment problem. (To be sure, the improvement in production techniques is causing similar unemployment problems even in industrialized nations.)

Furthermore, the use of capital-intensive technology has brought about the unanticipated consequence of economic dualism, a dichotomy between the traditional and modern forms of production in both the agricultural and industrial sectors. Clark Reynolds's study of Mexico reveals that "even in the same area, primitive forms of cultivation are applied across the road from modern commercial farms. Medieval artisanry is being carried on in the shadow of modern factories. . . . Not just dual but multiple techniques have survived in the same sector of economic activity for decades, and although the proportion of traditional to modern technology in the total output of these sectors has

TABLE 8

Levels of Technological Sophistication in Latin American Employment and Production, about 1970 (in percent)

	Productivity Level		
	Modern	Intermediate	Primitive
Total Latin America			
All Sectors Combined			
Employment	12.4	53.3	34.3
Product	53.3	41.6	5.1
Agriculture			
Employment	6.8	27.7	65.5
Product	47.5	33.2	19.3
Manufacturing			
Employment	17.4	64.9	17.6
Product	62.5	36.0	1.5
Mining			
Employment	38.0	34.2	27.8
Product	91.5	7.5	1.0
Central America			
All Sectors Combined			
Employment	8.1	33.6	55.0
Product	42.6	48.0	9.4
Agriculture			
Employment	5.0	15.0	80.0
Product	43.9	30.6	25.5
Manufacturing			
Employment	14.0	57.4	28.6
Product	63.6	30.4	3.3
Mining			
Employment	20.0	60.0	20.0
Product	57.2	40.0	2.8
Argentina			
All Sectors Combined			
Employment	21.3	65.8	5.3
Product	58.6	40.5	0.9
Agriculture			
Employment	25.0	57.0	18.0
Product	65.1	32.3	2.6
Manufacturing			
Employment	25.6	70.6	3.8
Product	62.1	37.5	0.4
Mining			
Employment	50.0	40.0	10.0
Product	77.8	21.6	0.6

Sources: CEPAL, *La mano de obra y el desarrollo económico de América Latina en los últimos años* (E/CN.12/L.1), as summarized in Anibal Pinto, "Notas sobre estilos de desarrollo en America Latina," working paper ECLA/ IDE/Draft/103, Dec. 1973; David Felix, "Latin American Power: Take-Off or Plus C'est la Même Chose?" presented at the annual meeting of the International Studies Convention, Toronto, 1976, p. 9.

fallen sharply over time, the transition has been very uneven from sector to sector and region to region."[29] Within this dualism, the modern sector increases its contributions to the structure of employment. Table 8 indicates that 65.5 percent of the agricultural workers in Latin America still use primitive techniques and therefore only produce 19.3 percent of the total agricultural products.

And yet policymakers continue to pursue the irrational policy of encouraging the use of capital-intensive technology by granting excessive fiscal, credit, and foreign exchange advantages to domestic and foreign entrepreneurs. These policies have combined with the entrepreneurs' fears of unions to render the opportunity cost of this type of investment extremely low. Latin American entrepreneurs can sometimes borrow money from their governments during inflationary periods (the usual condition) to finance capital investment at what turns out to be negative interest rates. Ignacz Sachs is especially critical of the capital-intensive bias of these policies: "What really counts is getting access to credit and government favours. For those who manage it—and it is a matter either of public relations or of a solid financial position—capital is neither scarce nor expensive. The trouble is that the bulk of government support thus accrues to entrepreneurs, who really could manage without it, while small-scale industries and workshops are really starved for capital."[30] Obviously, what is needed are incentives for entrepreneurs to increase their work force so as to reduce the unemployment rate.

The ISI strategy has accentuated another absurdity in Latin America, namely, an unhealthy concentration of wealth among certain social groups and regions of a country. We have already dealt with the problem of income distribution; here I want to stress the fact that in geographical terms, modernization has been highly concentrated in Latin America. The spatial impact of ISI strategy did not overcome the legacy of the Spanish colonial system in which political and economic power were concentrated in a few cities; instead, ISI enhanced this concentration.

The problem can clearly be seen in table 9 which ranks the city-size distribution of ten Latin American countries. On the basis of urban development in the West, most geographers believe that in a healthy rank-size hierarchy the primate city is approximately twice as large as the second city, three times larger than the third, and four times the population of the fourth.[31] It is claimed that such a distribution of cities can help serve as growth centers in different parts of the country. However, in Latin America only Colombia has what can be considered

TABLE 9
City-Size Distribution of Major Cities in Ten Latin American Nations, 1938–70 (in thousands of persons)

	City Rank									
	1	2	3	4	5	6	7	8	9	10
Argentina										
1950	4,500	570	426	325	256	—	—	—	—	—
1970	8,400(1)	803(2)	791(3)	573(5)	566(4)	—	—	—	—	—
Brazil										
1940	1,764	1,326	348	290	272	211	206	180	140	106
1970	5,979(2)	4,316(1)	1,255(6)	1,084(3)	1,027(4)	903(5)	873(8)	643(7)	624(9)	546(–)
Chile										
1940	952	210	86	66	50	49	43	42	38	36
1960	1,907(1)	253(2)	148(3)	115(4)	88(6)	84(10)	72(8)	68(5)	65(7)	61(11)
Colombia										
1938	326	150	144	88	73	51	42	37	31	30
1964	1,622(1)	911(3)	618(4)	493(2)	218(5)	217(7)	190(6)	148(9)	147(8)	125(12)
Ecuador										
1950	259	210	40	31	30	19	16	15	14	14
1962	511(1)	355(2)	60(3)	53(4)	42(5)	34(6)	33(11)	32(7)	29(17)	28(10)
El Salvador										
1950	162	52	27	18	18	13	10	10	10	10
1961	256(1)	72(2)	40(3)	27(4)	24(6)	24(5)	15(7)	15(12)	13(10)	13(8)
Mexico										
1940	1,757	236	190	148	115	104	104	103	98	93
1970	6,874(1)	1,196(2)	830(3)	522(4)	545(8)	436(21)	390(24)	364(13)	359(10)	335(–)
Nicaragua										
1950	109	31	21	17	13	10	—	—	—	—
1963	235(1)	45(2)	29(3)	23(4)	22(5)	15(6)	—	—	—	—
Peru										
1940	614	77	41	37	32	32	27	21	21	19
1972	3,318(1)	305(2)	242(4)	190(6)	159(–)	127(10)	121(3)	116(7)	111(5)	74(9)
Venezuela										
1941	354	122	55	54	33	32	26	20	18	16
1961	1,336(1)	422(2)	199(4)	164(3)	135(5)	98(6)	90(9)	76(10)	70(7)	63(8)

Source: Alan Gilbert, *Latin American Development: A Geographical Perspective* (Baltimore: Penguin Books, 1974), p. 93.
Note: Figures in parentheses show each city's rank at the earlier date.

a healthy rank-size hierarchy; the other Latin American countries suffer from excessive concentration of the population in one or two cities. The primacy of Lima in Peru, Santiago in Chile, São Paulo in Brazil, Mexico City in Mexico, Caracas in Venezuela, Guatemala City in Guatemala, Santo Domingo in the Dominican Republic, and Montevideo in Uruguay, exhibit strong elements of parasitism and internal colonialism which attract investment and talented people to these centers at the expense of other regions and cities. In a sense, the ISI strategy has succeeded in modernizing a number of primate cities in different countries, but has failed to develop the secondary regional centers of development—that is, the equivalent of Pittsburgh, Chicago, or Houston.

The impact of the ISI strategy on the geographical concentration of manufacturing can be seen in table 10. ECLA estimates that "the area of less than 5,000 square kilometers represented by the metropolitan areas of Buenos Aires, the Municipality of São Paulo, and Mexico City accounts for over a third of the total value of Latin American production, although it contains only about 8 or 9 percent of the region's population. Within each country the two main industrial centers usually constitute a very high proportion of the nation's industry."[32] New industry has tended to develop where industry already exists because of external economic advantages and because that is where the demand is concentrated. The incentive for industry to be located in capital cities has been intensified by a political factor, namely, the growing importance of government decisions upon the daily operations of companies. Under the ISI strategy, industrial profits are often a function of administration decisions concerning a license to import, a change in the multiple exchange rate, a subsidy, a loan, and so forth. Given the nature of Latin American governments, most business leaders want *personal* access to government decision makers; this requires proximity. Many of these cities have become more pockets of parasitism than centers that spread development.

The growth-retarding costs of such concentration can be seen clearly in Mexico City. Since 1960 the population of Mexico City has doubled so that the present population is 12 million and the predicted population by the year 2000—assuming the continuation of present trends—is 30 million. Mexico City has 20 percent of the country's population, 35.6 percent of its industry, 41.2 percent of its commerce, and 50.1 percent of its services.[33] The absurdity of this situation is that Mexico City is located 7,400 feet above sea level so that water has to be

TABLE 10

Geographical Concentration of Industrial/Manufacturing Workers in Seven Latin American Countries, 1930–68 (in percent)

Argentina	1935	1946	1954	1965
Federal Capital	47.0	40.2	32.2	26.0
Buenos Aires	25.2	29.5	33.2	39.9
Córdoba	4.3	4.8	6.2	8.0
Santa Fe	9.6	9.2	9.5	9.7
Total Workers	467,315	1,107,829	1,498,115	1,370,500
Brazil	**1940**	**1950**	**1960**	**1968**
São Paulo	35.0	38.6	45.6	50.2
Guanabara (Rio)	15.8	13.2	9.6	9.3
Minas Gerais	9.5	8.8	8.0	n.a.
Rio Grande du Sul	7.8	7.9	7.4	7.3
Rio de Janeiro	5.8	6.1	6.4	n.a.
Pernambuco	7.3	6.9	4.2	n.a.
Total Workers	781,185	256,807	1,425,886	2,218,278
Chile		**1940**	**1952**	**1960**
Central region		68.5	70.6	71.8
Concepción and La Frontera		14.9	15.0	14.3
			1947	**1964**
Santiago			51.5	60.3
Valparaiso			18.1	11.8
Concepción			12.6	11.8
Bio-Bio			1.1	2.3
Valdivia			2.5	1.8
Tarapaca			0.6	4.9
Total Workers			160,900	241,700
Colombia			**1945**	**1967**
Bogotá and Soacha			16.7	24.3
Medellín complex			21.9	22.8
Cali			7.1	12.5
Barranquilla			19.5	8.3
Total workers			135,400	293,825
Ecuador		**1950**	**1955**	**1965**
Guayas (Guayaquil)		38.9	42.0	38.8
Pichinicha (Quito)		38.3	36.8	30.7
Total workers		n.a.	30,370	47,629
Mexico		**1930**	**1950**	**1965**
Mexico City		24.6	30.3	33.9
Mexico		2.9	4.9	12.1
Jalisco (Guadalajara)		6.4	4.4	5.4
Nuevo Leon (Monterrey)		n.a.	n.a.	7.1
Total Workers		197,109	808,561	1,409,489
Peru			**1940**	**1961**
Lima/Callao			13.7	38.1
Arequipa			3.8	5.0
Cajamarca			13.0	5.1
Cuzco			19.4	6.9
La Libertad			5.4	5.2
Total workers			380,281	410,981

Source: Alan Gilbert, *Latin American Development: A Geographical Perspective* (Baltimore: Penguin Books, 1974), pp. 55–56.

Note: n.a. = not available.

pumped up to the city at costs that are five times greater per capita than in any other urban center in the nation. Moreover, because the city is surrounded by mountains, the location of so many factories there, especially the petrochemical plants of the nationalized oil industry, PEMEX, means that Mexico City is the most polluted city in the Western Hemisphere—perhaps in the world. Despite this fact, a half million migrants per year are still moving to Mexico City in hopes of finding employment.

The final disappointment concerning the impact of ISI policies involves balance of payments difficulties. It will be recalled that one of the original incentives for pursuing ISI was to avoid the humiliating constraints of this external bottleneck. Before 1929, Latin American economic growth was externally oriented, that is, exports generated a significant proportion of national income. The proponents of ISI succeeded in shifting the policy orientation from expanding the export of primary goods to internal industrialization. One measure of the success of ISI in this shift was in reducing the import coefficient (the ratio of imports to the GNP) from 25 percent in 1929, to 14.5 percent in 1949, and 10.3 percent in 1970.[34] The declining import coefficient indicates that Latin America was substituting internally produced manufactured goods for the previously imported goods from the industrialized countries. In spite of this change from one of the most "open" regions (with a high import coefficient) of the world to one of the most protected (with a low import coefficient), Latin America did not shake loose from other kinds of external dependence.

The success of ISI in achieving horizontal integration, combined with the increasing difficulty of attaining vertical integration, caused many countries to shift their growth strategies in the 1960s and 1970s. In the absence of a domestic capital goods sector, the construction of industrial plants was an import-intensive activity. As ISI advanced, there was an increasing dependency on export income to finance the importation of intermediate and capital goods, raw material, and fuel. The failure of exports to generate sufficient funds to finance advanced industrialization produced a negative balance of payments, burdensome foreign debts, and soaring inflation. For the oil-importing nations, these problems were exacerbated by the steep rise in oil prices in 1973 and 1979. Hence, many countries eventually had to alter their strategies of development by becoming more concerned with controlling inflation, reducing unnecessary imports, expanding and diversifying their exports, and obtaining loans from international lending agencies and private commercial banks.

Many of these neoliberal policies are extremely unpopular and only a few countries, such as Colombia, could make this transition under a democratic political system. Often, policymakers in other nations felt that their present regimes lacked the capacity to resolve the political and economic problems of promoting advanced industrialization, and thus have supported the creation of bureaucratic-authoritarian (BA) regimes. Examples of such regimes include the post-1964 period in Brazil, the 1966–70 and 1976–83 periods in Argentina, the post-1973 period in Chile and Uruguay, and perhaps contemporary Mexico.[35]

Bureaucratic-authoritarian regimes are based on a tacit alliance among the military, the technocrats, the domestic bourgeoisie, and foreign capital. Through a combination of repression, to hold down the demands for distributive social policies (see chapter 5), and an economic rationality designed by technocrats, BA regimes try to promote the orderly advance of economic development. The technocrats believe that a "deepening" of industrialization—what Hirschman calls backward linkages—requires a more stable and predictable economic and political environment. The advanced phases of ISI necessitate higher levels of technology, greater managerial expertise, and more capital. Some of these resources, which can only be acquired from multinational corporations, international lending agencies, and foreign commercial banks, will not be available if xenophobic nationalism is influencing public policy. Thus, many of the BA regimes have emphasized more orthodox, neoliberal economic policies—such as reducing budget deficits and promoting a more favorable balance of payments—in order to obtain the support of the World Bank, the International Monetary Fund (IMF) and the Inter-American Development Bank. However, after 1979, the rising cost of borrowing money, and the slowdown in international trade brought about by recessions and rising protectionism in Western Europe and the United States, created major barriers to increasing exports and preventing skyrocketing foreign debts.

The important point is that Latin American exports have not expanded rapidly enough to finance the necessary imports to promote economic growth. This is a critical handicap because "prior to import substitution a decline in imports implied mainly a tighter belt for consumers; after import substitution a reduction of imports meant unemployment and a lower rate of growth."[36] The weight of this handicap is displayed in tables 11 and 12. Between 1960 and 1980, as measured by constant 1980 U.S. dollars, the region's external debt increased from

TABLE 11
External Public Debt Outstanding in Latin America, 1960–79
(in millions of U.S. dollars)

	1960	1970	1975	1979
Argentina	1,275	2,455	5,217	10,963
Bolivia	179	549	1,222	2,759
Brazil	2,407	4,680	17,368	47,522
Chile	562	2,534	4,388	5,461
Colombia	377	1,850	3,011	5,419
Costa Rica	55	227	732	1,869
Dominican Republic	6	290	662	1,533
Ecuador	95	352	779	3,110
El Salvador	33	126	383	734
Guatemala	51	176	282	836
Haiti	38	45	106	346
Honduras	23	144	449	1,186
Mexico	1,151	3,792	13,821	36,016
Nicaragua	41	222	821	1,456
Panama	59	290	1,128	2,571
Paraguay	22	158	433	1,111
Peru	265	1,092	4,002	7,983
Uruguay	132	351	1,033	1,327
Venezuela	363	924	1,393	10,239

Source: Inter-American Development Bank, *Economic and Social Progress in Latin America, 1980–81 Report* (Washington, D.C.: IADB, 1981), p. 438.

about $18 billion to over $150 billion. Since the 1973 and 1979 oil crises, the rate of increase in external debt has accelerated, with a growing proportion of the debt owed to private Western banks. The causes of this expansion include rising interest rates, declining commodity prices, a sluggish international economy which stifled export growth, and increasing protectionism within many Western nations. By September 1982 Mexico had the largest external debt in the Third World, owing in U.S. dollars about $80 billion, of which $56 billion was obligated to private foreign banks. Similarly, Brazil's external debt in early 1983 was about $90 billion. By the end of 1983, Latin American nations had accumulated over $300 billion in foreign debts, half the total of all foreign debts owed by Third World nations. Nations such as Argentina, Bolivia, Brazil, Chile, Costa Rica, Ecuador, Mexico, Panama, and Peru have seriously mortgaged their future to pay for their present development. Many of these countries were compelled to negotiate nationally humiliating agreements with the IMF in order to reschedule old loans and to receive new loans. The price for these agreements were austerity packages—that is, policies designed to sta-

TABLE 12
Ratio of External Public Debt Service to Value of Exports of Goods and Services in Latin America, 1960–79 (in percent)

	1960	1970	1975	1979
Argentina	20.5	21.8	22.5	16.1
Bolivia	27.6	11.0	14.6	29.6
Brazil	38.7	12.6	17.4	37.4
Chile	14.2	19.2	28.7	26.8
Colombia	13.9	11.9	11.5	13.4
Costa Rica	4.8	10.0	10.6	23.4
Dominican Republic	n.a.	4.7	5.0	14.1
Ecuador	7.1	9.3	4.5	30.0
El Salvador	2.6	3.5	9.1	2.5
Guatemala	1.5	7.4	1.7	2.2
Haiti	3.6	7.5	7.5	4.1
Honduras	2.8	3.0	4.9	13.1
Mexico	15.5	24.2	25.5	65.5
Nicaragua	3.8	11.2	12.5	8.3
Panama	1.6	7.6	8.5	35.1
Paraguay	6.8	11.2	10.5	9.3
Peru	10.5	11.7	26.1	22.6
Uruguay	5.8	21.7	41.4	10.3
Venezuela	4.4	3.0	5.8	10.4

Source: Inter-American Development Bank, *Economic and Social Progress in Latin America, 1980–81 Report* (Washington, D.C.: IADB, 1981), p. 443.
Note: n.a. = not available.

bilize the economy by reducing national consumption and increasing exports. The unanswered question for Latin American nations threatened by the debt crisis is whether stabilizing their economies will destabilize their political systems.

Unless most Latin American countries increase their exports dramatically, especially those who must import oil, the balance of payments problem will get worse. For as the per capita income of a nation increases, "the structure of demand changes and the demand for goods with a higher import content increases more rapidly. This occurs because the middle and higher income sectors . . . keep wanting more complex goods as their simpler needs are satisfied and their incomes increase."[37]

Thus a dilemma: given the distribution of income in Latin America, the consumer-oriented growth that does take place does not generate a sufficient amount of foreign exchange to sustain that growth rate for a continuous period of time. Instead, most nations endure a stop-go pattern of economic expansion brought about by a limited capacity to import. Each time the pace of economic growth quickens, increased prosperity registers an increased demand for imported foreign goods or goods produced domestically either by foreign subsidiaries or by local firms who frequently hold foreign patents. As imports expand, profits and royalty payments flow out of the country, and the nation inevitably confronts a balance of payments crisis in which the government is forced to step in and put on the brakes by severely restricting credit. Too often under the ISI strategy and the terms of international lending agencies, the balance of payments problem can be "solved" only at the expense of a serious slow-down of economic growth over several years.

Conclusion

The term "politics of accumulation" refers to the choices and policies that officials in Latin America have followed to promote economic growth within their nations. The goal of economic growth is clearly a public responsibility in Latin America and a component of national security. A growing economy is an ally of the ruling government; a declining economy is an adversary. Because of the pressures of nationalism, soaring population growth, and the conviction that rational policymaking is capable of bringing about rapid economic development, the regime that fails to produce economic growth is likely to lose its legitimacy and be overthrown. Thus, promoting economic growth is a matter of political survival for the top policymakers in Latin America. However, achieving economic growth is only one of their aims. Other goals that also influence decision making, sometimes at the expense of economic growth, might include: preservation of the social status quo, changes in the social status quo, a more equitable distribution of income (Castro's Cuba has championed this goal at the expense of economic growth), and a reduction of national dependence. These diverse and frequently inconsistent aims of Latin American policymakers mean that no government can focus solely on economic growth as a policy goal.

In any case, Latin American nations have tried to accelerate their rate of economic growth, especially since the end of World War II. The strategy selected to pursue this goal, first in an ad hoc manner, later in a more systematic way as ECLA formulated a coherent package of policies, was import substitution industrialization. This policy was based on substituting the domestic production of manufactured goods for what was previously imported. It was assumed that after substituting national production for previously imported light con-sumer goods, there would be a steady progression of national produc-tion replacing foreign production in ever more sophisticated products until even capital goods were predominantly made in Latin America. With the unanticipated "aid" of multinational corporations, the ISI strategy was able to transform the economies so that most countries now produce most of their manufactured goods within their borders, but—with the exception of Argentina, Brazil, and Mexico—most capital goods still have to be imported. And even these three large countries are technologically dependent upon the industrialized coun-tries. Latin American nations do not create—and frequently do not even adapt to their own purposes—the technologies used in their in-dustrial sector.

It is part of the style of Latin American policymaking that the ISI strategy is frequently evaluated as being a total failure, when in real-ity it has made some significant contributions to the region's develop-ment, despite enormous obstacles. The ISI strategy had to overcome the antidevelopmental legacy of 300 years of Spanish and Portuguese colonialism, the political instability of the nineteenth and twentieth centuries, and the problems caused by a rapidly expanding popula-tion. It is therefore not surprising that the results of ISI policies have been disappointing.

In summary, the ISI strategy can be criticized for the following rea-sons: it neglected agriculture and population control; it engaged in horizontal rather than vertical specialization, which resulted in an ex-cessive diversification and insufficient exports of manufactured goods; it did not lead the Latin American nations into developing their own technology, thus forcing them to pay premium prices for foreign tech-nologies that are not suited to their needs; it overprotected entrepre-neurs; it led to an overemphasis on consumerism; it failed to change the skewed income distribution; it failed to reduce the unemployment rate; and it did not liberate the region from balance of payments difficulties. ISI policies have produced economic growth but in a spo-radic, stop-go pattern. The lack of continuous growth is caused by a combination of the following reasons: new industries grow until their expansion is checked by the fact that anywhere from 40 to 60 percent of the national population do not have the money to buy industrial products; entrepreneurs in overly protected markets are reluctant to risk exporting in the far more competitive international field; and when Latin American nations suffer from balance of payments crises, they have to restrict imports of the capital goods that make growth possible. In brief, critics can point to evidence indicating that because of the ISI strategy privileged groups got richer, the poor remained poor, and foreign debt increased.

The inability of exports to produce adequate funds to finance advanced industrialization has caused a number of nations to change their strategies of development and to embrace neoliberal policies that are more concerned with controlling inflation, expanding and diversifying their exports, and receiving loans from international lending agencies and foreign private commercial banks. These policies have been stymied by the debt crisis of the early 1980s which now threatens to impede economic growth for the next several years.

However, these economic growth policies have also helped to create social and political conditions that engender growing pressures for greater social justice in the distribution of goods, services, and income. Thus, while policymakers were stressing the politics of accumulation, they were also increasingly forced to shift gears and play the politics of distribution. We turn to this subject in chapter 3.

The Politics of Distribution

Most regimes in Latin America have stressed the accumulation of wealth instead of its equitable distribution. This has led many scholars to ignore how often and in what manner Latin American governments have responded to the ever expanding demands for distributive justice. Perhaps the labeling of so many governments in Latin America as conservative or reactionary has led scholars to assume that the prevailing response to popular demands for a better life is repression. While this frequently has been the reaction, another response has been the formulation of distributive policies that, although inadequate to meet the growing needs of an expanding population, can hardly be called "reactionary." It is worth noting that Latin American military expenditures are a small percentage of total expenditures. In fact, most Latin American governments engage in a wide range of distributive policies—from subsidizing public transportation to providing public health programs.

The purpose of this chapter is to analyze and compare distributive policies in Latin America. Its sections will deal with the concept of distributive policies, income distribution, agrarian reform, education, social security, and health care.

Distributive Policies

Added to the traditional functions of the state, such as providing law and order, is the relatively new responsibility of providing a more equitable distribution of wealth, property, and human services. The distributional patterns established by tradition or the market are no longer considered sacrosanct; all are aware that they can be changed, for better or worse, by public policy. All public policies have distributional consequences. Conversely, all distributional policies have a political foundation. In the words of Almond and Powell, "While the actual distribution of benefits and values in a society is the product of the economic and social systems as well as the political, the political system is a peculiarly important factor because it is the most comprehensive instrument of collective goal attainment in a society and may employ compulsory means."[1]

In the West, the distributive patterns that resulted from nineteenth-century capitalism are no longer politically acceptable in the twentieth. The response of Western nations during this century has been the welfare state. Beginnng with Bismarck's Germany in the 1880s, the creation of the welfare state has essentially been an attempt to humanize the consequences of capitalism by increasing the social responsibilities of the government. According to Harold Wilensky, "The essence of the welfare state is government-protected minimum standards of income, nutrition, health, housing, and education, assured to every citizen as a political right, not as charity."[2] Asa Briggs defines the welfare state as

> a state in which organized power is deliberately used (through politics and administration) in an effort to modify the play of market forces in at least three directions—first, by guaranteeing individuals and families a minimum income irrespective of the market value of their work or their property; second, by narrowing the extent of insecurity by enabling individuals and families to meet certain "social contingencies" (for example, sickness, old age and unemployment) which lead otherwise to individual and family crises; and third, by ensuring that all citizens without distinction of status or class are offered the best standards available in relation to a certain agreed range of social services.[3]

It is this idea of the welfare state, combined with the fear of what happened in the Russian and Chinese revolutions, and most recently, in the Cuban Revolution, that has influenced the evolution of distributive policies in Latin America.

Just as many Latin Americans believe that the state must intervene to promote economic growth, similarly, many believe that the state must intervene for distributive purposes. The assumption is that neither economic growth nor distributive justice will occur spontaneously. Reformers in Latin America are especially sensitive to the inadequacy of the free market as a means for achieving a more equitable distribution of income. Obviously, trading in international markets has not brought about an equitable distribution of income between Latin America and its Western trading partners. Even the supporters of the market economy stress that "the function of the market is efficiency in the allocation of resources (and rewards), not distributive justice."[4] Consequently, the idea has spread and intensified among many Latin American policymakers that distributive policies are at least as important, and sometimes more so for the sake of political survival, than growth policies. For example, the 1970 Colombian development plan stated, "The problem of lesser developed countries today is to combine marked social welfare with the achievement of growth."[5] Similarly, President Echevarria of Mexico in his 1970 inaugural address proclaimed, "Those who maintain that we must grow first in order to distribute afterward are either mistaken or lying out of self-interest. . . . Employment and productivity must be increased more rapidly, and to accomplish this, it is indispensable to expand the domestic market and share income more equitably."[6]

The idea that a developing nation should accumulate wealth first and then distribute it later is based upon the experience of Western nations whose economic development occurred at an earlier time. The post–World War II literature, as summarized by David Felix, stressed the "universality of a long-run bell-shaped relationship between growth and distributional equity, along with the notion that rising inequality increases savings and capital accumulation. The two notions were readily combined by many into a comforting model of self-limiting inequality. The initial growth of inequality accelerates economic growth, which accelerates the growth of demand for labor, which leads more quickly to excess demand in the labor market, rising wages, and a reversal of the inequality trend."[7] Unfortunately, the development of the various Latin American economies has not followed the path of the older Western economies; the Latin nations continue to be plagued by a population explosion, an excess supply of labor, and social inequality.

Under these circumstances, the state's legitimacy in the eyes of its citizens is now increasingly contingent upon the promotion of economic growth and distributive justice. The undisputed idea that economic growth is of absolute value had a much shorter period of ascendancy in Latin America than in Western Europe and the United States. Whereas in the 1950s the ideal norm of public policy in Latin America might have been summarized by the notion of *crecimiento con estabilidad* (growth with stability), by the mid-1960s the new ideal was *desarrollo compartido* (shared development). Intellectuals who had supported *desarrollismo* (developmentalism) in the 1950s turned the word into a pejorative term by the mid-1960s. Raúl Prebisch bluntly states, "Any system which fails to imbue the economy with the required degree of dynamism, and to promote more equitable income distribution, will have irrevocably forfeited the right to survive."[8] Western nations in the nineteenth century did not have to provide for both of these goals to maintain their legitimacy, but Latin American nations do today. Moreover, it is difficult to achieve either goal, and it is immeasurably harder—some would say impossible—to achieve both simultaneously. W. Arthur Lewis captures the complexity of these policy problems with his "two horse" metaphor: "The less developed countries have awakened into a century where everybody wishes to ride two horses simultaneously, the horse of economic equality, and the horse of economic development."[9] Nations pursuing economic growth policies, which frequently promote social inequality, are also issuing "inequality-reduction" social policies; the possibilities of foul-ups are obviously enormous. The models for these social policies are taken from the more developed Western nations, who often supply Latin America with expert advisors to help plan and implement such policies. The problem is that the political, economic, and administrative conditions are so different in Latin America that distributive policies taken from the Western democracies frequently do not function effectively. Political legitimacy in Latin America can no longer be achieved through legality; it can only be obtained through public policies that successfully fulfill at least minimum standards of well-being for most citizens.

For an idea of the complexity of the issues involved, let us review the requirements of a successful distributive policy. First, from an economist's point of view, "The challenge is to strike a balance between the extremely great, often distorted, socially untenable, and economically too costly inequalities and the utopian complete equality, which is consumption promoting but incentive stifling and investment depressing."[10] Second, distributive policies should be designed so as not to increase external dependence by augmenting chronic balance of payments problems. Third, it is necessary to figure out the particular determinants of income distribution—which will vary from country to country—and distinguish which of these factors is susceptible to manipulation and control by public policy. Fourth, the beneficiaries—the target social groups—should be precisely identified. Fifth, because of the wide variety of rural and urban poverty groups, no single policy (agrarian reform or social security) will achieve an extensive social impact; there must be a well-coordinated *set* of distributive policies designed to alleviate the effects of poverty for different social groups in different parts of the nation. Sixth, channeling resources to the marginal sectors of a developing society demands the creation of an administrative infrastructure. Seventh, "For these policies to exercise a tangible and definitely progressive influence, they should fulfill certain fundamental conditions; a substantial margin of resources should be mobilized; the services provided should give clear preference to the 'poorest,' and their cost should be mainly financed by the 'richest.' "[11] Finally, the decisive political support necessary for these policies is often lacking. Foxley points out, "The problem may reside in the fact that the social groups to be benefited by redistribution are usually those with the lowest level of organization, internal cohesion, and ability to pressure the state apparatus. It is necessary, then, to design policies that open the way for these groups to participate in power so that the advances they attain become irreversible."[12] In reviewing this list, one can understand why it is likely that most distributional policies will not be successful.

Income Distribution in Latin America

The manner in which a society distributes its income is perhaps the most important measure of its real attitudes toward social justice. Weisskoff and Figueroa describe the measurement of income distribution as "a type of social scorecard, the resolution of claims by competing groups for the economy's outputs."[13] The tragedy for social justice in Latin America is that since colonial times only a few privileged groups have been free to compete for shares in the economy's output, with the result that most Latin nations are characterized by a highly skewed income distribution. That is, a few are rich and many are poor. As a result of development, the structure of the original income distribution established during the colonial period has become more complex, but its essential characteristics remain entrenched. There is still too wide a gap between the rich and poor, and most important, still too many are poor. ECLA estimates that the proportion of the population living in poverty is about 10 percent in Argentina; between 10 and 25 percent in Costa Rica, Chile, and Venezuela; about 40 percent in Mexico; between 40 and 55 percent in Brazil, Colombia, and Peru; between 60 and 70 percent in Honduras, El Salvador, Guatemala, and the Dominican Republic; and over 80 percent in Bolivia and Haiti.

The income distribution in a nation is determined by a number of economic and public policy factors. According to Ricardo Ffrench-Davis,

The most visible among them are degree of concentration of ownership and earnings of capital on the one hand, and employment and wage levels on the other. The distribution determined by these factors—often called the functional distribution of income—is altered by taxation on capital and labor and by the social security system. The resulting profile—called personal distribution of income—is mainly a reflection of earnings in monetary form. This portrays only part of the distributive situation, for in various Latin American countries, state provision of collective goods and services, such as education, health care, and mass housing, has been growing in importance.[14]

The dilemma for Latin America is that concentrating the earnings of capital in the hands of large landowners and protected industrialists, combined with high unemployment, underemployment, and low wage levels in traditional occupations, maintains gross inequalities. It would take enormous efforts to overcome the inequalities resulting from this "original," functional distribution of income.

According to the neoclassical view of economics, during the early stages of industrialization income inequalities are functional because (1) growth depends on investment in physical capital; (2) this investment depends on savings; (3) savings in nonsocialist societies are contingent upon having a large proportion of the limited national wealth concentrated in the possession of a small number of people rich enough to be able to save even after fulfilling their consumption desires. Under the logic of this reasoning, income transferred from the rich to the poor will inevitably be consumed by the poor and thus such a transfer of income will impede the capital formation that is indispensable for economic growth. In Latin America this reasoning rests on a questionable base because it assumes that the rich have a reasonable propensity to save which can be channeled into the accumulation of capital. But if a high proportion of the rich consume imported luxury goods and refuse to save or invest within their own country because of economic and political insecurity, the economic justification for allowing these inequalities breaks down. Under these circumstances—and these *are* the circumstances that prevail in Latin America—the unequal distribution of income is dysfunctional for capital formation. However, this neoclassical view does remind policymakers that they should search for distributive policies that will not interfere with capital formation.

Most social scientists familiar with Latin America condemn the unequal income distribution as "bad," something that ought to be changed by public policy or revolution. But they are uncharacteristically reticent about what a "good" and desired level of income distribution should be. They stress that social justice requires a more equitable level of income distribution, but they avoid being specific, although greater precision is possible; there are measurements of income distribution. One popular measure is the Gini Index, a figure defined as one minus the area beneath the country's cumulative income curve divided by the area under the hypothetical complete equality line. The limits to the Gini Index are 0.0 (complete equality) and 1.0 (complete inequality). For advanced economies of the socialist or mixed-market type, the index ranges from 0.25 to 0.40.[15] As we shall see, the index is considerably higher among Latin American nations; in Mexico, for example, it was above 0.60 during the 1960s.

Although precise evidence is not available, it may well be that income distribution in the Western nations was never as unequal as it has been in Latin America from the colonial period to the present day. In any case, in the market economies of the West, the tendency for income to become concentrated in the hands of a few has been counterbalanced to some extent by (a) allowing the working class to mobilize in pursuit of higher wages, and (b) implementing national distributive policies to protect the needy (special cases of bypassed sectors—old people, minorities who have suffered from discrimination, the handicapped, and so forth). The evidence suggests that allowing the working class to mobilize is far more significant than distributive policies in altering the distribution of income within a nation.[16] The immense sums of money spent on distributive programs in Western nations "appear to have very marginal impacts on the overall structure of inequality among income groups," writes Hugh Heclo. "This does not mean that the redistribution achieved is unimportant, only that it is fairly meager compared to the capacities of modern societies to generate and preserve inequality."[17] Thus in most Latin American countries the income distribution structure remains fairly rigid because of the initially skewed system established during the colonial period, the weak and usually repressed working class (see chapter 5), and the inability of most distributive policies to change the basic pattern of income distribution.

We should also be aware of a crucial point, namely, that there are major differences between the poor in the industrialized countries and in Latin America. In the former, the poor are composed of what can be labeled "special cases," that is, the elderly, the temporarily unemployed, the sick or injured, and the very young worker. According to ECLA, "In Western Europe about half those in the first and second deciles [that is, those with the lowest incomes] are not active members of the labour force. On the basis of family incomes the two major groups at the bottom are the old and families with a female head. The very rapid rise from the minimum income level in the industrial countries is, for the most part, a reflection of moving from these special cases to those who are normal members of the labour force. Even the lowest incomes received as active, full-time members of the labour force tend to be sharply higher than the minimum."[18]

The situation in Latin America is starkly different; therefore, when the Latin American nations imitate and adapt the distributive policies of the industrialized West, the effects are frequently unexpected and inappropriate to the problems they are meant to solve. For example, in Latin America much higher proportions of the population are unemployed or underemployed. Moreover, large proportions of the urban work force and even more rural workers receive very low incomes. In contrast to incomes in Western Europe, in Latin America there is no steep rise from the minimum income level to the average. Most of the very poor are not "special cases," as they are regarded in the industrialized countries, and their plight is not amenable to social security and welfare programs: pensions, unemployment benefits, sickness or accident benefits, assistance to women with dependent children, and so forth. Such programs "will do little or nothing to raise minimum income levels," reports the ECLA. "Most of those at the bottom are active members of the labour force and do not qualify for benefits of this kind."[19] Indeed, as we shall see, some distributive policies in Latin America protect the better-off members of the labor force rather than those poverty-stricken workers who need help the most.

For the most part, the distribution of income in Latin America is more uneven than in the industrialized countries. In the United States and Great Britain, countries with a middle degree of income inequality, the top 5 percent receive 20 percent of total income. In Norway and Sweden, the top 5 percent receive less than 20 percent and in France the top 5 percent receive about 25 percent of the total income. By contrast, in most Latin American nations, the top 5 percent receive more than 30 percent of total income. While in the industrialized nations the bulk of the population has an income fairly close to the national average, in Latin America usually some 70 to 80 percent of

TABLE 13
Distribution of Income in Latin America, 1965

Income Group	Percentage of Total Income Received	Average per Capita Income[a]
Top 5 percent	33.4	$2,600
15 percent below the top 5 percent	29.2	750
30 percent above the median	24.1	310
30 percent below the median	10.3	130
Lowest 20 percent	3.1	60

Source: ECLA, *Income Distribution in Latin America* (New York: United Nations, 1971), p. 35.
a. These values are for 1965 but are expressed in terms of 1960 U.S. dollars.

the population receives an income lower than the national average. From another perspective, in the United States and Great Britain, the top 5 percent receive about four times the national average income; in most of Latin America the income of the same group is about six to seven times the average national income.[20]

An overview of the distribution of income in Latin America is provided in table 13. Hidden within these figures are the entirely different social realities experienced by the few rich and endured by the many poor in Latin America. While the rich enjoy a consumption-oriented life style comparable to that experienced in the United States, the poor battle for survival. While the rich take their children to Florida to visit Disney World, the children of the poor struggle to avoid disease and malnutrition. Carlos Díaz-Alejandro writes:

While the strictly economic growth justification for redistribution is shaky, the ethical and political cases for it are very strong. Income and wealth disparities tolerated yesterday become increasingly objectionable. A social system in which the brains of masses of poor children are permanently damaged by malnutrition while a few citizens enjoy luxuries found rarely even in industrialized countries is not only repugnant but also anachronistic. . . . Furthermore, Latin America is already at an income level where extreme poverty could be eradicated.[21]

TABLE 14
Distribution of Income in Selected Latin American Countries, 1970

	El Salvador	Costa Rica	Mexico	Venezuela	Argentina
Top 5 percent	32.9	35.0	29.0	26.5	31.2
15 percent below top 5 percent	28.4	25.0	29.5	31.5	22.9
30 percent above the median	22.6	22.0	26.1	27.7	25.4
30 percent below the median	10.5	12.5	11.8	11.3	15.3
Lowest 20 percent	5.5	5.5	3.6	3.0	5.2

Source: Richard Weisskoff and Adolfo Figueroa, "Traversing the Social Pyramid: A Comparative Review of Income Distribution in Latin America," *Latin American Research Review* 11, no. 2 (1976), 93.

However, the available data from different Latin American countries given in tables 14 and 15 indicate that, despite economic growth, poverty is by no means being eradicated. In Argentina the lowest 20 percent of the population receives only 5 percent of the national income. Within Latin America, Argentina is unique in that the middle 60 percent of its population receives 40.7 percent of the total, a figure higher than in any other country in the region. In the industrialized countries, however, this same group receives about 50 percent of the total income. In Argentina, "the top 5 percent received 31.2 percent of all personal income in 1961, and had an average income over four times that of even the 15 percent below the top. . . . Even within this top group the inequality is extreme. The top one percent alone received 16.3 percent of total income, and had an average income of

TABLE 15
Income Concentration in Urban and Rural Sectors of Six Latin American Countries, 1965

	Gini Index Coefficient	
	Urban	Rural
Argentina	.461	.496
Brazil	.629	.458
Chile	.440	.393
Colombia	.553	.570
Mexico	.512	.462
Venezuela	.427	.440

Source: Albert Berry and Miguel Urrutia, *Income Distribution in Colombia* (New Haven, Conn.: Yale University Press, 1976), p. 41.

some 27,000 dollars in 1961."[22] The same ECLA study reports that agriculture now accounts for no more than one-fifth of the income of the top 5 percent; instead, since the end of World War II, the possession of capital and commercial and financial positions in the cities has accounted for most of the income of the top 5 percent. The urban self-employed dominate the top income group.

The problem of income distribution and distributive public policies in Argentina is summarized by Gary Wynia:

> One of the principal shortcomings of Argentine policymakers after 1945 had been their failure to institutionalize a process of continuous income redistribution, especially through the tax system. In fact, less than 1 percent of the national income had been redistributed annually through income taxes. . . . Nor had the much publicized transfer of income through other means done much better. Income subsidies, for example, transferred only 0.4 percent of total family purchasing power from the upper 80 percent of the income scale to the lower 20 percent, while social security shifted only 3 percent of family income in favor of the lower 90 percent. This sad fact was due primarily to large-scale evasion and under declaration of income as well as government timidity in the area of progressive tax reforms; it is estimated, for example, that throughout the period only about 25 percent of the taxable income of entrepreneurs and rentiers was declared for tax purposes.[23]

In Colombia there was little interest in the issue of income distribution or the impact of major policy decisions on income distribution until the late 1960s; however, Colombian scholars, foreign scholars, and government officials have by now accumulated evidence which shows that the country has an extremely uneven distribution of income. A study by Albert Berry and Miguel Urrutia reveals that in the urban areas 1.5 percent of the labor force controls about 15 percent of total income, and those in the top two deciles control 60 percent of the income. The poorest 30 percent of the labor forces earns a meager 4.5 percent of all income. The situation is worse in the countryside where 1.5 percent of the work force controls 27 percent of the income, and the top two deciles have 65 percent of the income. Comparing Colombia to Great Britain, Berry and Urrutia note that the proportion of total income received by the poor in Colombia is about half the proportion received by a similar group in the United Kingdom, while the rich receive twice as great a proportion.[24] The redistribution of 8 percent of the national income of Colombia would double the income of the bottom quarter of the population and eliminate Colombia's extreme poverty. But the Colombian figures also suggest that the poorest sectors of society generally do not benefit from the kind of economic growth (a respectable 5 percent per year since the 1950s) the nation has been experiencing.[25]

Mexico has experienced steady and impressive economic growth rates since the 1940s, but the results have been disappointing from the perspective of distributive justice. Despite Mexico's heritage of violent revolution and extensive agrarian reform, the material conditions of the poorest 40 percent of Mexican families have changed little since 1910. Mexican development has benefited the upper 60 percent of families, but the proportional gains have been far greater for the top 20 percent. From 1940 to 1975, Felix reports, "The share of national income of the upper 80th–95th percentiles of households rose as much as that of the top 5 percent, and even the 40th–80th percentiles, whose share of national income fell moderately, had, nevertheless, a substantial increase of real income. Only the poorest 40 percent had no real income gain and suffered a severe drop of income share."[26] Between 1950 and 1969, the ratio of the average income of the top 5 percent to that of the bottom 40 percent increased from 22:1 to 34:1. Regional disparities in income levels were also not changed during this period of economic growth. Beneath these figures is a social reality: over half the Mexican population suffers from malnutrition. In brief, the developmental record of Mexico suggests that economic growth does not automatically reduce income inequalities. Given the power relations in Mexico, and in Latin America generally, little of the economic surplus generated by growth "trickles down" to the bottom 40 percent of the population. Power relations are more important in distributing income in Latin America than market relations.

Neither the export economies of the nineteenth century nor the import-substitution policies of the twentieth have brought about—nor were they intended to bring about—a more equitable income distribution. Instead, the uneasy grafting of modern sectors onto primitive economies has made the distribution of income more complex but still basically unequal. According to the ECLA, the "rapid growth of a modern sector which has reached a substantial size, but which exists alongside a still large primitive sector, can be expected to introduce great inequality among wage and salary earners themselves. The total inequality in such a case, and even the concentration at the top of the scale, may then be explained in part by the split between wage and profit income, and the great inequality in the distribution of the latter; but it will also be due to an important extent to the inequality which comes to characterize wage and salary incomes themselves."[27] The principal recipient of profit income in Latin America is not the *rentier* or the corporation, but the self-employed. It is easy and *customary* for the self-employed—who dominate the top 5 percent in each country— to evade taxes, which makes the redistribution of income under present conditions nearly impossible.

Here we should again make it clear that a small transfer of income from the tiny rich minority at the top of the scale could have a significant impact on the very poor. For example, Richard Webb has amassed data showing that in Peru "a selective transfer of 5 percent of the national income, taken from the top 1 percent, and given to the first (poorest) quartile, would reduce absolute incomes at the top by only 16 percent and would *double* incomes for a third of the population. If the alternative to redistribution is growth, a highly successful development effort consisting of sustained 3 percent per annum real growth in all incomes would require over 20 years to achieve the same improvement for the bottom third and much longer if one discounts for the waiting involved."[28]

The limited evidence accumulated so far suggests that the process of economic growth in Latin America during recent decades has not benefited the largest sectors of the population. Weisskoff and Figueroa distinguish between two patterns of redistribution associated with growth: "first, the transfer of income shares from the bottom 90 percent to the top 10 percent [as in Brazil]; second, the 'twisting' of the distribution away from the bottom-most 60 percent and top-most 5 percent toward a greater share for the middle 61–95 percentiles [as in Mexico]. Whichever the pattern of redistribution during growth, one fact is clear from these findings: So called development implies a loss of relative shares from the bottom 60 percent."[29] Similarly, in *Income Distribution in Colombia*—probably the most careful and cautious income distribution study for any Latin American nation—Berry and Urrutia conclude that in Colombia between 1930 and 1970 income distribution in agriculture worsened throughout the period, and "non-agricultural income distribution probably worsened from the mid-1930s until some time in the 1950s, then improved till some time in the mid-1960s, and then tended to level off."[30]

In short, the nations of Latin America came into existence with an inequitable income distribution due to the nature of their colonial experiences. Neither the policies of export growth in the nineteenth century nor the import substitution strategy of the twentieth has created a more equitable distribution. Consequently, the bottom 40 percent in every Latin American country, and sometimes even the bottom 60 percent, remains stuck in unyielding poverty. It is difficult to believe that any government in Latin America will be able to attain legitimacy and stability until these gross disparities in income distribution are reduced.

Agrarian Reform

Scholars interested in Latin America have probably studied agrarian policies more than any other policy area. Most agree that the persistence of archaic agricultural patterns has had a disastrous effect on the region; traditional agriculture has prevented—or, at best, slowed down—the modernization of Latin American societies. Since the colonial period, agriculture has been dominated by large estates, or latifundios, which have stifled development. The latifundio system has been held responsible for the initial unequal distribution of income; the stagnation of agriculture; the tradition of evading taxes; the creation of the *minifundio* system (which provides a surplus pool of cheap labor for the owners of the large estates [hacendados]); holding a large proportion of the rural population in debt peonage; attracting investment funds into land speculation as a hedge against inflation (which reduces the capital available for industrialization); widespread malnutrition; and finally, the fact that, even with significant portions of the population working in agriculture, many Latin American countries have to import food. "The *latifundio* is at the root of the social problem in Latin American culture," writes Jacques Lambert, "while the *minifundio* is responsible for its economic problem."[31]

As a society modernizes, economists assign three major roles to the agricultural sector: to produce more food for the growing population, to increase rural income so as to stimulate demand for the products of the new industrial sector, and to generate exports. With the possible exception of Argentina, agriculture in Latin America has failed to fulfill any of these three roles. In terms of production, the 40 percent of the labor force that worked in agriculture in 1980—compared to the 48 percent in 1960—produced less than 15 percent of the gross domestic product. Between 1960 and 1975, the rural population expanded from 101 million to 115.5 million while the urban population exploded from 98.7 million to 186.9 million. Despite the fact that 38 percent of its population (a declining percentage) lived in the rural areas, there were 42 million Latin Americans (a rising figure) suffering from malnutrition in 1975.[32] According to the UN Food and Agriculture Organization, "Latin America needs to increase food production 3.6 percent annually for the next 15 years just to keep up with its population growth and to maintain its trade balance. In order to eliminate malnutrition in the region, the area needs a 4.5 percent increase in annual production during the same period. Until now, Latin America has failed to sustain even the lower growth figures over a period of several years."[33]

The picture is equally bleak for the other two roles assigned to agriculture: increasing income and generating exports. The few rich members of the rural sector are far more skilled in evading taxes than they are in scientific farming. Moreover, their life styles are characterized by conspicuous consumption, which means that their capital is not utilized to modernize farming or to invest heavily in the industrial sector. The many poor people in the rural regions live at a subsistence level. For the most part, they are not part of the money economy and so do not increase the demand for industrial goods nor generate an economic surplus for themselves. In the early 1970s per capita peasant incomes in Latin America, except for Argentina where they are higher, averaged from an equivalent of less than US$40 to little over US$80. In 1970 it was estimated that there were 8,700,000 landless peasants (agricultural workers), 5,300,000 peasants (*minifundistas*) who owned altogether 4 percent of the agricultural land, 7,000,000 who owned small and medium-sized farms, or 56 percent of the land, and 440,000 large landholders who owned 40 percent of the land.[34] Under these conditions, the most viable strategy for raising incomes of the rural poor entails a major land redistribution whereby the large landholders yield some of their property to the peasants.

Given the traditional power of the large landowners, democratic reformers such as Uruguay's José Batlle y Ordoñez hoped that agrarian modernization could be induced without painful interventions by the state in the countryside. However, it is exactly because of the traditional power of the great landowners that the state was forced to initiate agrarian reform policies during the 1960s. No matter how harmful *latifundismo* was for national interests—and particularly for the bulk of the rural population—this system was not going to self-destruct or spontaneously reform itself as the process of industrialization continued. Indeed, one of the tragedies in Latin America is that virtually no institution spontaneously reforms itself. The rich and powerful do not willingly give up their wealth and power, least of all the hacendados.

Mexican sociologist Edmundo Flores has described an agrarian reform policy as essentially a revolutionary measure that transfers property, power, and status from one group to another. An authentic agrarian reform policy, in his words, "is a redistributive measure which transfers the ownership of land and, therefore, its income, . . . from the landlord minority which monopolized it, to the peasants who worked it but received only a minimal fraction of its produce. Its ultimate purpose is the same as that of all other redistributive measures . . . to reduce the income and consumption of the group that is taxed and to shift elsewhere the resources released."[35] For Flores, colonization projects on previously unused lands (as in the Amazon basin), new hybrid seeds, the construction of rural roads, irrigation projects, rural literacy and health campaigns do not constitute agrarian reform policies. Worse, they are frequently used as *substitutes* for authentic agrarian reform programs. These efforts to increase efficiency, though necessary, do not alter income distribution or the social structure and should more properly follow land reform rather than replacing it.

Most Latin American countries, encouraged by the financial and political support of the United States in the Alliance for Progress, enacted agrarian reform bills during the 1960s. Only Mexico (1915), Bolivia (1953), and Cuba (1959) passed such laws before that time. Venezuela enacted land reform legislation in 1960; Haiti, Panama, the Dominican Republic, and Colombia in 1962; El Salvador, Costa Rica, Nicaragua, and Paraguay in 1963; and Brazil and Ecuador in 1964. Most of these laws were passed in a defensive reaction to the growing militancy of peasants and in increasing fear on the part of urban elites of agrarian revolutions such as those of Mexico, Bolivia, and Cuba. These laws were passed over the vehement protests of conservative landed interests; they reflected *not* the government's commitment to agrarian reform, but the government's calculation that such laws would prevent the violent mobilization of peasants. A review of the land reform legislation of the 1960s, in which there are striking similarities among the laws of various countries, supports this generalization.

The constitutions of all Latin American countries, with the exception of Cuba, are dedicated to the preservation and protection of private property. Most agrarian reform statutes employ the concept of the "social function of land"—instead of "land to the tillers"—as the formal grounds to justify the expropriation of land from large estates. According to these laws, land fulfills its social function when it is efficiently and productively used; it does not when it is not utilized or is inefficiently exploited. Ernest Feder points out, concerning land reform laws:

> Expropriation is in the public interest if land in estates is not used in the public interest. Identifying the social function of land with the use of land means that attention is now focused on efficiency and intensity of land use, or, better, on output and productivity on individual enterprises, rather than on the social inequities inherent in an unequal distribution of land. . . . A further consequence is that expropriation now need not be undertaken on a large scale to wipe out these inequities, but only on an estate to estate basis, *each case* being judged on its own merits.[36]

Phrases such as "efficiently used" or "adequately managed" are vague and usually undefined in the laws, a vagueness that leaves it up to the discretion of agrarian reform institute bureaucrats to decide their meaning. Over the long run, decisions are more likely to favor the large landowners than the peasant. Given the nature of Latin American bureaucracies in general, and agrarian reform institutes in particular, case-by-case decisions regarding whether land should be expropriated from large estates and given to the peasantry ensure that land distribution will move at either a snail's pace or not at all.

The social function concept has other negative consequences for agrarian reform. First, it makes it likely that the best farm land will not be available for expropriations while the least productive land, frequently at a great distance from markets, will be available for a small number of peasants. Under these circumstances, in which the peasant farmers are doomed to failure, the fiction can be maintained that the peasants are incapable of being productive farmers on their own. Second, the concept allows landowners to fulfill their "social function" by transforming their estates into more productive farms—sometimes by firing rural laborers and buying modern machinery—and thus to avoid expropriation. Finally, the laws do not specify the times when the use, nonuse, or inadequate use of land will be considered relevant.

All Latin American agrarian reform laws allow the large land-owners, even when land is expropriated from them, to retain a portion of their estates in reserve. The estate owners can usually select this land, and they obviously choose to reserve for themselves the best land, as well as the land that contains the home, barns, and other buildings. Thus, the estate owner retains a going concern, although reduced in size, while the peasants receiving the expropriated land do not. In Colombia, each owner can retain 100 hectares of good land and up to 200 hectares of poor land (1 hectare equals approximately 2.5 acres). The 1964 Nicaraguan law was even more generous; it allowed owners to retain 500 hectares of good land plus a forest reserve. The 1964 Peruvian law allows owners to hold on to 100 hectares of irrigated land or up to 1,500 hectares of pasture. The 1967 Chilean law declares that an owner can retain between 80 and 1,000 hectares of irrigated land depending on the number of sons working on the estate and whether or not the estate is efficiently managed. In brief, even if the agrarian reform laws were rigidly enforced, which they are not, the large landowners would still retain their control over the best farmland in Latin America.

Most of the agrarian reform laws are also generous to the hacenda-dos in terms of compensating estate owners for expropriated land. The value of an estate can range from its commercial price, the maximum, to its declared tax value, the minimum. Feder notes that "the declared tax value is always a small fraction of the 'real' value of the estate, to allow an estate owner to avoid the payment of taxes. On the other hand, the 'market' value estimated by the owner tends to be above the 'real' productive value of the farm, because he tends to include factors such as his control over the land, people and farm inputs, his political influence and role, and the land's capacity to absorb inflation."[37] Most of the reform laws enacted during the 1960s employed appraisal tech-niques favorable to the estate owners, which meant that the expropria-tion price was weighted toward the market value of the estate. The major exception was the 1967 Chilean law which utilized the tax-declared value of the land plus any improvements not included in this appraisal to determine the expropriation price. In addition, the owners prefer to be paid off in cash and not in bonds, which they fear will rapidly decline in value because of inflation.

The significance of the compensation issue is that the higher the compensation, the less the state can afford to engage in land distribu-tion. Moreover, the more compensation is paid to the large landowners, the less redistribution of income can take place. In short, high compensation conflicts with—and can defeat—the manifest goal of redistribution. For Latin American revolutionaries, paying large estate owners adequate compensation is as self-defeating as compensating high-income earners for the extra taxes they pay in a progressive income tax system. However, one should also consider that giving the large landowners grossly inadequate compensation or no compensation will bring about, at the least, declining agricultural production. This in turn will cause rising food prices hurting the urban poor, increased balance of payments problems, and, at the worst, reactionary violence.

Agrarian reform laws are also weakened by a long list of unconditional and conditional exemptions. Unconditional exemptions exist in the 1964 Ecuadorian law, which exempts estates up to 2,500 hectares, plus an additional 1,000 hectares of pastures for estates located on the coast. In the mountains, the law exempts up to 1,800 hectares. Conditionally, the Ecuadorian law exempts estates that are efficiently managed. In Colombia the law requires that the Land Reform Institute expropriate privately owned land only if it is usable for farming or livestock "on a small scale." In Chile, the president can authorize exemption up to twenty years for estate owners who prepare investment plans for the improvement of their farms. Feder complains that when one reviews the land reform legislation of the 1960s, and especially the manner in which it was implemented, one must conclude that "there is a tendency for the exceptions (i.e., exemptions) to rule, and for the fundamental measure of land reform, the expropriations, to be allowed only occasionally."[38]

In brief, the significant land distributions envisaged at the beginning of the 1960s have not taken place. With admittedly unreliable data, Feder estimates that, between 1961 and 1968, only about 50,000 families received expropriated land in Latin America (excluding Mexico, Bolivia, and Cuba). In his words, "Since . . . the annual increase in new [rural] families—of whom 75 to 90 percent were estimated to be poor and therefore potential land reform beneficiaries—is estimated at . . . about 220,000 families, . . . it becomes evident that . . . the annual increase in potential land reform beneficiaries would be much larger than the number of families benefiting from land reform settlement, and, in fact, no dent would be made in the poverty status of the immense number of farm families before adding new generations of rural poor."[39] In a more comprehensive review, the Inter-American Development Bank concludes,

On the whole, during the past decade between 1 and 1.2 million landless families obtained possession of, or access to land through public programs, or an average of 100,000 to 120,000 annually. But two countries, Mexico and Venezuela, account for over half of this total. Considering that in the middle of the past decade there were some 10 million potential land reform beneficiaries, and in the light of the fact that the rural labor force is growing at a rate of more than 500,000 annually, the rates of progress for most countries are disappointing. Moreover, a substantial proportion of the total number of recipients of land rights—about two-fifths—were squatters and migrants to virgin public territories. Thus, relatively little progress has been made in the redistribution of rights to an income from the underutilized crop and grazing lands where, according to most studies, the bulk of the potentially income-producing resources lies.[40]

Whatever the correct figures, the bottom line is that there are now more rural poor and landless peasants than in 1960. However, these policies that offered expropriated and colonization land to a select number of peasants did succeed in preventing the peasants from mobilizing on a massive scale. Many peasants *competed with one another* to receive the parcels of land available through legal means rather than form class-based organizations that would have employed violent methods to achieve massive land distributions. Little land was distributed, and the very concept of agrarian reform was given a new meaning by emphasizing the need for technological improvements (the green revolution) to feed the expanding population, especially in the cities, and to increase agricultural exports, thus easing balance of payments difficulties. This decline in the demand for agrarian reform can best be understood by looking at some individual countries.

Mexico is probably the best example of the weaknesses and achievements of agrarian reform in Latin America. One of the major causes of the Mexican Revolution in 1910 was the land hunger of the peasants. Pressured by an armed and mobilized peasantry under the leadership of Emiliano Zapata, the Carranza government accepted Article 27 of the 1917 constitution which sanctioned the *ejido* system and land distribution. Under the *ejido* system, land tenure rights are granted to a village by the state; in turn the *ejido* community or village grants the right of ownership of a plot of land to each villager. This plot of land cannot be sold; it cannot be mortgaged; it cannot be taken over by a hacendado. Should the individual villager cease to work the land, it can be taken back by the *ejido* and then granted to another member. Additionally, legislation decreed that all landholdings in excess of 100 hectares were subject to expropriation.

Because of the revolution, "land distribution became the continuous obligation of every president of Mexico. Between 1915 and August 13, 1967, a total of 147.7 million acres of Mexican territory was distributed to 2.6 million farmers. The area covered by the program was 163.2 million acres, and the amount distributed between 1915 and 1967 amounted to just over 25 percent of the total area of Mexico."[41] The champion of land distribution was President Lázaro Cárdenas, who, during his term in office (1934–40), distributed an average of three million hectares annually. By 1960, there were 1,523,796 *ejidatarios* in possession of their own plots, and *ejido* land represented about 56 percent of all holdings and 43 percent of all arable land. By the early 1970s land had been distributed to about three million peasant farmers. The land that had been expropriated from the hacendados had been paid for in worthless bonds. Flores notes that only around 0.5 percent of the total value of expropriated land was paid for. In other words, Mexico's land reform was confiscatory for lands in excess of 100 hectares."[42] There was no other way a poor country could distribute large amounts of land to large numbers of peasants.

While these reforms ended the traditional exploitation of the peasants and promoted the political legitimacy of the government, Mexico is still plagued by agrarian problems. Almost three-quarters of a century after the Mexican Revolution began, 4 million peasants are still without land, and 5 million peasant farmers can barely feed their families from their subsistence plots. The peasant farmers given land on 28,000 *ejidos* were often given poor land, and they never received the credit, technical and marketing assistance, or machinery that would make their plots productive. In this arid and mountainous nation, "only one-fifth of the *ejidos* have irrigation and 15 percent produce food in excess of the immediate demands of the families that live on them."[43] Since many peasant families have five or more children, the plots have been subdivided into tiny inefficient units, thus forcing more and more young peasants to migrate to the cities, to attempt to slip into the United States as illegal aliens, or to join those demanding their own plots of land. The lack of agricultural productivity combined with the soaring population growth in the cities has meant that Mexico must import an increasing amount of food. Even so, 30 percent of the population consumes less than 2,000 calories a day (a normal level is considered about 2,600 daily). To feed the burgeoning urban population and generate export income, new farm estates have been created through legal fictions that circumvent the law establishing a 100-hectare limit on private property. During Miguel Alemán's administration (1946–52) amendments to Article 27 of the constitution were passed that allowed private landholdings growing cotton to have a maximum of 150 hectares; those dedicated to sugar, vanilla, and cocoa crops could have a maximim of 300 hectares. This has particularly affected the northwestern states where large agro-industrial farms have prospered thanks to government support through credit extensions and irrigation projects. Griffin points out, "In the northern part of the country commercial farms using hired labor occupy the rich irrigated land, while the majority of the rural population is confined to *minifundia* and *ejidos*. As a consequence, in Mexico 70.7 percent of the farmers account for only 6.6 percent of the marketable surplus, while at the other extreme, 55.4 percent of the total value of marketed agricultural commodities is supplied by commercial farmers who represent only 1.9 percent of the cultivators."[44]

The balance between growth and distribution that the Mexican government has tried to maintain in its agrarian policies is described by Clark Reynolds as follows:

> With one hand the government has advanced land distribution in densely populated areas on the high plateaus and in the south, and with the other has spent large amounts on irrigation projects in the north and west where water was needed to open up the desert. It has recognized agrarian reform as a political fact of life and has continued the process of land redistribution in small plots, while simultaneously channeling a growing amount of public investment into irrigation works to subsidize medium and large-scale private land-holdings. In so doing, it found itself able to meet the dual objective of peasant welfare and agricultural welfare.[45]

But the dual objectives of these agrarian policies are *not* being achieved. The demand for food is outstripping agricultural production because Mexico's population is now five times what it was in 1910. Mexico still has 4 million landless peasants but less land to distribute. The López Portillo government, inaugurated in 1976, announced that it would not confiscate the productive land of the larger irrigated farms in the north, but would concentrate its efforts on increasing the productivity of the *ejidos*. This will not be easy since, from an administrative point of view, the Mexican government has been far more capable of channeling its resources to benefit the large farmers than the *ejidos*.

Bolivia affords a second example of violent agrarian reform. Conditions in Bolivia in 1950 were reminiscent of conditions in the last days of Porfirio Díaz's Mexico. According to the Bolivian agrarian census of 1950, 8.1 percent of the landowners owned 95.1 percent of the cultivated land. The Indians were generally landless and still treated as a conquered, inferior race. The Indians had few dealings with the government; they were not part of the money economy; they were almost totally controlled by the hacendados. But, although the Bolivian Indians generally appeared to be docile, there was a land hunger among them reminiscent of the attitudes expressed by Zapata in Mexico.

The Bolivian Revolution, like the Mexican Revolution, was not initiated by the peasants, but by the Movimiento Nacionalista Revolucionario (MNR), a motley coalition of labor, middle-class groups, radicals, fascists, and the military. In April 1952 the MNR overthrew the government and nationalized the tin mines. Before the MNR knew what was happening, a second revolution took place in some parts of the countryside as Indians and peasants mobilized themselves to take land from the hacendados. The MNR made the strategic decision to support the peasants and even to encourage further rebellion through government agents. A commission was created on January 20, 1953, to draft an agrarian reform law which was hastily signed and issued on August 3, 1953, by President Victor Paz Estenssoro. By June 1970, over 30 million acres had been expropriated and distributed among 273,000 peasant families. Peasants now own about 75 percent of the land under cultivation. Peasant holdings average about ten hectares, but some own less than one hectare while others own more than twenty-five.[46] The former owners were supposed to be compensated in the form of bonds paying 2 percent interest for twenty-five years based on the tax evaluations of 1948. However, it quickly became obvious that inflation would wipe out the value of these bonds; indeed, the Bolivian government never even printed them. Similarly, a provision of the 1953 decree, requiring the peasants receiving land to pay the Agricultural Bank a compensation equal to five times the 1948 tax assessment on the property, has never been enforced.

Bolivian agrarian reform did help to end the terrible exploitation of the Indians by the hacendados. As a result of the reform, the Indians gained a somewhat higher status as campesinos with the right to organize *sindicatos*. However, because of the government's concentration on distribution and failure to follow through on the need to encourage increases in productivity, agricultural output fell significantly (13 to 15 percent) between 1952 and 1954. Part of this problem, undoubtedly, was due to the fact that the peasants were consuming more of their own production. Bolivia was thus forced to import food, which further damaged an already chronic negative balance of payments situation. Moreover, the lack of administrative rationality and the population growth in the highlands soon led to a proliferation of tiny plots of land. These plots, growing in number, cannot adequately support families, so there has been an increase in malnutrition and a high level of infant mortality. In brief, the experiences of Mexico and Bolivia suggest that land distribution by itself is not the magical key that opens the door to rapid development.

The agrarian reform experiences in Colombia, one of the few democratic and civilian-led nations in Latin America, have been particularly discouraging. In 1961 Colombia passed an agrarian reform law that allowed each large landowner to keep 100 hectares of good land and up to 200 hectares of poor land. Land that has been left idle for ten years could be expropriated by the Instituto Colombiano de la Reforma Agraria (INCORA) without compensation, but this provision could easily be evaded by putting some livestock on the land. The Colombian law required cash compensation for the estate owners in the case of inadequately and adequately managed land, as well as for land cultivated by sharecroppers or tenants. In 1968 amendments were added which provided that, when land is appropriated for the benefit of the tenants or sharecroppers on a particular estate, half of the expropriation price can be paid in negotiable bonds (2 percent interest over 25 years). The fact that in all other cases compensation must be in cash, with the bulk payable within a few years, means that INCORA does not have the cash to expropriate much land.

Moreover, the law makes it clear that most of the land to be distributed to the peasants is not to come from the large estates but from the public domain. This is more of a colonization project than agrarian reform. In Feder's words, "If 'it becomes necessary,' farm people can be settled on privately owned land which can be expropriated—but only in this sequence: first, on unused land; then, on land which is inadequately used; then, on land cultivated by small tenants and sharecroppers; and finally, on land which the owners voluntarily cede to the land reform institute. Only as a last priority can land which is 'well-managed' be expropriated. But the legal (quite apart from the political) obstacles to such expropriation are formidable."[47] This suggests that only the poorest land—the public lands in the remote parts of Colombia and the underutilized land of the hacendados—will be available for the peasants.

An evaluation of Colombia's agrarian reform highlights its inadequacies. The 1971 agrarian census indicated that 70 percent of the farmers owned 5.6 percent of the land in parcels of under twenty-five acres each, but half of which are considered too small or poor to support a family; but 6 percent of the farmers own 72 percent of the land. What is disturbing is that the concentration of land in the hands of a few families has been increasing, not declining during the past decade. By 1974, only about 100,000 peasants had received land under the program. Such a meager program cannot have a significant impact where there are a million peasant families without land, another million who possess an average of 2.6 hectares, and a thousand *latifundistas* with an average of 1,500 hectares.[48] Over 90 percent of the land distributed by INCORA was public land. An analysis of INCORA's budget during the 1960s reveals that only about a fifth was actually spent on acquiring and distributing expropriated land to peasants; the bulk of the budget was spent on infrastructural work projects, credit programs, and *asentamientos* (farm communities administered by INCORA) on public lands. What had started out as a program to aid the peasant class had become a program that distributed land to only a select few of the peasants while actually providing extensive help to the larger commercial farmers with its emphasis on increasing productivity through new credit facilities, irrigation projects, and the green revolution. This shift in emphasis was formalized in 1972 when President Pastrana's government and the National Agrarian Society (representing the large landowners) signed the Pact of Chicorral.

Peru experienced two major agrarian efforts in 1964 and 1969 that are worth examining. In the 1960s, Peru still had a rural economy that was socially and economically stifling. Along the coast, export-oriented commercial farms controlled most of the irrigated land; in the Andes Mountains, large haciendas were surrounded by *minifundia,* while Indian communities owned the poorest and most isolated land. About half of Peru's 12 million inhabitants lived in the rural areas, but they produced only 15 percent of the GDP, forcing the nation to spend over

US$100 million annually to import food. The land in Peru varies tremendously from region to region. The coast is primarily a desert except for fertile river valleys. Increases in production along the coast will require expensive irrigation systems. In the sierra, only 5 percent of the land is arable. Policymakers are thus confronted by a rural population of four million competing for about 800,000 hectares of cultivated land and an additional undetermined amount of grazing land.

On May 21, 1964, President Fernando Belaunde Terry signed an Agrarian Reform Law that had been passed by the opposition parliamentary coalition in control of the legislature. APRA, an important member of the opposition coalition, had succeeded in excluding from the jurisdiction of the law the sugar plantations along the coast, where the party was particularly strong among the sugar workers. APRA feared that agrarian reform implemented by the Belaunde government would weaken its electoral base among these coastal workers. The law also excluded efficient ranches and other agro-industrial estates from expropriation. It allowed owners to retain up to 1,500 hectares (depending on the use of the land), and required court issuance (an inevitably delaying mechanism) of all expropriation orders. Land valuations were to be determined by an incredibly complicated procedure that called for landowners to be paid for their expropriated land (part cash, part bonds) an amount equal to 70 percent of the average of three values: the tax value, the market price, and its potential income under efficient management. The law also included a section (Title XV) designed to enable sharecroppers to buy the land they worked. John Strasma analyzes this section of the law:

> Under this legislation, resident laborers and smaller sharecroppers could obtain title to the tiny plots they had been allowed to till in exchange for working on the estate free or for wages far below the "market" wage. Title XV required fewer formalities than formal expropriation, and it provided for repayment by beneficiaries on a long-term basis. Some 128,000 of these workers had applied for such titles by the end of 1966, and 54,800 of them had received provisional occupancy rights certificates by that time. . . . In addition, the Title XV program was legitimately criticized for "freezing" sub-subsistence *minifundia* that should have been combined instead. Also, many workers who demanded their Title XV rights got their plots but lost their small cash income from part-time employment on the estate, since the owners, in reprisal, substi-

tuted new full-time laborers who earned cash wages but did not have cultivation or grazing rights to estate lands.[49]

The 1964 law did not alter the agrarian structure of Peru. From 1964 to 1968, when the military overthrew the Belaunde government, only about 75,000 campesinos gained possession of small holdings ranging from two to ten hectares. Only sixty-one estates with a combined total of 651,419 hectares were expropriated. In addition. Strasma points out, "The 1964 law specified that land reform's budget should not be less than 3 percent of the total central government budget. However, a fiscal crisis began and the average land reform budget for 1964–1967 was closer to 0.6 percent, a third of which went into colonization programs instead of reform."[50]

The new military government, which came to power in October 1968, was headed by General Juan Velasco Alvarado and had much greater political motivations for bringing about agrarian reform in Peru. The military had squelched rural guerrilla movements in 1965 and believed that land distribution could insure stability in the country-side. The military was also willing to extend agrarian reform to the coastal region, hoping thereby to destroy the party strongholds of their historical enemy, the APRA party. Finally, the government viewed agrarian reform as the principal means of attaining mass support in the rural areas. President Velasco, perhaps because of his upbringing in an agrarian district in northern Peru, took a very personal interest in destroying the traditional rural oligarchy. The government went so far as to demobilize the National Agrarian Society, the pressure group that represented the large estate owners.

President Velasco, after firing his first minister of agriculture because of his qualms concerning significant land distribution, issued a new agrarian reform decree in June 1969. The new decree reflected a far more serious intent to bring about agrarian reform than the 1964 law it replaced. Under the new law, the large coastal sugar plantations are subject to total expropriation, the government is given a more extensive range of instruments to implement the reform, and the large estate owners are warned that sabotage, such as taking land out of cultivation or withdrawing products from market, would lead to arrest and trial in military courts. The valuation of expropriated land is based solely on the declared value by the hacendado for tax purposes (based on the self-assessment required of owners in a 1968 real estate tax reform), and extensive litigation over expropriation can no longer delay the reform process. Compensation will be paid in twenty-to-thirty-year bonds. These may be cashed before maturity if the money is used to finance at least half of a new industrial enterprise. Another reversal of previous policy under the new decree is that cash compensation for estate inventories and installations is no longer needed. Moreover, a new water code was adopted that declared void, without compensation, existing water allocations, some dating from the colonial period. Under the new code, farmers with ten hectares of land or less are to receive water before the larger owners get any more. Finally, agrarian courts were created in each of the twelve agricultural regions of the country to adjudicate the new law.

The chief goal of the 1969 Peruvian decree was to insure that "land is directly worked by its owner and is a source of production and not of rent. The legislation made it clear that medium-sized commercial farms employing wage labor would not be touched—about 200,000 of them."[51] The law called for the expropriation of all estates larger than 150 hectares on the coast and 15 hectares in most sections of the sierra. An attempt was made to overcome the *minifundia* problems caused by Title XV in the 1964 law by having the new law require "that other lands belonging to the same owner must also be distributed, in order to give each Title XV beneficiary at least a family farm unit [of at least three hectares]. Clearly recognizing the shortage of technical staff in the reform agency, the law obliged owners to turn over the extra land themselves by June 30, 1970, without waiting for official action, on pain of a fine of half the value of the added land required."[52] Finally, the law called for the creation of a number of different kinds of rural cooperative arrangements, including the Agrarian Social Interest Societies (SAIS), the Agricultural Production Cooperatives, and the Integral Rural Settlement Projects. Since 1969, the original decree has been altered fifty times, with the most important change being that the maximum farm size has been reduced from 150 hectares to 50 hectares in order to have more land available for distribution.

An evaluation of the impact of the 1969 agrarian reform indicates that by 1976 a total of 6.3 million hectares had been distributed to 260,000 families. Harding estimates that "about two-thirds of all cultivated land in Peru will be affected by the reform, but only 25 percent of the national pasture; only about one third of the rural population will benefit directly from the land redistribution, and very small peasant proprietors . . . are likely to be as badly off after the reform is completed as they were before it. About 43 percent of farmland will remain in private hands in 1976."[53] Cleaves points out that "the creation of agricultural enterprises (either cooperative or SAIS) had altered the community of beneficiaries from 3,782 families owning all properties over 500 hectares (with an average size of about 4,000 hectares) in 1969 to 200,000 families spread among 810 agricultural enterprises averaging 6,000 hectares in 1975."[54] Bourque estimates:

> The agrarian reform of 1969 will result in some income distribution when it is fully implemented (on the order of $86 million), effectively doubling the income of the permanent labor force on the expropriated farms. However, fully two-thirds of the benefits of redistribution will be realized by peasants and farmers in the Coast, not in the Sierra. The total income transfer is estimated at less than 2 percent of 1967 national income. Furthermore, even if it is fully carried out, the agrarian reform will benefit less than 40 percent of all farm families needing assistance and less than 10 percent of the Indian communities.[55]

Unlike most other Latin American governments, the Peruvian military government was serious about agrarian reform and was able to distribute land to several hundred thousand peasants. However, there are still anywhere from 600,000 to 800,000 peasants who have not received land. With an average of 20,000 new farm families a year, and with most of the good land already distributed, the arithmetic of the situation suggests that there will be continuing difficulties in the rural sector. Moreover, Harding explains, reformers with overly romantic notions toward peasants have been shocked that "closed allocations of land, limited to full-time workers on an estate, are liable to create both pressures to get in from those on the outside [the seasonal laborers] and an equal determination to keep them out and maximize their own incomes by the beneficiaries. The *egoísmo del grupo* has proved a serious problem for the authorities."[56] Another major problem—a typical one—is that so many of the 1,800 cooperatives have been poorly managed. Finally, food production has stagnated, causing an increase of food imports (80 percent of Peru's wheat consumption is imported), further exacerbating an already chronic balance of payments problem.

In 1975 President Velasco was ousted by General Francisco Morales Bermúdez who halted land expropriations and ended price controls on some farm products, to the benefit of private farmers. In 1980

Belaúnde was reelected president by offering private farmers a legal guarantee against further property seizures and promising to increase credit for private farmers and to remove the remaining price controls.

While the salience of the agrarian reform issue has declined in most of Latin America, its significance has soared in Nicaragua and El Salvador. In July 1979 the Sandinistas overthrew the Somoza dynasty and quickly expropriated 2.5 million acres of land from the Somoza family and its supporters. However, the peasants, who constitute over half of the country's 2.7 million inhabitants, were not given private landownership by the revolutionary government. Since the Sandinistas are more concerned with maintaining production for both internal and external markets than with satisfying the desire of peasants for their own land, they have tried to apply state capitalistic rather than populist criteria to the farming sector, first by preventing the fragmentation of estates into *minifundia,* then by forming even larger state-run administrative units. Thus the approximately 2,000 expropriated farms now belong to 170 production complexes and just 24 agricultural companies.[57] Private farmers still own 70 percent of the cultivable land, but they can be controlled through the rural credit programs directed by the nationalized banking system. Whether Nicaragua has the administrative skill to run these state farms productively remains to be seen.

In El Salvador, a tiny nation crowded with 5 million people, the right-wing dictatorship of General Carlos Humberto Romero was overthrown by a military coup in October 1979. Before the coup, less than 2 percent of the population owned more than half of the arable land. In the prior thirty years, population growth and changes in farming patterns had increased the proportion of the landless poor from 12 percent to 40 percent of the population. To prevent the mobilization of these peasants by leftist guerrillas aided by Cuba and Nicaragua, the ruling junta (headed by José Napoleon Duarte, a Christian Democrat, but dominated by the military), with the support and pressure of the Carter administration, decreed an extensive agrarian reform law which was designed to redistribute land, break the power of a small class of large landowners, and preempt the popular appeal of leftist guerrillas. To accomplish these goals, the law has three phases. Under phase one, which has been implemented, all estates larger than 1,235 acres were expropriated, with compensation in the form of bonds for the former owners. The new landowner is a public agency, the Institute for Agrarian Transformation, which now administers 282 cooperatives. Unfortunately, even the strongest proponents of agrarian reform agree that the institute has been inefficient and corrupt. About 260,000 people—10 to 15 percent of the rural population—live and work on these cooperative farms. The second phase requires the similar conversion of private farms larger than 247 acres. The third stage, usually labeled the "land-to-the-tiller law," stipulates that tenant farmers will become the owners of the small plots they have been working. About 150,000 families were expected to benefit from this provision but after one year only 500 land titles were distributed to tenant farmers. With the defeat of Carter by Ronald Reagan, and a decline in U.S. pressure regarding land reform in El Salvador, it now appears that neither the second or third phases of the law will be implemented. However, many large farmers are now trying to drive the renters from their land before the latter can claim they have a right to it.[58]

In evaluating agrarian reform policies in Latin America, one must remember that the latifundio system has dominated most countries for centuries. Attempts to uproot this system of privilege will encounter enormous political, economic, social, administrative, and legal obstacles. From a comparative perspective, it is analogous to the United States engaging in efforts to eliminate the consequences of hundreds of years of institutionalized racism. In either case, progress is likely to be slower than its proponents and especially its beneficiaries (nonwhites and peasants) would want. Nevertheless the results of agrarian reform policies have been particularly disappointing. In the first place, most development theorists have blamed the latifundio system as the major factor inhibiting the modernization of Latin America. They were hopeful that the elimination of the latifundio system would be the key to future progress. Everyone agrees that there have been three authentic agrarian revolutions in Latin America: in Mexico, Bolivia, and Cuba. Some might add Peru to this list. Many peasants benefited from these revolutions, but from a developmental point of view, agrarian reform did not prove to be *the key* that unlocked the door to rapid modernization. Once this door was unlocked, other obstacles were encountered.

Second, most Latin American nations passed agrarian reform laws during the 1960s. These laws have led to the gradual elimination of such traditional forms of land tenure as the *huasipungo* system in Ecuador, the *yanaconazgo* in Peru or the *inquilinaje* in Chile. Many of these traditional systems, in which the assignment of a plot of land, grazing privileges, and other noncash allowances were exchanged for a specified number of work days on the landlord's estate, have been altered into wage arrangements. These changes have proved to be a mixed blessing for the former *colonos* or resident workers on the haciendas. While many of these workers have acquired ownership of the land they already occupied, the plots have often been too tiny to constitute economically viable units, leaving the peasants as dependent on the large landowners for services and cash income as before. In addition, the introduction of the new cash wage arrangements has meant that thousands of campesinos have lost the assigned plots of land on which their subsistence depended.

The agrarian reform laws of the 1960s have not resulted in significant land distribution to the peasants. Feder summarizes: "The laws have tended to restrict land reform to a small portion of the land potentially available for redistribtuion to peasants, and to relegate reform to the outlying and poorer agricultural areas. This has been achieved principally by four types of provisions: the priorities established in the legislation with regard to where land reform is to begin; the condition or requirements necessary for the expropriation; the exemption from expropriation that takes land out completely from the reform program; and the rights accorded owners of expropriated land."[59] Instead of the massive land distributions envisioned by the proponents of agrarian reform, one generally finds "an atomized program of small land reform projects."[60] The limited amount of good land, the large and growing number of peasant families, the limited administrative and financial resources of agrarian reform agencies, the lack of autonomous and mobilized strength of peasant organizations, and the political power of the large landowners and their claims that only large farms can produce the surplus needed to feed the exploding urban population and earn export income have all combined to insure that only a portion of the eligible peasant populations actually recieved land. But even this small distribution of land was sufficient to forestall the agrarian revolts that many were predicting at the beginning of the 1960s if significant land reform were not achieved. The implementation of land reform policies reflects the Latin American policy style of the *selective* rather than the *general* applicability of the law.

Third, the fact that the landholding elites successfully stifled land distribution in the latter part of the 1960s has been explained by proponents of agrarian reform in terms of continuing political domination of Latin American governments by hacendados. A more accurate view is that the traditional landholders no longer control these political systems: witness the emphasis on industrialization and exchange rates that discriminate against agrarian products. But the great landowners do maintain a veto power in this policy area to prevent, or at least dilute, the kinds of changes that are the most threatening to their way of life. However, sporadic peasant agitation and land invasions and the large landowners' fears that a new revolutionary government might actually implement an authentic agrarian reform create an atmosphere of insecurity in the rural areas that probably makes the capitalist development of agriculture difficult, if not impossible.

Opponents of land reform now emphasize that land distribution results in a decline of production that Latin America cannot afford politically or economically. This argument assumes that the size of a given farm or estate is the key to production; "If this were true," says Frances Foland, "Latin America should be world leader instead of laggard in crop yield."[61] But whatever the logic of the arguments, agrarian productivity and distribution remains one of the major problem areas in Latin American public policy.

Educational Policy

Education is of primary importance in distributive public policy but it can also be viewed as an investment in human resources required for future economic growth. To a great extent, public policy determines access to schooling, the construction of educational facilities, the availability and training of teachers, and the nature of the curriculum. As a society modernizes, educational policies become a source of dispute because the demand for education exceeds the supply of resources needed to advance it. Hence, controversial allocative decisions must be made. For the individual, educational policy is important because it affects self-esteem, social mobility, and job opportunities. For governments, educational policy affects the ideas and attitudes of the population (and thus the legitimacy of the political system), levels of employment (both by delaying the entrance of youth into the job market and providing employment for teachers and administrators), and the availability of skilled workers. An educational system performs both static and dynamic functions. Its static function is to transmit prevailing cultural values to a new generation; its dynamic function is to stimulate changes in cultural values so that future social aspirations can be attained. Educational policy reveals what a particular society wants to be in the future—that is, what is to remain the same, and what is to be altered.

Traditional Latin American education was tied to a socially conservative, status-conscious society. The school system was designed to provide elite males with a cultural background and middle-sector males with the skills necessary for the colonial and postcolonial bureaucracy and economy. The function of this system was to preserve, not to change, society. As education performed this static function, structures and patterns of behavior were created and maintained that have made it very difficult for Latin American school systems to play a more dynamic, developmental role in the twentieth century.

In the nineteenth century most Latin American nations adopted the basic structure of the French and Iberian models of education, and these structures are still in operation today. The system is centrally controlled. Curricula, teacher qualifications, textbooks, and the number of hours students spend in school are usually determined by national legislation and administered by the Ministry of Education. Primary education begins at age six or seven and lasts for six years; secondary school also has a six-year program. Most secondary schools prepare students for university training by the granting of the *bachillerato* (bachelor's degree). There are also secondary schools (*escuelas normales*) that provide vocational education and special education for those planning to become primary teachers. Many of the students attending secondary school are in private schools; most of these are church schools that receive public subsidies.

Higher education in the New World was initiated in 1551 by Charles V of Spain, who authorized the creation of the first two universities in Lima and Mexico City. The Portuguese monarchy did not allow the establishment of higher education in Brazil until the royal court was moved to Rio de Janeiro in 1808. During the colonial period, Spain founded twenty-five universities, all of which were dominated by the Catholic church. These universities were modeled after the Spanish universities of the sixteenth century with four faculties: theology, law, medicine, and the arts. During the nineteenth century the national governments added eleven new universities and attempted to secularize them. The secularized universities dropped the faculty of theology and gradually added schools of engineering, dentistry, pharmacy, architecture, and secondary school teaching. During both the colonial period and the nineteenth century, universities were established for the education of select members of the upper classes, and were reluctant to incorporate the intellectual and scientific currents originating in Europe and the United States. These conservative institutions were also hesitant to broaden the curriculum so as to provide wider and more practical course content to satisfy the needs of new professions, or to engage in research directed toward solving the economic and social problems of Latin American societies.

Students attending these universities would enter a particular faculty, depending upon which profession they intended to pursue—medicine, law, engineering, or the humanities. Each year of the curriculum had a required number of subjects that had to be passed before students could register for the next year and thus fulfill the requirements for the title or degree. Reflecting a paternalistic administrative style, in most universities all subjects comprising a certain curriculum were required for all students in that faculty. Each faculty represented a profession and operated autonomously within the university, a situation that was often symbolized by the location of different faculties in different parts of the city. Teaching at the university level was mainly a part-time activity; the motivation for becoming a university professor was often the status acquired, not the pay (which was low) or the vocation of teaching. Eminent lawyers, doctors, writers, and architects acquired a chair (*cátedra*) or professorship for each of the courses required for the professional degree and would then deliver the same lectures for years. The inefficiency of this traditional structure is captured by Harrison: "The faculties were entities unto themselves, each with its own professors of mathematics, chemistry, literature, or history. The student had no contact with professors outside his own faculty and completed a rigidly prescribed curriculum that only action by the national government could change."[62]

Similar rigidity is found in primary and secondary schooling. The most frequent criticisms leveled against the traditional curricula used in Latin American schools are summarized by Oscar Vera:

> They are encyclopedic, overladen with material, excessively ambitious and rigid; . . . quite remote from the daily lives and experiences of the pupils, they tend to lose sight of the basic aims of general education and encourage memorization, verbalism and intellectualism rather than the development of personality, initiative, powers of observations, the acquisition of the habit of scientific inquiry and the application of skills and knowledge to the problems met in everyday life; . . . they include topics of doubtful value and exclude others which would be of greater use and efficiency educationally; . . . [and] there is little co-ordination between subjects, or between the content of primary education and the first years of secondary education.[63]

These charges against primary and secondary schooling bear a strong resemblance to criticisms, already described, of university education.

Latin American educational systems have also been attacked as retarding economic growth and development. By the 1950s, when most Latin countries were becoming more concerned with development, their educational systems were criticized for miseducating the established elites and failing to educate the bulk of the rural population. In terms of developmental needs, the system miseducates by promoting a disdain for manual labor, attracting the most educated to the few largest cities in each country (*El Dorado Urbano*), creating a reluctance to work (or teach) in rural areas, and maintaining a highly stratified society. Furthermore, it orients students toward occupations that are not related to the human resource requirements of development. The most notorious examples are the lack of middle-level technicians and agricultural experts produced by Latin American schools, which partially accounts for the region's technological dependence and disappointingly low agrarian productivity. Lawyers do not reduce a nation's technological dependence or increase its agricultural production.

The traditional style of teaching also miseducates. Most teachers, using formalistic teaching methods based on memorization, follow a text word for word. The pupil copies and repeats. Innovative teaching is hampered by the lack of training of so many teachers and either the absence or deficiency of physical facilities such as libraries and laboratories. In the words of Robert Arnove, "The tendency is for the modal school in Latin America to develop competitive and authoritarian relationships, while alienating students from their environments. Generally, the teacher is the sole source of authority and knowledge in the classroom. The learning process centers on the transmission of information, the variety of which is not questioned, in a direct line from the teacher to the student—the so-called 'banking' concept of teaching—learning where information is deposited in empty minds."[64] This style of teaching has contributed to the chronically high attrition rate in Latin American education.

The traditional educational system noneducates through a funneling process—both academic and social—whereby the school selects who will succeed, rejects others, and encourages dropouts. The traditional school environment promotes early school desertion, high absenteeism, alienation, and frustration. Such problems are particularly severe in rural areas where there are the fewest schools, the highest proportion of incomplete schools, the lowest-paid and least trained teachers, the greatest shortage of teaching materials, and the least adequate programs for helping the student with books and materials, food, clothes, and health problems. During the 1960s in Mexico, for example, only 26 percent of the rural primary schools went beyond the first four grades, and only 9 percent of all rural students completed the four grades. Similarly, in Colombia, 85 percent of rural schools had less than the first four grades, which largely explains why the average length of schooling of the rural population was 1.7 years (according to the 1964 census) as against 5.1 years for the urban population.[65]

In the twentieth century, beginning with the university reform movement of 1918 (to be discussed), and continuing through the 1950s and 1960s, there have been increasing demands for educational reforms at all levels. The need for such reforms was amply demonstrated in figures indicating that in 1950 about 49 percent of the population fifteen years of age and over in Latin America had either not attended school or had left school before completing the first grade; 44 percent had obtained some primary education, but only about 8 percent had completed primary school; 6 percent had received some secondary education, and only 1 percent had begun or completed any form of higher education.[66] The variations among educational systems are revealed by a UNESCO study which shows that in the 1953–58 period the percentage of seven-to-fourteen-year-olds enrolled in schools was 89 percent in Argentina, 86 percent in Panama, 84 percent in Chile, 77 percent in Costa Rica, 69 percent in Uruguay, 64 percent in Cuba, 63 percent in Brazil, 61 percent in Ecuador, 60 percent in Mexico, 59 percent in Peru, 59 percent in Venezuela, 53 percent in Colombia, 50 percent in El Salvador, 44 percent in Bolivia, 35 percent in Guatemala, and 32 percent in Haiti.[67]

For the rising middle sectors, educational reform was believed to be one of the magical keys that would unlock the door blocking national development. The goals of educational reformers were not modest; by increasing educational expenditures and enrollments, proponents of educational reform hoped to transform their nations. Improved education was expected to rapidly reduce and eventually eliminate illiteracy, supply the trained human resources necessary for economic development, promote social mobility, encourage political democracy (since it was believed that an enlarged and educated middle class would be less likely to support caudillos and authoritarian governments), and increase both technological and cultural autonomy. The demands for reform were strong because Latin American culture respects education, and the population associates doing well in school with obtaining

higher-paying and higher-status employment. The need for more and
better education was also echoed by a variety of politicians. Responding favorably to educational demands was easier than catering to other
demands (such as agrarian and tax reform) because it involved less of a
zero-sum conflict. Educational reform promised to provide a multitude
of jobs for teachers, administrators, and construction workers; it was
strongly supported by most segments of the population and thus produced less group and ideological strife. Hence, even Colombia, with a
socially conservative political system, could agree to a 1957 constitutional amendment that allocated at least 10 percent of the national
budget for public education.

Tables 16, 17, and 18 reveal some of the progress various Latin
American countries have made in primary, secondary, and higher education. Since 1950 most governments have increased their educational

TABLE 16
Total Expenditures on Public Education in Latin America, 1960–74

	Percent of Total Public Expenditures			Percent of GNP Devoted to Education
	1960	1970	1974	1974
Argentina	13.3	14.0	18.8	4.0
Bolivia	19.4	26.2	30.6	3.3
Brazil	10.5	10.5	15.2	2.9
Chile	14.8	10.6	12.5	3.8
Colombia	20.1	25.5	21.2	3.3
Costa Rica	29.6	35.0	31.3	5.2
Cuba	n.a.	n.a.	n.a.	9.3
Dominican Republic	7.3	16.3	16.4	2.6
Ecuador	21.0	21.8	19.8	3.2
El Salvador	20.5	24.9	28.4	3.6
Guatemala	16.7	17.5	16.7	1.7
Haiti	11.7	11.7	11.2	1.1
Honduras	16.6	19.5	21.7	3.3
Mexico	19.1	20.1	13.1	3.2
Nicaragua	14.5	18.6	15.6	2.2
Panama	21.2	34.6	21.7	5.9
Paraguay	16.0	13.2	17.2	1.4
Peru	17.6	23.4	21.7	4.2
Uruguay	26.4	26.1	n.a.	3.6
Venezuela	14.5	23.1	21.8	5.3

Sources: UNESCO, *Evolución reciente de la educación en América Latina* (Santiago, Chile: 1976), p. 43; *Statistical Abstract of Latin America,* vol. 19, Latin American Center, University of California, Los Angeles, p. 86.
Note: n.a. = not available.

TABLE 17
Enrollment in Latin American Schools and Universities, 1950–75
(in percent)

	Primary Education			Secondary Education			Higher Education		
	1950	1960	1975	1950	1960	1975	1950	1960	1975
Argentina	94.1	98.3	98.1	10.4	27.0	50.5	5.2	11.3	28.0
Bolivia	35.0	53.8	92.9	4.9	9.9	18.0	1.6	3.6	5.9
Brazil	39.3	59.7	85.5	5.7	9.5	19.6	0.9	1.5	9.4
Chile	74.0	88.7	90.0	10.7	21.5	47.2	1.6	4.0	16.2
Colombia	36.0	54.8	88.5	3.9	10.2	20.1	0.9	1.7	8.4
Cuba	66.2	94.5	107.0	4.7	12.3	27.4	n.a.	3.3	9.0
Dominican Republic	53.5	82.0	94.4	1.7	11.6	25.5	0.9	1.5	5.7
Ecuador	56.7	72.6	93.7	4.4	10.6	27.5	1.3	2.6	8.3
El Salvador	61.1	66.7	93.4	2.9	9.6	19.1	0.6	1.1	n.a.
Guatemala	27.7	39.9	53.3	2.4	4.8	10.1	0.7	1.6	4.1
Haiti	19.0	30.8	35.2	1.0	3.8[a]	5.0[a]	0.2	0.5	0.5
Honduras	28.1	56.9	73.4	0.6	5.7	11.9	0.6	1.1	4.4
Mexico	53.0	70.1	98.5	2.7	10.0	30.2	1.6	2.6	9.6
Nicaragua	38.5	48.7	71.4	2.7	5.4	19.3	0.7	1.2	6.7
Panama	76.0	80.5	106.9	9.2	25.0	48.4	1.9	4.6	18.3
Paraguay	74.3	84.7	86.4	1.5	9.4	17.7	1.2	2.3	4.8
Peru	66.8	72.5	95.2	6.4	13.5	33.9	2.1	3.6	22.8
Uruguay	89.8	93.8	90.6	17.0	30.5	62.4	5.7	7.7	15.0
Venezuela	51.1	83.5	84.5	3.0	17.7	31.9	1.3	4.3	19.8

Source: For 1950, classifying primary education as covering ages 7–13: UNESCO, *Statistical Yearbook 1963;* for 1960 and 1975, classifying primary education as covering ages 6–12, secondary education ages 13–19, and higher education ages 20–24: OREU, UNESCO *Statistical Yearbook 1975;* CELADE, *Estimaciones de Población, para los tramos de edad.*

Note: For 1960 and 1975, grades 1–6 are considered primary and grades 7–12 secondary; n.a. = not available.

a. Data from UNESCO, *Statistical Yearbook 1976.*

expenditures both in total amounts and as a proportion of the government budget. Peru, for example, expanded its educational expenditures (within an expanding national budget) from 14 percent of the budget in 1955 to 21 percent in 1963. During the 1960s educational expenditures for Latin America as a whole increased by an average of 9 percent a year, attaining a level of $4 billion in 1970. This figure represents about 3.4 percent of the GDP and 20 percent of the national budgets.[68] The major portion of educational expenditures—usually at least 70 percent—has been allocated for teachers' salaries. But the increased educational budgets have also been used to improve enrollment ratios at all three levels of schooling, to increase the number of teachers, and to reduce illiteracy rates. Table 17 shows that in 1950 only Argentina and Uruguay were educating about 90 percent of the primary-level children.

TABLE 18
Illiteracy among Latin Americans Age Fifteen Years and Older, 1950–76
(in percent)

	1950	1960	1970	1976
Argentina	13.6	8.0	6.0	7.4
Bolivia	n.a.	n.a.	60.2	40.5
Brazil	50.7	39.5	33.0	18.8
Chile	10.2	16.4	11.6	10.3
Colombia	37.7	27.1	22.0	22.4
Costa Rica	20.6	15.6	11.0	11.6
Cuba	n.a.	22.0	15.0	10.0
Dominican Republic	57.1	35.5	32.8	23.3
Ecuador	44.3	32.5	28.0	25.0
El Salvador	61.6	51.0	42.0	40.5
Guatemala	70.6	62.1	55.0	52.7
Haiti	n.a.	n.a	78.0	75.3
Honduras	64.8	52.7	43.0	42.0
Mexico	44.1	37.8	23.8	23.7
Nicaragua	61.9	50.2	42.0	47.4
Panama	30.1	23.4	21.7	16.0
Paraguay	34.1	25.6	20.0	19.5
Peru	n.a.	38.9	32.2	21.1
Uruguay	n.a.	9.7	n.a.	10.2
Venezuela	49.0	36.7	n.a.	22.9

Source: America Latina en Cífras, Revista Progreso, 1977.
Note: n.a. = not available.

By 1975, nine other nations had reached this mark. The average yearly growth of primary school enrollment has generally exceeded general population growth since the 1950s. Whereas in 1960 the average enrollment rate for primary education in the whole region was about 70 percent, by 1970 it had increased to 86 percent. As of 1975, the two countries with the poorest records at the primary level were Haiti, with only 35 percent of this age group attending school, and Guatemala, with 53 percent attending. At the secondary level, whereas only about 15 percent of the fourteen-to-nineteen-year-old age group were attending school in 1960, by 1970 it was almost 29 percent, and by 1975 it was 42 percent. Similar advances were achieved in higher education. In 1960 only 3 percent of those twenty to twenty-four years old were attending school, but by 1970, almost 7 percent were attending, and by 1975 almost 12 percent were attending. We should also note that increasing numbers of women are participating in both secondary and higher education. Women constituted at least 40 percent of secondary education students in most countries in 1975 and over 40 percent of higher education students in Argentina, Brazil, Panama, the Dominican Republic, and Uruguay.

As for reducing illiteracy (table 18), virtually every country except Haiti has made significant progress, although much remains to be done. The countries still plagued by major proportions of illiterates (over 40 percent of the population) are Bolivia, El Salvador, Guatemala, Haiti, Honduras, and Nicaragua. In Nicaragua, the Sandinistas launched a massive literacy campaign on March 24, 1980, in which 110,000 youths were expected to teach 700,000 illiterates how to read and write. Most other countries continue to have large pockets of illiterates among their Indians, peasants, and urban poor. In Guatemala, for example, illiteracy in the various departments ranges from a high of almost 90 percent to a low of 20 percent. In Mexico, the range of illiteracy rates by states varies from a high of almost 50 percent to a low of 10 percent. In Colombia, illiteracy rates are almost three times higher in the rural areas than in the cities.[69] Unfortunately, there are still 50 million illiterates in Latin America.

The university reform movement, which eventually influenced higher education throughout Latin America, was launched in 1918 at the University of Córdoba in Argentina. According to Kenneth Walker, "The major impetus for the movement was a reaction against the archaic and oligarchic structure of the university, characterized by nepotism, an emphasis on formalism in lectures and an absence of practical training, and the domination of the university by a self-perpetuating governing council with little concern for the interests of students or lower status professors or for the cultural needs of the nation, and with little or no support of original research, development of new fields of study or new methods of teaching."[70] In the "Córdoba Manifesto" the striking students called universities "the secular refuge of mediocrities" and "faithful reflections of a decadent society, offering a sad spectacle of immobile senility." The students demanded and—with the help of the Radical party government of President Hipólito Irigoyen—eventually achieved the following reforms: free tuition at the university, with admission conditional only on successful completion of secondary school studies; representation by students, professors, and graduates on the governing councils of the university and of the faculty; *ex officio* membership, by election, of the rector and deans of faculties on the superior council of the university—the deans elected by majority vote of faculty councils, and the rector elected by the university assembly, composed of equal representation of students, faculty, and graduates; and freedom for professors to teach and students to attend classes without compulsion or restriction. The *reformistas* believed that, by gaining university autonomy from the national government and by having students participate in the university decision-making process (co-government), the university would become an instrument of, rather than an obstacle to, national development.

The major accomplishment of the reform movement was to open up the universities to a broader segment of the middle class. Between 1956 and the mid-1970s the Latin American university population soared from about 440,000 to almost 3 million. In Brazil the number of university students increased from about 13,000 in 1929 to over 9 million in the early 1970s. By the mid-1960s in Latin America there were more than a thousand universities, teacher training schools, technical institutes, and colleges. Before 1958 in Venezuela there were only six institutions of higher education; by 1976 there were nine public universities, five private universities, four teachers' colleges, three polytechnic institutes, seven technological universities, and five junior colleges.

Students are now studying a much greater variety of subjects in a larger number of universities. Whereas there was not even an economics program at the National Autonomous University of Mexico until 1929, by the mid-1970s this university was awarding degrees in twenty-six technical careers, fifty-four careers at the bachelor level, sixty-three postgraduate specialist degrees, seventy-seven master's programs, and thirty-seven doctoral programs.[71] Similarly, the National University in Colombia now offers sixty-eight different courses of study. However, the traditional fields of law and medicine continue to attract nearly a third of Latin American students, compared to less than 5 percent in the United States. Increasing numbers are studying engineering (which in Latin America is primarily civil engineering), administration, accounting, economics, and statistics, but very few students major in the natural and agricultural sciences. For example, during the mid-1960s, in the five Central American countries where the agricultural sector represents more than two-thirds of the population, only 1.7 percent of the university students were enrolled in agriculture, and Honduras had not yet initiated any university programs in agriculture.[72] In 1974, the Venezuelan president, Carlos Andrés Pérez, created the Gran Mariscal de Ayacucho scholarship program to send abroad 6,000 students to study in what are called priority fields for national scientific and technological development. The list of priority fields includes: oil and petrochemicals, agriculture and livestock, metallurgy and steelworking, oceanography and fishing, aeronautics, and naval industries.[73] This list illustrates that although Venezuelan universities have adapted to increasing numbers of students, they have not yet adapted to the growing complex needs of a modernizing nation. Universities have certainly improved, but students still complain about part-time teachers, lack of responsibility and poor performance among the faculty, and the university's negligence in updating the curricula. In the early 1970s about 37 percent of the university faculty in Chile and Colombia were full-time, which was the *highest* percentage in Latin America. Only 3 percent of the faculty of Mexico's National University were full-time.[74] Part-time faculty, because of their uncertain and degraded positions, are less likely to devote themselves to teaching, research, or recent developments in their fields, than regular, full-time faculty. A study of Colombian higher education concludes, "University teaching emphasizes three things—theory, long class hours, and memorizing information. As a result, the student's attitude inclines toward passive learning rather than creative or critical thinking. He tends to regard his studies as an obstacle course leading to graduation."[75] Under these conditions, many university students drop out and never complete their studies. In Colombia and Mexico the dropout rates among university students are approximately 50 percent.

It is ironic that some claim that the very success of the 1918 reform proposals have contributed to the universities' inability to perform a more modernizing function in their countries. While university autonomy and student participation in university governance have sometimes played a progressive role, such as helping to overthrow corrupt dictatorships during the 1950s in Colombia, Cuba, and Venezuela, they have also contributed to the politicization of the university, resulting in violence, strikes, and sometimes the closing down of the university for a period of time by government authorities. The majority of students in Latin American universities are most concerned with earning their degrees, but ideologically motivated students are likely to control student organizations and exercise a disproportionate influence over student elections. Consequently, many Latin American universities are fragmented by different groups who want the universities to provide humanistic education; education for the traditional professions regardless of national needs; technical education for the occupational needs of a modernizing nation; a place for serious research, critical reflections, and discussion; and a haven for revolutionary critics and urban guerrillas, so that the university will become the first liberated territory in the revolutionary struggle. These mutually incompatible goals have inhibited universities from playing the role envisioned for them by the 1918 reformers. A Venezuelan professor writes,

> It is important to note that . . . two of the most important of the Córdoba reforms—co-government and the inviolability of the campus—have had an adverse effect on the progress of academic freedom in that they have greatly increased the politicization of the Latin American state university. Political parties, as well as politically motivated student groups, have been encouraged to use the university campus both as a recruiting ground and as a headquarters for demonstrations and activities . . . Like other contending socio-political forces they want the university to support them, not to be "free."[76]

University autonomy and student participation have also contributed to the relative independence of the various faculties or schools. The administrative separateness of faculties, often reinforced by physical separation, reduces the university's capacity to make changes designed to make itself more responsive to the requirements of a developing nation. Instead, the loyalties of teachers and students are often limited to their own schools, resulting in bitter conflicts and inefficient use of institutional resources. To illustrate this problem, Arthur Liebman et al. presented a case study of the failure of the University of Chile in its attempt to set up an Institute of Science in the 1960s. It was hoped that the institute would train undergraduates in modern physics, biology, chemistry, and mathematics; the graduates could then help modernize the teaching of science at all levels of the educational system. However, the institute found it could not compete successfully within the university against such powerful traditional faculties as medicine and engineering. When university officials went so far as to veto a direct grant to the institute by a North American foundation to buy needed equipment, several members of the institute resigned to accept better-paying jobs in private industry and outside the country.[77] Attempts to adapt Latin American universities to the needs of contemporary science and technology are often interpreted by the traditional faculty and radical students as penetration by U.S. imperialism and as threats to the humanistic traditions of the nation. Harrison laments, "In practice, the very word 'modernize' has come to be synonymous, for many of both the right and the left within the university, with North American cultural imperialism or dominance. . . . One of the lamentable by-products of the Plan Camelot embroglio of 1965 was that anyone using the quantitative and data-collecting aspects of modern social science . . . could be labeled as anti-national or pro-U.S. by the traditional Chilean professors uninterested in research."[78] By refusing to buy modern equipment and utilize new techniques, contemporary universities are following in the footsteps of their nineteenth-century counterparts in that they are not creating knowledge, but instead teaching what has been learned in the more advanced countries.

Because it is so difficult for established universities to adapt to new conditions, many countries have found it easier to create new universities and research institutes. For example, writes Richard Pelczar, in Colombia "initial changes came in newly-founded institutions like the University of Los Andes (1948) or the University of Del Valle (1945). In both places, reformers were influenced strongly by the land-grant model of the North American university and fortuntely did not have to overcome old prejudices, archaic practices, or recalcitrant traditions."[79]

The impact of educational reforms on development has also been disappointing. One problem that now plagues educational reformers is that they can no longer claim that improvements in education will automatically promote democracy and economic development. Argentina and Uruguay have long been committed to education and have had much success; however, in both nations education has suffered because of political instability, dictatorship, and severe economic problems. But while a commitment to education does not automatically bring development, it is clearly one of the prerequisites. Haiti's lack of commitment to education is related to the fact that Haiti is overwhelmed by the worst poverty and the most corrupt political system in the region. The Latin American experience suggests that educational improvements are a necessary but not sufficient means of promoting development.

Educational reforms have also not been able to equalize educational opportunities. Although opportunities for education have grown, the traditional functions of selection and rejection are still operating. As an example of this propensity, Robert Halpern notes that during the early part of this century kindergarten and social welfare programs together served less than one percent of Latin American children. By the end of the 1970s such programs were serving less than 10 percent of the preschool children, and most of the participants were from middle- and upper-class families least in need of such social services.[80]

For many poor children, such programs are necessary to overcome the correlates of poverty—malnutrition, debilitating diseases, lack of parental supervision, being out on the street on their own at very early ages, the lack of reading materials in the home, and the absence of a place to study. Unless compensatory mechanisms are employed by the schools, these conditions ensure that large percentages of the poor will fail at early ages. The daily struggle for survival is not compatible with success in formal schooling.

Just as damaging is evidence compiled by two Latin American scholars concerning the percentage of students enrolled who are not able to complete the cycle of compulsory primary schooling. According to Rama and Tedesco, "Data on drop-outs among recent cohorts show . . . that out of every 100 students enrolled in first grade only the following reached the 6th grade of primary education: 16 in Brazil, 19 in Nicaragua, 21 in the Dominican Republic, Honduras and Guatemala, 30 in Paraguay, 32 in Colombia, 38 in Peru, 42 in Ecuador, 53 in Argentina, 54 in Venezuela, 60 in Panama, 61 in Bolivia, 64 in Uruguay, and 76 in Costa Rica. In most countries, the highest drop-out rates occur during the first three years of school. For this reason, learning of the basic skills of reading and writing is not duly achieved and it is lost in a few years due to lack of practice."[81] This evidence reflects the persistence of such problems as inadequate or nonexistent schools in the countryside and a school environment that alienates large numbers of the poor and thus encourages dropouts. Educational reforms have widened the traditionally narrow bridge across the social gap and created "a stratified educational system which, while it cannot provide for the population as a whole at a basic educational level, offers possibilities of a long education to those who overcome the barrier of primary school."[82]

Reform efforts have also been overwhelmed by the disparity between the magnitude of educational needs and the inadequate amounts of money available for educational expenditures. Because of the great preponderance of young people in most Latin American populations, the spectre of numbers haunts educational policymakers. The traditional structure only accommodated a minority of the school-age population; reformed school systems have been attempting to universalize schooling for an expanding school-age population. The problem of coping with an expanding population was summarized by Oscar Vera during the 1950s: "The average annual increase in population in Latin America is estimated at 2.6 percent as compared with the world average annual increase of 1.6 percent. This means that the Latin American countries must make an effort 60 percent greater than that of the average country elsewhere in the world in order to increase their educational facilities if these are to do no more than keep pace with the annual increase in their population."[83] This educational burden is reflected in the fact that in 1970 the number of U.S. adults (ages twenty to sixty-four) per child of primary school age (five to fourteen) was 2.74, while in Mexico it was 1.25, that is, for every five adults there are four children in Mexico. Of the nations with such rapidly expanding populations, perhaps only Venezuela has the financial capacity to universalize schooling.

Educational costs are also rising because universities and normal schools are graduating increasing numbers of teachers who then demand incomes commensurate with their educational qualifications. In addition, major advances are now being made in most countries not at the primary level but at the secondary and university levels, and the average cost of educating a secondary student is twice that of a primary student, while educating a university student costs ten times more. University enrollments are not only growing more rapidly than enrollments at the two lower levels, but also accelerating.[84] In many nations, higher education now accounts for one-third or more of educational expenditures and is thus inhibiting the capacity of the system to universalize basic education.

The combination of increasing numbers of students and a shortage of money has caused problems at the primary level and an alleged decline in the quality of public secondary and university schools. At the primary level, schools have adjusted through larger classes, multiple shifts, and low investments in equipment, books, and maintenance. At the secondary and university level, many well-to-do parents have preferred to send their sons and daughters to private schools. In recent decades private universities have grown faster than public ones, which is changing "the traditional image of the non-denominational, non-paying Latin American university of the liberal republican governments."[85]

School systems have also not responded adequately to the increased demand for technically trained personnel required by nations concerned with accelerating development. One major weakness has been the failure of secondary schools to train middle-level technical and managerial talent. The educational system instills in the students the notion that "success" in school means becoming a university graduate (*titularse*—to title oneself), although this is possible for only a small portion of the population. At the secondary level, practical courses are often not available; but even when they are, they often do not attract students. Thus, most students end up working in jobs for which they are not trained. Both students and faculty tend to see this issue in terms of "Humanism versus Technology in a culture in which the former is clearly the side of the angels."[86] Many humanists wince at the idea the one of the major functions of a nation's educational system is to develop a broader and more qualified stock of human resources— that is, trained workers. This problem is reflected in Colombian secondary schools where students are offered three choices in curricula— traditional academic studies, commercial or technical programs, and agriculture. Although few students will enter the university, about 80 percent of Colombian secondary students enroll in the academic program, which supposedly prepares students for higher education. Recognizing the resistance of the traditional educational bureaucracy toward vocational education, the Colombian government in the 1960s created the National Apprenticeship Service (SENA) *outside* the Ministry of Education to provide intermediate-level technical training. SENA is financed by a 2 percent payroll tax from businesses employing ten or more persons. Although SENA has successfully trained hundreds of thousands of workers, one Colombian journalist lamented, "In our country the university gives 'status' and technical studies—as offered by SENA—are not considered as prestigious."[87] As is often the case in Latin America, the existing value system is not compatible with developmental needs.

One might expect that central control of educational policy would facilitate educational reform, but this has not proven to be the case. Formal, central controls have been inadequate to counter the power of cultural values, the status attraction of traditional occupations, and the inertia of inefficient and uncoordinated educational bureaucracies. In most countries, primary and secondary public education have separate administrative components that are not well coordinated in spite of their normal control by the minister of education. Similarly, higher education jealously guards its autonomy, vocational education often has its own administrative machinery either inside or outside the ministry of education, and private schools are often in a powerful position to defend their own interests. Whereas we frequently hear about the centralized authority of Latin American presidents and ministers of education, the reality is that most of these officials would not be able to deliver a speech on a university campus because of political opposition. Nor can they implement many of the reforms they have decreed. Latin American school systems have developed in a haphazard manner and are subject to contradictory pressures, reflecting the different demands of governments and social sectors. In 1966 the ECLA complained that although education appears to be the social policy area most susceptible to planning, "one cannot . . . as yet find an example of an integrated program effectively applied to the *whole* of a school system, determining priorities and controlling educational output in accordance with an over-all conception of national education objectives. . . . Aside from the difficulties common to all areas of planning and programming, the educational systems present rigidities that derive from their historical development and their peculiarly close relationship to existing social structures."[88] In 1977, a leading Latin American scholar concluded that educational policy remained "extraordinarily confused as regards objectives and priorities."[89]

Ideally, education is a unique policy area where well-planned improvements can promote *both* economic growth, by providing the skilled personnel necessary for increased productivity, and social justice, by eliminating illiteracy and enhancing social mobility. Most countries have made significant gains in raising both literacy rates and the proportion of youth attending the three levels of education, but the progress has been more difficult to achieve than expected. Only Cuba (as we will see in chapter 6) has been able to mobilize its educational system as an instrument to achieve its developmental objectives. For the other nations, the educational system has not been efficiently synchronized with the needs of either accumulative or distributive policies.

Social Security Policy

Social security is also one of the most important components of a distributive public policy. A social security system is designed to help individuals cope with old age, sickness, invalidism, maternity, work-related injury, and unemployment by providing cash benefits and/or services. As a society modernizes, the state assumes—some would say has thrust upon it—greater social responsibilities for the maintenance of individual security against life's inevitable risks and problems. When a nation becomes more industrial and urbanized, individual and family self-reliance declines, and the state's social responsibilities increase.

In the last quarter of the nineteenth century the industrializing nations of Western Europe began to deal with the problems associated with the urban working class. The pioneer in developing social responsibilities was Bismarck's Germany, which, in order to gain the political support of the working class and prevent the growth of the Social Democrats, initiated sickness insurance in 1883, industrial accident insurance in 1884, and pension insurance in 1889. Confronted with similar problems, other European nations adopted similar policies—which became known collectively as welfare state policies. The ideas associated with social security then spread—or "diffused" as students of comparative public policy prefer to say—to Latin America. In pre-industrialized Latin American nations, social protection and charity were the responsibilities of the family, mutual aid associations, and the Catholic church. The first Latin American countries to adopt social security policies were Argentina, Chile, and Uruguay (the southern cone countries), which were characterized by higher levels of urbanization, middle-class reform parties, and trade unions. However, these three countries initiated their social security systems with lower income levels and a lower proportion of industrial wage earners than existed in the European countries. Argentina, like most Latin American countries, had established pension benefits for the military and civil servants in the nineteenth century, but it passed its first pension law for workers (railroad workers) in 1915. Chile also established a pension program for railroad workers in 1911 and a pension and health program for all blue-collar workers in 1924. Uruguay passed its first work injury law in 1914 and its first old age, invalidism, and death law in 1919. From these beachheads, the idea of social security was eventually adopted in every Latin American country, with Honduras being the last nation to establish its program in 1962.

Social security systems in Latin America have taken two main forms. The southern cone countries and Brazil established separate funds (*cajas*) for individual categories of employees and workers, each with its own legally defined sources of income, conditions of entitlement, range of benefits, and administrative apparatus. These systems have grown by accretion until most of the economically active population is now theoretically covered. The exclusion of some groups for many years was a function of their lack of political power and the administrative problems of trying to collect contributions from a multitude of widely dispersed small economic units (farms, families, vendors), many of whom did not earn enough to contribute. It was also expected that traditional paternalism would take care of these people, not the state. Outside of these four countries, says an ECLA report, "Most of the countries that embarked on social security during the 1930's and 1940's enacted legislation setting up a single institution to provide limited benefits to certain categories of workers and employees for a beginning, but with the intention of gradualy expanding coverage in respect of occupations, geographical areas and types of coverage; such expansion by stages was generally provided for in the basic legislation itself. Pre-existing pension systems for public employees and the armed forces generally retained their separate administrations."[90] Some of the nations that established their social security systems during this period were: Ecuador, 1935; Peru, 1936; Panama, 1941; Costa Rica, 1941; Mexico, 1943; Venezuela, 1944; Colombia, 1946; Guatemala, 1946; the Dominican Republic, 1947; and El Salvador, 1949.

During and after the 1930s, all social security systems were influenced by the recommendations and standards of the International Labor Organization (ILO). Beginning in 1936, the ILO sponsored a series of regional conferences over the next decade which advocated that every country accept the principles of compulsory coverage for all citizens, standardization of contributions and benefits, and administrative unification of social insurance funds. They also pressed for the extension of benefits into a full range of medical and social assistance programs. These reforms were to be financed according to the ideal of "social solidarity," that is, a method of finance that implied a substantial redistribution of income. The ILO provided skilled actuaries and training programs for civil servants in countries that were organizing social security programs. Consequently, a regional network of experts was created that worked within national contexts for social security reform. The ILO view of reform was incompatible with preexisting systems of multiple funds and corporate representation of interest groups in the administration of decentralized social security agencies.

Rosenberg and Malloy describe the situation in this way: "As they were originally conceived in Latin America, social security programs were not granted on the basis of citizen 'right' but rather on the basis of a group-specific contractual obligation. . . . Therefore, even at its outset, social security was neither mass based nor egalitarian in Latin America. It was limited to those who were privileged with employment in the modern sector."[91] Before 1940 these programs were developed around "funds" that granted protection to specific groups usually identified in terms of economic function and/or occupational criteria. The governing boards of these funds were organized into a tripartite corporate structure composed of representatives of employers, employees, and the state. New funds were created for newly recognized groups. The typical pattern was to extend social security benefits to the military and public employees, then to those working in vital infrastructural activities (such as miners), then to those in critical urban services (like bank employees), then to those in industrial services, and only in recent decades to the urban self-employed and to rural workers. Both Chile and Peru set up separate programs for white-collar workers (*empleados*) and blue-collar workers (*obreros*), with the higher-status *empleados* generally receiving better benefits. This particularistic, piecemeal policy style, so typical of Latin America, helps to explain why Carmelo Mesa-Lago has labeled the evolution of social security policy in each country "a mirror that reflects the overall societal stratification."[92]

In Latin America the initiation and evolution of social security policy has responded more to power (or feared potential power) than to need. Mesa-Lago argues that the military "has granted itself or exerted pressure in order to receive the earliest, best, and cheapest social security protection." Similarly, "The more powerful a pressure group/subgroup, the earlier in time it gets social security coverage, the higher its degree of coverage by the system, and less it costs to finance that system (largely because of contributions from the state and from employers), and the more generous its benefits (more benefits available, more flexible requirements to acquire such benefits, and higher amounts granted)."[93] However, the initiation of social security policies was more often a preemptive gesture on the part of ruling elites rather than a direct response to the pressure of different social groups.

Many of the above generalizations are illustrated by the experiences of Brazil. In Brazil programs to protect the military were initiated during the colonial period and expanded during the nineteenth century. It was not until the 1920s that social protection was extended to the private sector. In 1923 the legislature passed the "Lei de Eloy Chaves," proposed originally by Eloy Chaves of São Paulo. Chaves argued that the elite were faced with new conditions in which they would have to stimulate productive labor and avoid the class conflict being encouraged by radicals. Social security was advocatd by Chaves as an example of an elite-sponsored reform that proved that class collaboration was more socially beneficial than class conflict. In Chaves's words, "It is our responsibility as witnesses of these extraordinary times to create solutions and heal the wounds and chaos originating from them. We are in new times: the underprivileged classes justly hope for a greater share from life and its comforts. It behooves us to attend to them with a friendly and liberal spirit."[94]

The Chaves law called for the obligatory creation in each railway company of a fund (CAP) for retirement and survivors' pensions. The Lei de Eloy Chaves became the model upon which the Brazilian social security system would be constructed and established the precedent of using social insurance as a means of coping with social questions. In this system, insured workers had a contractual obligation to contribute to their own protection. Workers were granted benefits proportional to their monthly contributions. The funds were to be financed from three sources: each employee was to contribute 3 percent of his or her monthly income; each company would contribute 1 percent of its annual gross income; and the government would provide funds derived from taxes levied on the users of railroad services. The funds were to function as autonomous semipublic organizations under the general supervision of the government. According to Malloy, this law

> embodied the concept that social insurance did not extend to broad social categories based on some abstract notion of class or citizenship but to specifically designated work-based groupings; in this case the stipulated category was railroad workers and the unit of coverage was each individual company. The effect was to divide workers horizontally (in a class sense); for example, the insured from the noninsured and each insured category (in 1926, dock and maritime workers) from one another. At this stage the division went even deeper, dividing workers within a category on a company by company basis. Within a category and a company, however, all employees regardless of job, status, or income belonged to the same CAP. Thus, even while the structure divided workers horizontally within classes, it united them vertically across class lines. This administrative principle—which persisted until 1966—was to prove an extremely useful device to control the working class after 1930.[95]

Social security benefits were extended to railway workers in 1923; maritime and dock workers, 1926; public service workers, 1931; mine workers, 1932; bank employees, 1934; commercial workers, 1934; and industrial workers, 1938. During the first Vargas regime (1930–45), a large and complex social insurance system was constructed as part of a general strategy to strengthen the national government and to divide the working class by creating separate funds for different categories of workers. In 1933 a new administrative structure was introduced called the Instituto de Aposentadora e Pensoes (IAP). Instead of constructing insurance around company-based CAPs, the IAPs would organize social protection into one institution covering all workers in specific categories. Both the CAPs and IAPs were to be autarchic public institutions under the supervision of the Ministry of Labor, Industry, and Commerce. By 1939 the Brazilian social security system consisted of ninety-eight CAPs, five IAPs, and totally separate systems for civil servants and the military. Both the CAPs and IAPs were financed according to the triple contribution formula in which the employer and the state contributed an amount equal to that of the insured. The state was supposed to finance its contributions from a variety of "user" taxes on services, such as railroads, shipping, bank transactions, electricity, and gas, and from general revenue. However, the state rarely contributed its full share and thus accumulated a soaring debt to the social security system.

As can be seen, by the 1940s Brazil had a multitude of different social insurance programs providing different benefits and services to their members, with some groups (bank employees, for instance, who were the beneficiaries of earmarked user taxes) receiving better protection than others (industrial workers did not receive any earmarked taxes). Before the 1950s industrial workers, covered by the Institute of Industrial Workers (IAPI), were provided with only three major cash benefits covering sickness, invalidism, and survivor pensions. Unlike several other institutes, IAPI did not provide maternity benefits, old-age benefits, and time-of-service benefits. Thus, the system contained groups with a vested interest in blocking many reforms proposed by ILO-inspired technocrats that might threaten their privileged position. But during the 1950s and early 1960s populist politicians overcame some of their opposition by granting new benefits and by extending benefits previously enjoyed by one or two institutes. The powerful institutes were able to thwart the principle of administrative unification, but the number of institutes was reduced from ninety-five in 1940 to thirty-five in 1950 and to six by 1960. In the Social Insurance Organic Law of 1960 the only CAP fund still in existence became an institute, and the same system of benefits, services, and financing, together with the identical administrative structure, were established for all six institutes. Meanwhile, the numbers and percentages of the economically active population (from 20 percent in 1950 to 23 percent in 1960) steadily increased along with the aforementioned increase in benefits. In 1963 President João Goulart proposed the creation of a rural workers' fund for which there were woefully insufficient funds. With the government failing to meet its financial obligations, with many of the employers either avoiding making their payments (sometimes in collusion with workers) or delaying them in order to take advantage of the accelerating inflation, and with some of the institutes subject to corrupt political and union practices, most of the social security institutes were in serious financial trouble by 1964.

After Brazil's military coup in 1964, the military government gave the social security technocrats a relatively free hand in reorganizing the system. In 1966, over the objections of groups such as the bank employees, the six IAPs were unified into the National Institute of Social Insurance (INPS) headed by social insurance technocrats. In 1967 INPS assumed full responsibility for workers' compensation from the private insurance companies. In 1971 the government extended a separate program of social insurance for the rural sector entitled FUNRURAL. FUNRURAL was unique in that it was *not* based on such concepts as the triple contribution and the amount of benefit being determined by the amount of contribution. The persons insured, which theoretically included almost all rural workers, made no direct contribution. Instead, FUNRURAL was supported by a 2 percent tax on rural products paid by wholesalers (which made the program easier to administer than taxing the much more numerous producers) and by a 2.5 percent tax over the wage bill of urban organizations that contributed to INPS. INPS collected these funds and then turned them over to FUNRURAL. As for benefits, Malloy writes, "Curative medical assistance is available to all, but in practice delivery is determined by availability of funds, availability of clinics and hospitals to be contracted by FUNRURAL, or the ability to build, equip, and staff its own clinics and hospitals. Four flat-rate cash benefits accrue to all: a monthly retirement benefit (65 years of age), a benefit for invalidity, a monthly survivor's pension, and a one-time funeral benefit. All are one-half the national minimum salary (in 1975 approximately U.S. $30.00)."[96]

By the mid-1970s, social insurance protection was approaching universalization with close to 93 percent of the total population covered (including the insured and their dependents). However, there were still six major systems covering the military, federal civil servants, state-level civil servants, INPS (urban workers), and FUNRURAL (rural workers). The benefits for the military and federal civil servants were superior to the other systems' benefits, while the situation for state-level civil servants varied from state to state. INPS was the largest social security instituion; it employed over 120,000 persons and covered over 80 percent of the urban population. INPS was financed by equal employee and employer contributions and a government contribution to cover administrative costs. The 15 million urban workers contributed 8 percent of their monthly income up to a maximum income of twenty times the minimum salary. The normal retirement age was sixty for women and sixty-five for men, but a long-service pension was payable at any age after thirty years of work. To qualify for a pension, a beneficiary had to have contributed for at least 60 months. The urban basic old-age pension was 70 percent of average covered earnings in the thirty-six months prior to retirement.

Malloy emphasizes that glaring inequalities remain between the urban and rural social insurance systems:

> INPS provides its insured with at least thirty different cash benefits while FUNRURAL provides only four; and these four rural benefits set at one-half the minimum salary are rather small indeed. Moreover, FUNRURAL's medical program is rudimentary, provides limited types of care, and suffers from the same distribution problems as INPS. The magnitude of the extreme differences between the two systems stands out clearly in the fact that in 1973 INPS spent close to Cr. $19 billion to service an insured population roughly similar in size to that of FUNRURAL which spent only around Cr. $2 billion. Compared with INPS, FUNRURAL is a most modest program.[97]

Further administrative reform took place in 1977 when the National Social Security and Assistance System (SINPAS) was created under the control of the Ministry of Social Security and Assistance. Within SINPAS two autonomous organizations were established: the National Medical Assistance Institute (INAMPS) and the Institute for Financial Administration of Social Security and Assistance (IAPS). Two institutions—the Assistance Fund for Rural Workers (FUNRURAL) and the Pensions Institute for Civil Servants (IPASE)—were eliminated, and the urban National Social Security Institute (INPS) was profoundly altered. Under SINPAS, the benefit programs of the urban and rural workers and of federal civil servants—previously administered by the former INPS, FUNRURAL and IPASE, respectively—

are now run by the new INPS, financed through the same employee/employer contributions, to be collected by IAPAS (the government continuing to bear administrative costs).[98]

The achievements—and problems—of the Brazilian social security system are paralleled by the experience of other Latin American countries. Of all the world's developing regions, Latin America has achieved the greatest progress in social security programs. All of its nations have established compulsory social security systems that provide income maintenance and health protection for growing proportions of their population. These programs are increasingly adopting the ILO principle of universality (total coverage), but the actual implementation of such noble objectives is still decades away for most countries. Progress has also been made in limiting the proliferation of social security institutions for different categories of workers and in improving coordination among them. The number of such agencies in Latin America, which had reached 150 by 1960, has been significantly reduced by a number of consolidation programs. Unfortunately for the proponents of participatory democracy, the most successful consolidation efforts have been achieved in such nondemocratic states as Castro's Cuba, and the military dictatorships of Argentina, Brazil, and Peru. Despite Allende's commitment to equality, his administration refused to reform the chaotic and unequal Chilean social security system because of the opposition of labor groups who benefited from the status quo.

As should be obvious by now, social security in Latin America has been promoted by a variety of political leaders with very different ideologies. In Argentina Perón increased his popularity by expanding social security coverage from about 500,000 persons in 1945 to about 5 million in 1955. Dictators (Vargas, Odría), democratic reformers (Battle, Alfonso López, Cárdenas), Christian Democrats (Frei), Socialists (Allende), Communists (Castro), and corrupt politicians (Miguel Alemán) have all supported increased social security programs. There is no major ideological opposition in Latin America to the concept of social security.

The social security programs in Latin America are generally of the "insurance" type in which the contributions and benefits are earnings-related. The programs are financed by contributions of varying amounts payable by workers and employers and representing a percentage of remuneration. There is also a state contribution in most schemes. Cuban social security under Castro's reforms takes the unique form of a single, noncontributory program run by the state and centrally financed out of the national budget.

It is difficult for Latin American countries to maintain adequate financing for their social security programs because they have been gradually extending them in three directions: to cover more risks, to protect more categories of persons, and to expand benefits geographically from the capital city to the provinces and to the rural areas.

Argentina, Chile, and Uruguay supply thirty-five kinds of social security benefits ranging from old age pensions to dental care. The least covered social risk is unemployment. In 1979, the only countries to have unemployment programs (usually small) were Argentina, Brazil, Chile, and Uruguay. The extent of coverage for the elderly, invalids, and survivors of deceased persons varies considerably from one country to another but is steadily increasing. Virtually the entire economically active urban and rural population, including self-employed and domestic workers, are now covered in Argentina, Brazil, Costa Rica, and Uruguay. In other countries coverage is less universal. For example, during the 1970s, only 30 percent of the whole population and 72 percent of the economically active population of Chile were covered by old-age and invalidism insurance; for the Dominican Republic, the figures were 5 to 12 percent, respectively; in Ecuador, 6 and 16 percent; in El Salvador, 4 and 14 percent; in Honduras, 8 and 27 percent; in Nicaragua, 6 and 21 percent; in Panama, 16 and 45 percent; and 32 percent of the economically active population of Venezuela was covered by insurance for invalidism and old age.[99] In Bolivia only 20 percent of the population of five million was covered by social security. In Mexico the social security system was initiated in 1943; by 1952 only 5 percent of the labor force was covered; by 1964, 18 percent; by 1970, 25 percent; and by 1978 almost 40 percent. In Colombia the social security system was created in 1946; by 1958 14 percent of the labor force was covered; and by 1974 almost 30 percent.

Despite these achievements, Latin American social security programs have been plagued by problems since their inception. Most of these programs were introduced with inadequate technical and administrative expertise, and their subsequent development has often been ruled by politically inspired improvisations instead of planning. Where one would expect to find an abundance of statistics and data regarding this program, one quickly learns that little data—a basic prerequisite for planning—is available. Indeed, not until recently did many of these systems utilize demographic projections to estimate the future costs of given types and levels of benefits. While social security is a policy area that appears naturally suited for unified administration and coherent programming because it has significant and multiple effects upon other social and economic policies and offers an instrument for the potential attainment of many policy objectives, the social security systems of a number of countries have grown by accretion. As a result, they are too complex, too costly, and uncoordinated. In the late 1960s ECLA described social security as "a sector characterized by administrative autonomy and compartmentalization, the focus of strong and complex political pressures, and the preserve of well-entrenched bureaucratic interests."[100] Describing the activation in the 1970s, Mesa-Lago writes:

> Each of the pressure groups/subgroups that has been capable of obtaining social security protection is covered by a separate fund, public, autonomous, autarchic, with its own legislation and ad hoc contingencies covered, conditions for granting benefits, amount of their benefits, and sources of financing. This proliferation . . . of institutions and variety of regulations has created a legislative labyrinth with resultant confusion for the insured, cumbersome procedure for employers, . . . difficulties for control resulting in a high rate of evasion and fraud, conflicts of jurisdiction among funds, duplication and waste of human and material resources which increase administrative costs, and lack of continuity in protection for the insured who change occupations. The whole system usually lacks a central agency empowered with policy-making, coordinating, filing, supervising, and auditing. National planning has only recently begun to include social security but with little or no effective strategies and control for implementation.[101]

These problems have been particularly severe in Chile. In the 1970s Chile had more than 160 social security funds including 31 systems of old-age retirement, 30 of seniority retirement, 30 of disability, 35 of health-maternity, dozens of family allowances and unemployment compensation programs, and 55 of social welfare. There are also hundreds of laws that remain uncompiled and uncoordinated affecting the administration, financing, benefits, and supervision of different groups.[102]

The problem of financing social security programs is also a major concern. Social security revenues have grown in several countries to the point where they are almost equal to total government revenue, but they are frequently squandered and rarely invested wisely. The squandering is reflected in high administrative costs. The cost per member of administering a social security program is usually in inverse proportion to the number of persons insured. Multiple social security programs within a single country results in higher costs because of the duplication in administrative structures and less efficient use of electronic equipment. Administrative costs are also inflated by corruption. For all these reasons, administrative expenditures are considerably higher in Latin America than in the United States. Whereas in the United States, administrative costs for social security in the 1970s were only about 1 percent of the social security budget, in Chile they were about 14 percent, in Brazil about 11 percent, and in Mexico between 16 and 19 percent.[103]

Social security funds are squeezed by the extensions of benefits and coverage, excessive administrative costs, corruption, overly generous benefits for the employees of social security agencies, and widespread evasions and delays in government contributions. Increases in employer and employee contributions, which in countries like Uruguay have reached levels equivalent to almost half the size of the wage bill, increase the incentives to evade. In inflationary periods employers can reduce their burdens by delaying their social security contributions for a year or so. Employer contributions alone are often equivalent to 25 or 30 percent of wage costs, which encourages capital-intensive, instead of labor-intensive, development. Under these circumstances, employers try to maintain their profits by hiring fewer workers, deflecting social security costs onto consumers, and pressuring policymakers for greater protection from foreign competitors. Governments sometimes exploit social security reserves to make up their own deficits by inducing the funds to buy government bonds, while inflation is permitted to reduce the real burden of payments to beneficiaries. Unfortunately, there may be an association between extensive social security coverage and severe chronic inflation. Mesa-Lago points out, "In countries such as Uruguay and Chile the gradual extension of social security protection and privileges has resulted in social security costs that reach a proportion of GNP [nearly 15 percent] surpassed only by that of some developed Western and Eastern European countries."[104] He suggests that this may partially explain the stagnation and economic crises of Uruguay and Chile. In 1966, President Eduardo Frei of Chile warned his nation that current trends would bring about not only the bankruptcy of the social security funds but also the bankruptcy of the country. There is now considerable concern that Costa Rica will not be able to meet its social security commitments because of rising oil import prices and falling coffee exports.

Latin American citizens are also plagued by the administrative problems of social security agencies. Because of the size and complexity of social security programs, this policy area is particularly dependent upon efficient administration translating legal provisions into tangible and readily available benefits and services. At the simplest level, efficient administration is contingent upon information, and one is therefore surprised to learn that most agencies have no data banks compiling information on insured persons. Applicants for benefits must supply the social security agency with a series of documents such as employers' certificates of contributions and certification of marital status. The Kafkaesque trials of citizens seeking their rights from the bureaucracy are a source of great frustration. A common practice is to hire intermediaries or use influential connections to reduce the administrative delays. Hence, most citizens must wait an excessively long time before acquiring benefits. Some of these delays serve the purpose of reducing actual benefits paid out to the system's level of resources.

Finally, social security policy in Latin America does not alleviate the income distribution problem. According to the principle of social solidarity, social security should be able to achieve a more equitable income redistribution by taxing the wealthy to aid the poor. But the guiding principle of social security policy in the region has often been a political one: "to gain the electoral support of a particular clientele, to legitimate a spurious political regime, and to satisfy the needs and coopt powerful pressure groups which threaten the status quo."[105] Hence, social security policy often reflects the power structure in which those with the most power and the least need receive the best protection, and those with the least power and most need are either underprotected or unprotected. A social security system cannot redistribute income if the contributions of the state are financed by regressive taxes or if the costs of the contributions of the employers are passed on to the consumers through higher prices. Because benefits are tied to the contributions of the individual, those who contribute more receive more from the system. The income transfer is more horizontal—that is, *within* income groups, from the healthy to the sick and the young to the old—than vertical, from the rich to the poor. Thus, in terms of income distribution, the effects of social security policies are probably either neutral or retrogressive.

In brief, policymakers have used social security policy to maintain the incomes of the increasing number of social sectors needed to preserve the social order rather than to promote income distribution. However, a considerable amount of social justice has been achieved through these programs, flawed though they may be, and social groups continually pressure governments for more and better coverage.

Health Policy

Another major area of distributive public policy is health policy. Health policy includes: preventing illness, curing the sick, and providing health personnel resources and facilities. Health policy is primarily a distributive policy but the improvement of health in a society can significantly contribute to economic growth. It is increasingly recognized that prevention of disease, medical care, proper diet, and environmental sanitation are essential requirements for socioeconomic growth. Healthy workers and farmers can be productive; sick workers and farmers cannot. Similarly, healthy children are more likely to do well in school. Reformers in the field of health policy have tried to get policymakers to view health costs not as consumer expenditures but as investments in human capital.

As a society becomes more urban and industrialized, health policy becomes more of a public responsibility. Whatever their ideologies, most governments acknowledge a major responsibility in assuring that their citizens have access to health services. Whereas in the nineteenth century providing health services for the poor who could not afford to pay was a function of charity, in the twentieth century the rise of the equalitarian idea that all citizens have the right to adequate health services means that the absence of health facilities for the poor can no longer be morally justified. Health policy is an area where elites can provide greater services to the less privileged without threatening their power position. Health policy is not the zero-sum game that agrarian reform and income redistribution policies are; nor does it raise potentially unrealizable occupational and social aspirations that educational reforms do. However, few nations in Latin America have been able to satisfy the health care demands of their expanding populations.

Health policy in Latin America reflects a variety of historical influences. The original Indian culture depended upon various primitive "nonscientific" medicines for its health needs which are still used by many Indians and some peasants today. Traditional healers (*curanderos*) and midwives still employ combinations of magic, herbs, and physical measures to cure the sick, ward off the evil eye, and aid in childbirth.

A second influence is the tradition of charity hospitals. In the colonial period, the Catholic church of Spain originated many of the charitable or *beneficencia* hospitals to care for the urban poor. These hospitals were originally financed by the bequests of wealthy people, by the operation of cemeteries, by lotteries, and by donations. Today these hospitals are usually semipublic institutions heavily subsidized by the government. The typical *beneficencia* hospital is an old building, poorly designed for modern medical purposes, with large wards to serve the poor who are seriously ill. According to Milton Roemer, most of these hospitals are run by "a board of leading citizens from the local city; while these men and women may be kind and public spirited, their knowledge of modern medical requirements is usually very limited. Nor is there a trained hospital administrator, except rarely, to compensate for these deficiencies. The top direction is often in the hands of a busy doctor, who does clinical work in the hospital, and maintains a private practice in town, and can give little attention to administrative matters."[106] Some of these charitable hospitals have provided the teaching facilities for medical schools attached to universities. In the twentieth century many of these hospitals have been taken over by the national government and operated by the ministry of health. The Mexican government nationalized these hospitals after the 1911 revolution, and the Chilean government took control of them in 1952 when it created the National Health Service. In brief, each government has evolved a somewhat different pattern in its use of public money, between support of these charitable facilities and complete replacement of them by public hospitals.

Third, from colonial times to the present, the wealthy have bought their health services from the private medical sector. Given the skewed income distribution in Latin America, only a minority of the population has been able to afford this fee-for-service system.

A fourth historical influence was provided by the United States through the Pan American Health Organization, which, beginning in 1902, promoted public health programs, especially environmental sanitation and mass campaigns against such vector-borne diseases as malaria and yellow fever. In 1961, the Kennedy administration established the Alliance for Progress, and, through the Charter of Punta del Este, the Latin American governments pledged to improve their health conditions over the next decade. Specifically, they each promised to:

increase life expectancy by at least five years; provide adequate potable water and sewage systems for not less than 70 percent of the urban population and 50 percent of the rural population; reduce existing mortality rates for children under five years of age by at least one-half; intensify the control of communicable disease; improve nutrition; and train medical and health personnel to meet at least certain minimal requirements.

Finally, the concept of social security, developed by Bismarck in Germany, spread to the Americas and gave rise to a special subsystem of health services for insured workers. Social security programs, including health benefits, were eventually established in all Latin American countries. Today, medical care is provided to insured workers along two general patterns. The first pattern, established in Chile after 1924, was to use social security money to buy medical, hospital, and related services from existing facilities and personnel. Such services are paid for on the basis of contracts involving various forms of remuneration. According to the second pattern, originating in Peru in 1940, the social security agency would create its own facilities and employ its own personnel who would be paid salaries to provide services to the designated beneficiaries. Neither pattern has been able to achieve medical coverage for the bulk of the population. In Roemer's words, "The programs in Chile and [Castro's] Cuba have reached much higher proportions only by shifting from social insurance to predominantly general revenue financing. Because of this minority coverage and because social security everywhere in the developing world has been able to support a higher quality of medical care for the minority than that available to most of the national populations, serious questions of equity have arisen."[107]

In 1952 Chile created the National Health Service (NHS) by combining the *beneficencia* hospitals, the social security program of medical care for workers (*obreros*), and the Ministry of Health programs of preventive and curative services. The original NHS covered about 70 percent of the population, including insured manual workers and low-income rural people. Remaining outside the NHS were insured white-collar employees (Employees' National Medical Service—SERMENA), railroad workers, civil servants, the military, and the wealthy. SERMENA preferred not to join the NHS because of its opposition to joining the health care system created for workers and medical indigents; however, the increasing demand of white-collar employees for curative services brought them under NHS coverage by 1969, although they were still permitted to choose a private doctor if they were willing to pay half of the private fees.[108] By the early 1970s, 90 percent of Chilean doctors worked at least part-time for the NHS.

The combination of these historical influences means that most Latin American countries have a number of different and uncoordinated health delivery systems that provide medical services differing widely in quantity and quality for different social groups. Medical personnel and facilities tend to operate in autonomous, vertical systems. There is a lack of horizontal cooperation among medical personnel and facilities within local communities. Dieter Zschock captures the institutional anarchy of Latin American health systems:

> In addition to public health services and private medical care facilities, they have separately organized social security services for salaried employees and for wage earners, quasi-public charity hospitals (governed by boards of private citizens or church authorities, and financed by donations and income from state lotteries), and special facilities for military and police forces. Many national, regional, and city government agencies also frequently operate independent medical care services, either for their employees, or as part of their principal functions, for example, in agriculture and education. Moreover, all but public health facilities and charity hospitals, which provide services to the general public where they exist, serve relatively small privileged segments of the population for whose benefit they were created. Large segments of the countries' low income population, on the other hand, particularly in rural areas, receive few if any modern health services.[109]

An overview of health policy in Latin America is provided by tables 19 and 20. As is often the case in the region, much of the health data is not as reliable and comparable as we might prefer. This is especially true in the less developed countries (Haiti, Bolivia, Honduras, Guatemala, Nicaragua) and the rural areas of most Latin American countries. It is also difficult to compare public health expenditures because some countries submit only Ministry of Health expenditures, while others will combine Ministry of Health expenditures with social security costs and still others will include local and state health expenditures. Nevertheless, enough data over time is available to make the following observations.

TABLE 19A
Latin American Mortality Statistics, 1960–80

	Deaths per 1,000 Inhabitants			Infant Mortality per 1,000 Live Births			Life Expectancy		
	1960	1967	1975–80	1960–62	1970	1977	1950	1960	1975–80
Argentina	8.7	7.9	8.9	61.0	62.0	51	59.2	66.0	69.4
Bolivia	15.1	12.9	17.5	103.0	157.0	155	49.7	n.a.	48.6
Brazil	n.a.	11.8	7.9	n.a.	90–100a	109	42.4	n.a.	63.4
Chile	12.2	9.5	6.7	117.8	40.1	61	51.9	57.2	65.7
Colombia	11.9	9.4	7.0	92.8	59.6	98	45.1	n.a.	63.4
Costa Rica	8.8	7.1	4.1	n.a.	22.3	38	55.9	63.4	70.0
Dominican Republic	8.9	7.6	4.8	94.1	33.9	96	62.1	57.9	62.4
Ecuador	14.1	10.6	7.8	99.4	71.5	70	52.0	53.8	62.1
El Salvador	11.7	9.3	6.9	72.5	50.5	58	51.2	58.5	62.2
Guatemala	17.3	15.2	10.9	89.3	82.9	77	43.7	49.0	57.8
Haiti	21.6	21.6	14.5	n.a.	150.0	140	32.6	42.0	52.0
Honduras	9.8	9.0	6.2	48.4	33.6	103	45.8	n.a.	57.1
Mexico	11.5	9.2	8.5	71.4	56.0	60	49.7	58.9	64.0
Nicaragua	8.5	7.2	12.2	63.1	12.3	122	59.9	n.a.	55.2
Panama	8.0	6.7	4.1	51.1	24.4	47	56.1	59.2	67.9
Paraguay	10.5	10.8	8.1	89.7	64.0	64	n.a.	n.a.	63.6
Peru	11.4	8.6	11.8	92.9	100.7	80	57.4	52.8	57.2
Uruguay	8.5	9.5	8.5	44.6	48.6	46	68.8	65.5	72.0
Venezuela	7.2	6.9	5.5	52.1	34.4	49	57.6	66.1	66.4

Source: Inter-American Development Bank, *Socio-Economic Progress in Latin America, 1969 Report; 1979 Report* (Washington, D.C.: IADB, 1970, 1980).

Note: n.a. = not available.

a. Estimated figure.

TABLE 19B
Latin American Health Statistics, 1960–77

	Population per Physician			Hospital Beds per 10,000 Population	Percent of Population with Safe Water
	1960	1972	1977	1977	1977
Argentina	680	495	521	524	66
Bolivia	5,756	2,342	2,631	228	34
Brazil	2,181	2,025	1,695	327	55
Chile	1,661	n.a.	1,613	359	70
Colombia	2,632	2,282	1,961	161	64
Costa Rica	2,729	2,663	1,389	345	72
Dominican Republic	7,149	2,088	1,887	233	55
Ecuador	2,609	n.a.	1,562	204	36
El Salvador	5,232	3,934	3,704	161	53
Guatemala	4,644	n.a.	2,500	187	39
Haiti	34,325	13,264	14,286	72	12
Honduras	5,132	3,503	3,125	137	41
Mexico	1,798	1,385	1,754	115	62
Nicaragua	2,809	1,516	1,667	207	56
Panama	2,701	1,441	1,282	386	77
Paraguay	1,996	2,279	1,299	135	13
Peru	1.975	1,751	1,562	184	47
Uruguay	821	911	719	418	92
Venezuela	1,513	997	934	292	75

Source: Inter-American Development Bank, *Socio-Economic Progress in Latin America, 1969 Report; 1979 Report* (Washington, D.C.: IADB, 1970, 1980).
Note: n.a. = not available.
a. Estimated figure.

Since the end of World War II, most Latin American nations have reduced both overall mortality and infant mortality, while increasing life expectancy. Because of earlier development, plentiful food, and good climate, Argentina and Uruguay had made excellent progress in the health field before World War II, and have continued to make moderate improvements. Progress in health care is general in the region. A Latin American born in 1950 could expect to live past sixty in only three or four countries, whereas a Latin American born in 1980 can expect to live past sixty in fourteen countries.

However, problems remain nevertheless. The infant mortality rate, deaths under one year per thousand live births, is generally considered to be one of the most sensitive indicators of public health achievements. In the United States this rate has remained around 25 per

TABLE 20
Latin American Public Health Expenditures, 1977–79
(in millions of U.S. dollars)

	1977 Expenditures	Expenditures Per Capita	Percent of Total Government Expenditure for Public Health (1979)
Argentina	375	14	3.0
Bolivia	33	7	8.2
Brazil	1,445	13	2.8
Chile	263	25	7.8
Colombia	174	7	8.0
Costa Rica	20	10	5.0
Cuba	310	32	n.a.
Domincan Republic	59	11	2.1
Ecuador	56	8	9.3
El Salvador	40	9	10.1
Guatemala	45	7	8.9
Haiti	7	1	13.7
Honduras	40	12	11.7
Mexico	525	8	10.1
Nicaragua	32	14	19.8
Panama	33	18	6.3
Paraguay	7	2	4.3
Peru	139	9	5.0
Uruguay	36	13	6.6
Venezuela	1,003	74	4.8

Source: Ruth Leger Sivard, *World Military and Social Expenditures, 1980* (Leesburg, Va.: World Priorities, 1980); Inter-American Development Bank, *Economic and Social Progress in Latin America, 1979 Report* (Washington, D.C.: IADB, 1980).
Note: n.a. = not available.

thousand for many years. In Latin America, Cuba and Costa Rica have achieved great success in reducing infant mortality rates, but the rates in Bolivia, Brazil, Colombia, the Dominican Republic, Haiti, Honduras, Nicaragua, and Peru remain shockingly high. Some idea of the large percentage of preventable deaths in the region is conveyed by the fact that in 1969 deaths among children under five years of age accounted for 44 percent of all deaths in the Latin American countries, compared to only 8 percent in the United States.[110] The health situation in Haiti is the worst in the hemisphere: mortality rates for Haitian children under five is ten times that of developed countries.[111]

As a society modernizes, the principal causes of death change. In the United States, the five principal causes of death in 1974 were: diseases of the heart, malignant neoplasms, cerebrovascular disease, accidents, and influenza and pneumonia. Countries that provide adequate food, sanitation, and health services (especially to mothers and children) will approximately duplicate the United States pattern. By the mid-1970s, Argentina, Chile, and Cuba had matched this pattern. In the other Latin American nations, large numbers of people are still dying from essentially preventable causes of death. Prenatal death (during the period from about three months before birth to one month after birth) is one of the five principal kinds of mortality in Costa Rica, El Salvador, Guatemala, Haiti, Mexico, Uruguay, and Venezuela. Similarly, enteritis and other diarrheal diseases are major causes of death in Colombia, the Dominican Republic, El Salvador, Ecuador, Guatemala, Haiti, Honduras, Mexico, Nicaragua, Panama, Paraguay, and Peru.[112] That so many preventable deaths still occur indicates how inadequate health policy is in most Latin American countries.

Latin America is also very deficient in medical personnel. The United States has more physicians, dentists, pharmacists, and graduate nurses than all of Latin America combined. The World Health Organization recommends one doctor per thousand people, but this ratio has been achieved only in Argentina, Cuba, Uruguay, and Venezuela. However, between 1960 and 1970 the number of medical schools has increased from 98 to 158, which has significantly improved the ratio of doctors to population in most countries. There is an even greater shortage of dentists. In 1970 the number of dentists per ten thousand inhabitants was about 5.4 in the United States and Argentina, 3.3 in Chile, 2.7 in Brazil, 2.1 in Colombia, 1.9 in Venezuela, 1.6 in Bolivia, 1.5 in Peru, and 1.2 in Ecuador.[113] The lack of trained pharmacists is important because pharmacies are the source of much self-medication in Latin America. Roemer reports, "Whereas drugs may typically constitute 10 to 15 percent of health care expenditures in the United States or Europe, they may consume 33 percent or more of health costs in Latin America."[114] The lack of trained nurses is particularly severe and is partly caused by cultural patterns. Many of the young women who graduate from secondary education are from the upper social classes; they are inhibited from becoming nurses by tradition and their families.

Public expenditures for health have generally increased since 1950. The percentage of total central governmental expenditure for public health is usually somewhere between 3 and 10 percent. Table 20 reveals that public expenditure per capita on health in 1977 varied from a low of US$1 in Haiti to a high of US$74 in Venezuela. One major criticism of health expenditures in Latin America is that not enough is spent on preventive measures. Usually about 80 percent of the health budget is spent on curative medical care despite the prevalence of diseases whose occurrence could be significantly reduced by preventive measures. One partial exception to this generalization is provided by Chile, which, as we have seen, was a frequent innovator in social policy until 1973. In 1938 Chile passed the Preventive Medicine Law which required the annual examination of all insured workers for early detection of tuberculosis, syphilis, and heart disease. Cancer was later added to the list. However, Roemer reports, "After a while the burden of performing these examinations became greater than could be borne by the resources of the Chilean health system as a whole, and the tests became applied only to selected groups of white-collar employees, mainly in governmental jobs."[115]

The poorly coordinated health systems in Latin America are confronted—and sometimes overwhelmed—by a variety of difficult problems. The major problem is that there are growing numbers of poverty-stricken people living in rural and urban environments that are not conducive to good health. In general, improvements in basic sanitation programs have a greater impact on reducing mortality rates and health problems than do improvements in health care delivery systems. In Latin America, however, most rural people have no sewage systems, and few have access to adequate water supplies. Explosive urban growth has meant that city governments have not been able to keep up with the demands for adequate water supplies and waste disposal systems. In countries like Bolivia, Ecuador, Guatemala, Haiti, Honduras, Paraguay, and Peru, less than half the population has access to safe water (see table 19). The consequences of unhealthy water can be seen in Haiti where only 12 percent of the population has access to clean water and the infant mortality rate is 140 per thousand births.

Malnutrition also contributes to significant health problems. Because of the aforementioned income distribution, most of the poor in Latin America cannot afford an adequate diet. Illiteracy and lack of education contribute to this problem because few of the poor have been taught to take advantage in a nutritional sense of what little money they have. In any case, if one assumes acceptable daily calorie intake to be about 2,500 to 2,750 calories, about one-third of the present population is suffering from malnutrition. The problem is particularly severe among children (the poor tend to have large families), where it is estimated that 35 million children under six suffer from malnutrition.[116] These children are not likely to do well in school and are also likely to fall prey to such diseases as pneumonia, tuberculosis, influenza, measles, whooping cough, diphtheria, various parasitic diseases, and severe diarrhea. Malnutrition is a major contributor to the large number of preventable deaths among children in Latin America.

Another severe problem is that the health care that is available is so unevenly distributed. Privileged segments of the population, such as the military, government employees, and strategically important workers, have been granted good medical coverage; but more than 100 million people lack adequate preventive and curative health care services. There are from six to twenty-five doctors for each ten thousand inhabitants in Latin American cities, but fewer than four doctors per ten thousand people in rural areas.[117] Lima, Peru, contains about 20 percent of the national population, but about 65 percent of all the physicians. About half of the health expenditures in Peru is spent for the care of only 10 percent of the population, while the other half must serve the needs of 90 percent of the population.[118] In Chile, 60 percent of the nation's physicians practice in Santiago, which contains one-third of the nation's population. Even during the Allende period it was estimated that the national health service received 40 percent of Chile's total health expenditures to serve 80 percent of the population, while 60 percent of the nation's total health expenditures went to private practitioners caring for 20 percent of the people. A health survey of 45,000 Chileans in 1968 revealed that the groups least likely to have their health needs satisfied were the rural poor, the urban poor, those who lack social insurance, and the elderly.[119] In the mid-1970s in Mexico the national ratio of doctors to population was 1:1,418, while in the capital it was 1:474. This ratio would be even worse if it were not for a 1933 law that requires new medical graduates to practice in rural areas for several years. However, Mexico has increased its number of medical students from 20,000 in 1967 to 80,000 in 1979, almost twice as many as in the United States. The health problems of about 20 million Mexicans are covered by the social security system, which in 1979 had a budget of US$4.5 billion. But the rest of the nation—about 45 million people—is "covered" by the Health Ministry which has a budget of only $660 million.[120]

In Colombia the central government has been bound by a 1973 law to allocate at least 15 percent of its total budget for education and health. The per-capita allocation of national expenditures for health more than doubled between 1965 and 1975.[121] Still only about one-third of the population have their health needs covered by a variety of social security programs. About half the rural population—more than 6 million people—have little access to the most elementary modern health services. This problem would be even more severe if it were not for the 1957 law requiring every graduating physician in Colombia to provide obligated service for at least two years, usually in a rural area designated by the minister of health. However, a large number of doctors manage to weasel out of this social obligation. A World Bank study reports:

> The uneven distribution of physicians in the United States has evoked much concern but nowhere does it approach the maldistribution recorded in Colombia where almost 3 out of 4 doctors reside in the principal cities and serve less than one-third of the total population; only 10 percent of the medical manpower in Colombia is available to the two-thirds of the population residing in places of 20,000 population or less. Probably of even greater significance is the observation that, with the resources at present in sight, it would take no less than 100 years for the medical training institutions of Colombia to produce the number of physicians required to approach current United States physician to population ratios.[122]

As is true of other Latin American countries, the abundance of doctors in Bogotá results in their inefficient use, while other parts of the nation have few health professionals to serve the public.

The lack of medical personnel and facilities in Colombia, combined with their inadequate distribution, means that only a small proportion of the population is protected against common infections by simple and relatively inexpensive immunization procedures. By the late 1960s only 13 percent of the susceptible population (under age five) had been immunized against whooping cough, 9 percent (under age fifteen) against diphtheria, and 5 percent against polio (under age five). A measles vaccination had not yet been distributed through public health channels and tetanus toxoid had been given to only about 1 percent of the general population. Even smallpox vaccination had been administered to only 56 percent of the population, a level of protection that is considered dangerously low by health experts.[123]

To summarize, we have examined health policy as primarily a distributive public policy but one which can also make significant contributions to socioeconomic growth. Protecting the health of the people is increasingly viewed as a public responsibility; citizens have come to see their access to health care as a social right. Hence, most Latin American governments have improved their health systems which has resulted in greater longevity. But these efforts have frequently been inadequate, in part because a variety of historical influences have led to uncoordinated and inefficient health systems that distribute health care very unevenly. Thus the combination of inadequate health delivery systems, unsanitary environments, and malnutrition means that there are still hundreds of thousands of preventable deaths each year, especially among children.

Conclusion

Most political systems in Latin America have emphasized the accumulation of wealth instead of its equitable distribution. However, when one looks at the structure of Latin American bureaucracies and national public expenditure figures, it becomes obvious that not only are these governments concerned with such traditional functions as maintaining law and order and managing the financial system, public works, and foreign affairs, but also they have become increasingly involved with such distributive programs as agrarian reform, public education, social security, and health care. Although some of these policies have achieved success in many countries in supplying schools, raising literacy rates, building hospitals, lowering infant mortality rates, and providing pensions and health care for workers, the effectiveness of many of these policies has been diluted by the poverty of most countries, too-rapid population growth, inflation, and the limited administrative skills of public bureaucracies. Many of these policies were begun with inadequate planning and poorly trained personnel, resulting in the institutionalization of inefficient, uncoordinated, and corrupt practices—a subject that we will examine in the next chapter. In promoting distributive policies, Latin American policymakers have been motivated by the needs of political survival (as illustrated in tactics like buying off some potentially threatening group such as land-hungry peasants or angry workers), bureaucratic aggrandizement (such as an education agency pressuring for more funds with which to build new schools), the desire to emulate social welfare systems in Europe, and, finally, an honest commitment to social justice.

The policy elites understand that their legitimacy is now dependent upon their promoting both economic growth and distributive justice. The main obstacle to the growth of distributive policies is *not* the political culture of the region, which is compatible with a paternalistic welfare state, but the soaring costs. Most Latin American countries have engaged in distributive policies for select groups (the military, the bureaucracy, the labor aristocracy) for a long time. By the 1960s, however, governmental and opposition rhetoric have contributed to citizens becoming more conscious of what they now perceive to be social rights. Hence, most governments are now pressured by demands for distributive justice as previous beneficiaries want more and potential beneficiaries desire universalization of social welfare programs.

Distributive policymaking in Latin America is often characterized on the one hand by grand rhetoric and utopian aspirations, and on the other by selective and piecemeal implementation. Many are promised land, education, social security, and health care, but only some receive them. When the distributive policies of Western industrialized nations, which promise universal application, are adopted by the paternalistic nations of Latin America, they are applied in a highly selective manner. Few of these policies aid the poorest sectors of society and many of them aid landowners, unionized workers, and the middle class. From the elite's perspective, this system has generally been functional because it has prevented whole groups—Indians, peasants, workers, urban squatters—from rebelling despite the fact that the bulk of each of these groups continues to endure the kinds of deprivations that radical leftists believe should produce both the objective and subjective conditions necessary for revolution.

In any case, both distributive and economic growth policies in Latin America are increasingly dependent upon the efficiency of a centralized bureaucratic system, which is the subject of chapter 4.

4

Bureaucracy and Public Policy

In the previous two chapters we discussed the strategic choice between accumulation and distribution; in this chapter we shall begin an analysis of the choice between building the public bureaucracy and mobilizing the people. Most Latin American policymakers believe that building and maintaining the bureaucracy should be stressed over social mobilization in order to promote an orderly process of modernization. It is believed that the state, dominated by bureaucratic institutions, is necessary to promote both economic growth and greater distributive justice. Whatever the political leanings of a government, state intervention has been an expanding part of the economic scene since the Depression. The paradox of this strategic choice is that Latin Americans have placed the burden of promoting modernization in the hands of public officials—both civilian and military—whom they distrust. Indeed, there is a mutual distrust between public officials and the mass public that sets up enormous obstacles to this strategy of modernization.

The purpose of this chapter is to analyze Latin American bureaucracies in terms of their influence on developmental policies. Our analysis will include, first, the reasons why Latin Americans have become committed to a strategy of development that emphasizes bureaucracy; second, the structure and functions of modern bureaucracies; third, the weaknesses of those bureaucracies; and, finally, the consequences of relying so heavily on centralized bureaucracies for public policy.

Reasons for the Stress on Bureaucratic Development

Most Latin Americans have never been attracted to the liberal state. The idea of the state playing the role of referee among the competing interests of society and concerning itself mainly with providing law and order and a minimum level of public services is not compatible with either the colonial heritage or the developmental aspirations of most policymakers since the 1930s. Latin America endured 300 years of Spanish and Portuguese colonialism, and this legacy still affects bureaucratic behavior today. The Spanish colonies were considered the *personal* property of the monarch. All laws were created in Spain by the Council of Indies which "set the stage for administration that was intensely personal at the same time it was intensely legalistic."[1] The Iberian monarchies, in establishing and maintaining their rule over people thousands of miles away, institutionalized a paternalistic style of administration. The colonial legacy has inclined the nations of Latin America toward a top-down approach to modernization, whose characteristics are variously described as a patron-client system, a corporatist tradition, and a patrimonial state. Solon Barraclough connects the colonial legacy with contemporary administration and policy in this way:

> Outsiders are prone to regard the complicated labyrinth of price controls, production limitations, import and export subsidies, prohibitive tariffs, state-protected monopolies, exchange-rate manipulations, and special tax exemptions as a recent development imposed by misguided disciples of state intervention in the economy. Actually, the mercantilist systems of Spain and Portugal have much more to do with the present structures than is generally realized. The networks of regulations, licenses, official monopolies or concessions, quotas, and red tape were already largely formed in the 18th century.[2]

In the twentieth century, the Latin American state has become the ultimate patron, from which citizens expect everything—except justice.

Proponents of a bureaucratic, state-centered style of development do not have to overcome a liberal heritage; there is no strong ideological limitation on statism in Latin America. Instead, there is an inherited belief system that holds that large numbers of people—Indians, peasants, workers, and urban squatters—do not have the capacity either to care for themselves or to influence the public policies designed to help them. The elites are inclined to stress that modernization is essentially an administrative problem rather than a political one. That is, public policy decisions should be made by elites with minimal political interference from those who are considered least able to provide constructive influence and most likely, if autonomously mobilized, to promote violence and chaos. This attitude is nicely captured by Guy Poitras's characterization of the Mexican elite:

Revolutionary leaders (the president, members of the party and government) believe that economic development and social change must be directed from the top by a fairly small group of public and private leaders. This preference has tinted the bureaucracy with semiauthoritarian paternalism, even though the government party (the P.R.I.) officially represents workers, peasants, and the popular (middle) classes. This notion, which underlies the entire system—that economic and social change should be accomplished on behalf of the masses but without their meaningful participation—is closely related to the assumption that unmanaged economic growth would jeopardize the political stability that the country has maintained for decades.[3]

In brief, Latin American elites are likely to reflect a low estimate of their citizens' ability to know what is best for them and a high estimate of their own capacity to decide what is best for the nation.

This belief in state-centered development is shared by practicing politicians of different political ideologies. The tradition of state-directed development is exemplified in the policies of Batlle y Ordoñez, Vargas, Cárdenas, Perón, Castro, Betancourt, Frei, and Allende. Each of these politicians substantially increased the role of the public bureaucracy in his nation's development. The view of the state held by Brazil's Getúlio Vargas reveals what the proponents of a bureaucratically directed style of modernization desire:

Vargas struggled mightily to make the state the pivot and regulator of national socioeconomic relations; as part of that strategy he sought to liberate the state from both internal and external pressures and to endow the state with as much autonomy as possible; finally, he instituted a process of modernization of social relationships which, at least after 1937, was based on a policy of industrialization. In a sense, the state became, under Vargas, both a means and an end; he sought to use the state to create a more coherent, modern and powerful nation which would express its power to the world in the form of a relatively autonomous and powerful state. One can argue it was a process of adapting the form of the traditional patrimonial state to the substance of the modern era.[4]

A second reason for the inclination of Latin American policymakers to pursue a bureaucratically directed style of development is their negative view of the domestic bourgeoisie. Whereas the commercial and industrial middle class in Western countries is often viewed as having promoted democracy, industrialization, and nationalism, in Latin America the belief has spread that the indigenous bourgeoisie needs help in state capitalist societies and should be eliminated as the major obstacle to development in state socialist countries such as Castro's Cuba. In Latin America the private entrepreneurial class is criticized for not promoting democracy, for fostering a process of industrialization that has been too open to the exploitation of foreign capital, and for developing a self-indulgent consumerism that is inimical to both the rapid accumulation of capital and social justice. An Argentine social scientist justifies the dominant role of the state in promoting development by condemning the Argentine bourgeoisie for its lack of asceticism; for its inability to take risks, to innovate, to develop its own technology, and to export; and for its commitment to quick and speculative profits.[5] Under these circumstances, reformers call for the state to supplement the role of the native bourgeoisie, while radicals demand that the state replace and eliminate the bourgeoisie. With the property-owning class unable to accumulate capital or exhibit the necessary managerial talents, the state has tried to perform the role of economic advisor, regulator, planner, and major entrepreneur in the process of modernization.

Structure and Function of the Bureaucracy

Thus Latin Americans have decided that their future should be determined by the administrative state. According to Milton Esman, "The administrative state as an ideal type is one in which the state is the dominant institution in society, guiding and controlling more than it responds to societal pressures, and administrative (bureaucratic) institutions, personnel, and values and style are more important than political and participative organs in determining the behavior of the state and thus the course of public affairs."[6] Since the Depression, and especially after World War II, virtually every Latin American government has shifted from a passive to an active role in promoting economic growth and involving itself in an expanding number of expensive distributive policies. Whether this type of regime is labeled paternalistic, corporatistic, or authoritarian, writes Merilee Grindle, it is

> typified by extensive state enterprises coexisting and supportive of the private economic sector, comprehensive responsibility for the provision of welfare services, . . . and functionally organized clientele groups dependent upon and even formally attached to the regime in power. Policymaking . . . is the exclusive prerogative of a small elite and is characterized by limited informational inputs, behind-the-scenes bargaining and accommodation, and low levels of public discussion and debate. Not only does the government of such a state claim responsibility for a wide range of activities; it also tends to reserve important policymaking roles for public administrators.[7]

Latin American nations do not have free enterprise–capitalistic economies. At first, entrepreneurs relied upon the state to make only the necessary infrastructural investments (roads, railroads, and port facilities), but now they are dependent upon a vast array of public policies that provide them with protection, investment capital, water, electricity, cheap transportation for workers, and state controls over labor unions. With the exception of Cuba, most Latin American countries have state-capitalist economies in which public investments and public enterprises play a far more significant role than in the United States.[8] Private enterprises are now more dependent upon state support than they ever were—or are—on foreign, private capital. Governments control or influence currency, credit, imports, public facilities, and labor, which means that the private sector operates in an environment where public decision making can make or break any firm. Operating in this milieu, where all things are possible—from Castro's Cuba to Pinochet's Chile—the insecure bourgeoisie cannot perform the functions they have traditionally performed in the Western democracies.

Latin America must now confront the problems that have emerged from import-substituting industrialization policies (ISI) and populist politics. These include: inflation, massive foreign debts, chronic balance of payments deficits, unemployment, skewed income distributions, inadequate economic growth (given population pressures), overdependence on foreign technology, soaring rates of urbanization, and the insatiable demands for social justice, as previous beneficiaries of selective welfare policies want more, and potential beneficiaries agitate for universalization of such policies. Such problems create an atmosphere of painful uncertainty and mistrust that inhibits further development.

Many bureaucratic, military, and private-enterprise elites believe that only a bureaucratic-authoritarian state can provide the social predictability necessary for what Guillermo O'Donnell labels "the deepening" of development. That is, for nations to move beyond the light industrial development nurtured by ISI, to attract foreign and domestic private capital, to raise public capital for infrastructural and heavy industrial investments, and to integrate and coordinate the unplanned industrialization that took place from the depression to the 1960s, the creation of the bureaucratic-authoritarian state is required. O'Donnell interprets such a political system as a reaction to the growing activation of the popular sectors and to the need "to rebuild, perfect, and stabilize the mechanisms of capital accumulation."[9] Based on the examples of Argentina, Brazil, Pinochet's Chile, Mexico, and Uruguay, O'Donnell defines the characteristics of the bureaucratic-authoritarian state as follows:

(a) higher governmental positions are occupied by persons who come to them after successful careers in complex and highly bureaucratized organizations—the armed forces, the public, and large private firms; (b) political exclusion, in that it aims at closing channels of political access to the popular sector and its allies so as to deactivate them politically, not only by means of repression but also through the imposition of vertical (corporatist) controls by the state on such organizations as labor unions; (c) economic exclusion, in that it reduces or postpones indefinitely the aspiration to economic participation of the popular sector; (d) depoliticization, in the sense that it pretends to reduce social and political issues to "technical" problems to be resolved by means of interactions among the higher echelons of the above-mentioned organizations; and (e) it corresponds to a stage of important transformations in the mechanisms of capital accumulation of its society, changes that are, in turn, a part of the 'deepening' process of peripheral and dependent capitalism characterized by extensive industrialization.[10]

By giving priority to the development of their bureaucracies, the advanced nations of Latin America have created more complex administrative structures than exist in the United States. In the mid-1970s, for example, the Mexican federal bureaucracy was composed of 18 regular ministries and departments, 123 decentralized agencies, 292 public enterprises, 187 official commissions, and 160 development trusts.[11] In contrast the *U.S. Government Manual, 1975–1976* listed 17 executive offices, boards, and councils, 11 departments, 59 agencies, 6 quasi-official agencies, and 64 other boards, committees and commissions. More important has been state intervention in the economy. According to Gary Wynia, "By 1970 the Mexican government was involved in over 400 enterprises, either as the sole owner or as a partner with private interests. It has also invested heavily in economic infrastructure, accounting for 30 percent of the gross domestic investment in the country since 1940."[12] The role of the Mexican state was increased even further in September 1982 when the outgoing president, López Portillo, nationalized the private banking sector. Public expenditures in 1982 accounted for almost half of the gross domestic product. The irony of this situation is that the U.S. bureaucracy, although far below Weberian ideals, has greater administrative capability than any Latin American bureaucracy, and yet is asked to do less.

Studies of bureaucracies in various Latin American countries tell a similar story; they are generally growing in size and extending their influence over many different sectors of society. In Venezuela, since the government nationalized the oil industry in 1976, the public sector has accounted for 60 percent of the gross domestic product and now directs over 200 agencies and companies. In Chile, the growth in the number of public employees from 1940 to 1970 increased nearly 400 percent to about 300,000 employees while the population increased only about 35 percent during the same period. One Chilean scholar comments about this 1940–70 period, "The bureaucracy's activities permeated all of society. Almost everything had to be done with the aid or at least the concurrence of a public agency."[13] In Brazil, Schmitter writes,

> The role of the state apparatus in Brazil has grown from almost nothing before 1930 to include a vast variety of functions. Public authorities in Brazil currently own all, or at least a substantial proportion of the maritime, river, and railroad transport, petroleum, steel and alkali production, mining of atomic minerals, and electric power generation. They intervene directly through institutes or indirectly through the Bank of Brazil in the commercialization of coffee, sugar, rubber, cacao, rice, maté, pinewood,

salt, cotton, beans, corn, soybean, wheat, manioc flour, and other products; they produce and export most of the country's iron ore; they regulate mining rights, communication and transport concessions, exchange rates, and insurance; they fix (or attempt to fix) prices on basic goods, interest rates, minimum salaries, rents, and minimum agricultural prices; they provide much of the country's short-term and virtually all of its long-term credit; they finance and control directly port facilities, storage areas for agricultural products and major housing projects. In addition, of course, they have the usual sorts of government controls over monetary, fiscal, investment, educational, health, national security, and foreign policy.[14]

The increasing functions performed by Latin American governments are reflected in the increasing structural differentiation of both ministries and decentralized agencies (analogous to the TVA in the United States). In many Latin American countries decentralized state corporations (also called autonomous agencies) are at least as important as cabinet-level ministries. The creation of such corporations is based upon the prevailing notion that regular line agencies cannot, or will not, adapt to performing new functions (that is, a ministry of agriculture resisting efforts to carry out an agrarian reform), and so a decentralized agency is established in those policy areas where the political elite is serious about implementing a particular program. In Colombia, for example, the traditional inefficiency of the Ministry of Education was countered by the creation of three decentralized corporations to build schools, to improve teaching methods, and to improve higher education.[15] Supposedly such decentralized agencies can recruit a highly qualified staff, pay higher salary schedules, and avoid ministerial red tape. The attractiveness of such agencies is such that they now number in the hundreds in several countries, and have larger budgets than line agencies. They regulate prices, wages, and production quotas; they manage steel, mining, electricity, railroad, utility, and petrochemical corporations; they administer social programs; and they are involved in national planning, agrarian reform, and regional development programs. The propensity of Latin Americans to create new autonomous agencies instead of making the regular ministries adapt to performing new programs reminds one of their similar inclination to write new constitutions when the old ones do not work or to create new political parties rather than reform the old ones.

Weaknesses in the Latin American Bureaucracies

The traditional Latin American bureaucracy provided (1) a channel for upward mobility for the educated middle class; (2) permanent incomes for that portion of the middle class who supported the regime; (3) a low level of certain services; and (4) opportunities for private entrepreneurship, based on the powers attached to certain offices.[16] The traditional bureaucrat was not imbued with the spirit of public service; bureaucracy served the personal and political needs of those who held public office. By emphasizing the bureaucratic approach to development today, Latin Americans must create a new, more development-oriented bureaucracy; administrators must use much greater rationality in making their public investment decisions, managing public enterprises, providing services to ever expanding cities, and administering a complex variety of social policies. In other words, they must replace the old bureaucracy—patrimonial, individualized, inefficient, eccentric, primarily devoted to the advancement of bureaucrats—with one resembling more closely the ideal described by Max Weber. According to Weber, the ideal bureaucracy is impersonal, legalistic, and hierarchically organized; efficiency and rationality are guaranteed by a high degree of professionalism, specialization, and division of labor.[17] As Weber pointed out, the movement toward an ideal bureaucracy involves both structural and behavioral changes. The dilemma for Latin America is that it has encountered what Schmitter labels "structural overbureaucratization" and "behavioral underbureaucratization."[18] Structurally, the bureaucracy has splintered into a proliferating number of departments, agencies, boards, and—especially—autonomous agencies. The result is the continuing rigidity of the old line departments and tremendous problems of administrative and policy coordination. In their behavior, most members of the bureaucracy also do not conform to Weber's ideal type; their primary goal seems to be self-aggrandizement—that is, obtaining benefits for themselves. Varying proportions of Latin American bureaucracies are characterized by *personalismo,* nepotism, job insecurity, high turnover rates, lack of expertise, inadequate use of existing expertise, failure to delegate authority, formalism, stultifying legalism, unsatisfactory information gathering and communication, use of the bureaucracy to relieve unemployment, and lack of coordination among agencies and departments.

Under these circumstances, the bureaucracy does not contribute what it should to increase the probability of rational developmental policymaking. This fact is widely known in Latin America. An advisor to the Colombian government complained in the 1960s, "The country simply cannot hope to achieve the desired economic goals without modernizing its manner of conducting public business and making it much more efficient. . . . The whole system of multiple responsibility (in which no one is responsible), multiple signatures, endless shuffling about of papers, preaudit, and post-audit, . . . monthly budget allotments, archaic tax enforcement methods, and complete disregard for the convenience of the public, is costing the country heavily in unnecessary bureaucracy, unnecessary delays, and a great waste of time on the part of anyone who has anything to do with government, which includes practically everybody."[19] In Argentina one hears complaints about the inefficiencies of the state-run railroads; in Bolivia the nationalized tin mines lose money; in Brazil billions of dollars have not been able to alleviate the misery of the Northeast; in Venezuela billions of dollars have not achieved success in modernizing the agricultural system; and throughout Latin America the administrative costs of running social security programs are usually from three to ten times higher than in the United States.[20] Perhaps the most discouraging case of bureaucatic greed and ineptitude is displayed in Uruguay where Batlle's democratic dream was turned into a fascist nightmare. Martin Weinstein's study concludes, "The economic stasis experienced by Uruguay since the mid 1950's is in almost diametrical opposition to the growth statistics of the public sector."[21]

This is not to say that there are no bureaucratic success stories in Latin America. Such a list would include PEMEX in Mexico, PETROBRAS in Brazil, the Venezuelan Guayana Corporation, the Cauca Valley Corporation in Colombia, the Ministry of Hydraulic Resources in Mexico, and probably many others that have not yet been studied. Nonetheless, most studies of development administration in Latin America have concluded that inefficient bureaucracies are a major hindrance to modernization and that efforts at administrative reform have proven to be inadequate.[22] Most bureaucracies are improving their administrative skills, but not fast enough to keep pace with the accelerated demands that are being placed·upon them by state-directed strategies of development.

One basic problem is that bureaucrats in Latin America operate in an environment that makes them feel vulnerable and insecure. Such an atmosphere inhibits rational decision making from a developmental perspective. According to Victor Thompson,

Personal insecurity in an authority position is likely to create personal needs of such magnitude as to dominate over organizational needs. Resulting behavior, then, will be pathological from the standpoint of the organization and so has been called "bureaupathic.". . . Bureaupathic behavior stems from needs that can be generalized as the need to control. It is manifested in such things as close supervision; failure to delegate; heavy emphasis on regulations, . . . precedents, and the accumulation of paper to prove compliance; cold aloofness; insistence on office protocol; fear of innovation; and restriction of communication. . . . In an extreme bureaupathic situation, it is difficult to see how development planning can take place.[23]

This situation is created because competition for government jobs is intense. In societies where there is high unemployment, public employment that offers adequate-to-good salaries, job security, extensive vacation time, and multiple fringe benefits—such as access to low-cost housing, free medical care and drugs, periodic pay bonuses, and good pension programs—are very attractive. Administrative costs are exceptionally high in Latin America, which reduces the ability of public agencies to fulfill their objectives. For good reason, one often hears the proverb, "He who divides and distributes keeps the lion's share for himself."

In the Mexican bureaucracy, employees are divided into two categories, base and confidence workers. Base workers are lower-level employees who are fairly safe from arbitrary dismissal. Confidence personnel are higher-level employees who "are directly dependent upon their hierarchical superiors for continued employment although their salaries are now generally set by statute or regulation. A chief who wishes to dismiss a confidence worker simply informs him 'you have lost my confidence,' and after receiving indemnification, the employee must seek another job. At the change of administration, many confidence workers follow their chiefs to new appointments."[24] Roger Hansen estimates that "every six-year change in presidential administrations witnesses a turnover of 18,000 elective offices and more than 25,000 appointive posts. Of those positions about half provide good to excellent incomes, licit and otherwise."[25] To be hired, promoted, or fired for personal reasons rather than for merit is an obvious violation of the norms of a Weberian bureaucracy.

The system of rapid bureaucratic turnover in Mexico serves to remind both aspirants and incumbents that they are operating in a very precarious environment. High- and middle-level officials cope with this situation in a culturally legitimated manner; they develop patron-client relationships. Such relationships are based upon enduring personal bonds of reciprocity and personal loyalty between individuals in superior and subordinate positions. These bonds promote security and career mobility in a fragile environment. But such responses cannot alleviate the pressures generated in a scarce resource and job society. Competition for advancement is intense, so there are numerous patron-client networks competing through the upward channels for the limited number of top positions. If your patron advances and you maintain his confidence, you advance as well. If your patron loses the trust of his superior or you lose his confidence, then you may be fired. Bureaucrats are given the contradictory advice to be loyal to their patrons but to avoid factions that are falling out of favor with higher-level patrons. Personal loyalty must be constantly tested and proven in this environment, since loyalty is far more important for career advancement than expertise or commitment to public policy. It is safer for subordinates to communicate deference to their superior rather than accurate information or critical evaluations of public policy. Moreover, the turnover of high- and middle-level personnel means that bureaucrats must administer policies and establish a record in areas they know little about. In Grindle's words, "Unprepared for their responsibilities, they are nevertheless expected to take charge quickly, to plan new activities for the unit under their command, to revise operating procedures, and to implement rapidly the directives of their superiors. These conditions place a premium on the availability of trustworthy subordinates."[26] Subordinates are advised: do things fast; don't make mistakes; don't embarrass your superiors. Such advice is a recipe for ulcers in a working environment made up of competing factions and limited information and expertise.

This insecure environment has negative consequences for the making and execution of rational public policy. A bureaucrat improves his income and status through vertical attachments rather than developing expertise in particular policy areas. Hence, there is often a divergence between career advancement and the needs of the organization in carrying out its function. Rotation in office means that individuals do not develop expertise or even responsibility for certain policy areas since problems can be blamed on previous incumbents. Such conditions help create the "syndrome of plazismo" for local governments in Mexico. In this situation, officials support the creation of public projects with low developmental importance. According to Fagen and Touhy,

> These take the form of a "beautification" effort: an improvement to the central plaza, a new fountain, benches, paved areas, stalls, or some other civic addition of marginal usefulness. The attractions of such projects to cautious officeholders are legion: they are physically and politically visible; they can be completed in a relatively short time and thus accrue wholly to the reputational capital of the incumbent; they are for all the people and thus require no hard choices as to what sector or project should receive scarce resources; they are uncontroversial in the tradition of "good works"; they can often be partially funded through the donations of others eager to have their names associated with civic improvements.[27]

Obviously, such attitudes are not conducive to good maintenance procedures, which helps to explain why so much of the capital stock in Latin America is allowed to deteriorate.

Another irrational characteristic of policymaking in Latin America, identified by Hirschman in Brazil and Grindle in Mexico, is the lack of acquired wisdom and serious evaluation of previous policies because of rotating personnel. The new bureaucrats often believe they have nothing to learn from former, discredited administrators and therefore old mistakes are repeated and some successful innovations are discarded. In Grindle's words:

> Each new administration is concerned with making its own impression on public programs quickly, and newly recruited officials take over their duties with little commitment to preexisting plans. As a result, old policies which have failed are reintroduced in the guise of new solutions; old mistakes are repeated by the inexperienced cadres; and many programs which prove to be promising in one administration are shelved by the next. The experience which is accumulated by individual administrators as they move from agency to agency during their careers is the subtle capacity to persist through the management of human relations and politics; it generally has little relevance to the more specific tasks of designing and implementing policy.[28]

Hence, too many Latin American bureaucracies do not accumulate the institutional memories from trial and error experiences necessary to enlarge administrative capabilities required to perform new tasks and to improve efficiency in carrying out old functions.

A second major problem of bureaucratic behavior concerns the issues of centralization and control. The overcentralization of Latin American bureaucracies has not brought about greater control; it has brought about less. Most agencies are organized like a monarchy in which little authority is delegated down the line and the chief administrative officer must sign everything. A recent treasury minister in Colombia complained that he had to sign 200–300 documents a day concerning subjects ranging from millions of dollars for public works projects to a $200 travel allowance for a dentist in the Ministry of Health.[29] Similarly, in Ecuador, a planning commission study of the Ministries of Development, Economy, Public Works, Education, and Social Welfare concluded, "The single-person regime that channels all work and responsibility through the minister himself, and the lack of technical agencies that could advise the ministry on decisions that require coordination with the local economic policy of the government, has reduced those ministries in practice to the fulfillment of routine administrative functions and has brought on an inertia to change that is not the fault of individuals, but the very weight of the system."[30] Centralized control is impossible in complex governments short on legitimacy and rich in patron-client networks.

In analyzing the Venezuelan bureaucracy, Bill Stewart found that the more authority is concentrated at the top, the less likely it is that policy can be carried out effectively by those below. With so little formal authority delegated downward, a tremendous number of requests for authorizations must flow upward. Few direct actions can be taken at the intermediate level. Bottlenecks inevitably occur as top executives find themselves inundated by details important to specific cases but not to general policy. Formal communication becomes too slow and cumbersome. Top executives become increasingly dependent upon informal personal contacts for important information. Routine decisions, unless lubricated by personal contacts, get bogged down in red tape. Top officials tend to become overly dependent on crisis management; lower officials tend to short-circuit official procedures by informally solving problems through the falsification of forms and reports. Stewart also finds that "the time and effort that must be expended in gaining the leaders' attention are so large that most bureaucratic executives outside Caracas find it expedient to send a messenger with routine requests and to travel to Caracas whenever an important decision is needed. Within Caracas the same system is followed, although here the advantage of a messenger over the mail service is obvious and less time is lost in traveling. The drain upon subordinates' time and energy is great and its effect upon efficiency can only be negative."[31] In brief, the concentration of authority at the top in Venezuela does not result in the Venezuelan bureaucracy's performing developmental functions in a more efficient manner.

Weaver observes similar problems in the Guatemalan bureaucracy. Again, the bureaucracy in Guatemala is highly centralized without effective control over its bureaucrats. Within agencies, directors are overwhelmed by the responsibility of checking and approving every petition, letter, and memorandum. Since top executives do not delegate authority, they cannot place responsibility. The administrative system lacks uniform procedures for collecting, integrating, and evaluating information. The high turnover of middle- and top-level officials is not conducive to accumulating policy expertise and is detrimental to effective control and management. Rapid turnover is accompanied by procedural confusion. Moreover, the bureaucracy is stifled by legalism, a "code fetish" that requires officials to be constantly consulting statutes, executive and legislative decrees, bulletins, and specific ministerial orders. In Jerry Weaver's words, "Where existing rules and regulations do not apply, long delays are incurred while a new circular or decree is prepared or a written opinion is obtained from the minister's office. Consultants to the government of Guatemala have produced studies demonstrating that thousands of revenue dollars are lost each year because of spoilage, theft, and destruction of goods held by Customs while awaiting rulings on tariff rates. Similarly, all manner of development programs are delayed, clients angered and rebuffed, and business opportunities lost while bureaucrats search the code books or await rulings from their superiors."[32] In such a system, compliance with the code books becomes more important (and safer for insecure bureaucrats) than performance. Weaver's portrait of the Guatemalan bureaucracy suggests that one cannot expect a strong developmental performance from such an organization: "We have a picture of top executives seated behind mounds of petitions, memos, and requests for rulings; beseiged by clients, friends, and subordinates begging assistance or opinions; and occasionally and hastily scanning a report which is probably largley fictitious and almost inevitably devoid of critical analysis. But a basic condition of centralization—control—seems to be absent from this picture."[33]

A complaint frequently heard in Mexico, and in many other Latin American countries, is that the overcentralization of authority in the capital results in inefficient administration at the local level. In Mexico the federal government exercises enormous controls over the initiation, financing, and construction of most local development projects. Although this system results in long delays, as local officials must develop and maintain their personal contacts in Mexico City, it persists because it provides national officials with power, prestige, and patronage. Tuohy correctly argues that "whatever benefits accrue to rationalization and coordination of policy through the centralized organizational forms are lost owing to the corruption, inefficiencies, and careerism that are the other side of Mexican centralism. Thus, developmental planning gets sacrificed to system maintenance, and patronage takes precedence over expert performance."[34]

There is an administrative style in Latin America that assumes that intelligence resides only at the top of the bureaucratic hierarchy in the capital city, that lower officials—especially in the provinces—must be tightly controlled by regulations and cannot be trusted with discretionary authority, and that citizens are lying unless they have documentary proof or personal connections. Top officials are thus overwhelmed by trivia about which they complain, but it is part of their status to be deferentially besieged by subordinates. Middle- and lower-level civil servants quickly learn that deference is far more likely to be rewarded than candor. Centralized authority may not mean effective centralized control, but it probably inhibits developmental innovations. The pathology of centralized authority and lack of effective control is thus summarized by Mark Cannon:

> A sense of exalted status accompanying a position of authority, a mistrust for peers and subordinates outside one's circle of personal influence, a sense of the inviolability of one's personal dignity, a readiness to take offense, a formalism emphasizing appearances—all these contribute to deference to authority and politeness which inhibit open communication of real feelings in Latin America. These features also contribute to a lack of skillful supervision which might help develop employees and mobilize their energy, skills, and commitment to institutional goals. Instead, supervisory situations sometimes become anarchic, partly

because confrontation is avoided, or they become one-way authoritarian command relationships.[35]

The facade that obscures the personalistic realities of Latin American bureaucratic politics is a highly formalistic legalism. The combination of the Iberian heritage and a constant stream of lawyers graduating from the universities and being hired as civil servants has burdened the region with an "overdeveloped" legal system that stifles the bureaucracy. Just as the conquistadores brought along notaries to certify the legality of their behavior in subjugating the Indians, contemporary bureaucrats display a meticulous and time-consuming concern with confirming the existence of formal legal authority for almost any decision. And discovering the operating law today is probably as difficult as it was for administrators in the colonial period. There is a lack of comprehensive digests, and the official gazettes are often not indexed. According to two legal scholars,

> Instead of amending basic code provisions, Latin American practice is generally to adopt supplemental legislation, which, in turn, is amended and reamended. Frequently, one is forced to read a host of separate statutes and decrees regulating a given subject . . . and then undertake the jigsaw job of piecing together the provisions still in force to find the governing law. Hence, it is quite common to discover that the authorities charged with administering a particular body of law are unaware of significant changes in the statutory or case law. Inertia, ignorance, and inability to keep abreast of rapid-fire legislative change frequently combine to produce substantial differences between the formal norm and the law actually being applied.[36]

But even in this situation, a formalistic legalism is preserved through the concept of the "rightfulness of command." Morse explains, "In a patrimonial state, to which command and decree are so fundamental, the legitimacy of the command is determined by the legitimacy of the authority which issues it. Hence the importance of sheer legalism in Latin American administration as constant certification for the legitimacy, not of the act, but of him who executes it."[37] In brief, the proliferation of administrative law has promoted neither bureaucratic efficiency nor respect for the law, but it has become one more obstacle retarding development.

A third major weakness of Latin American bureaucracies is their inability to coordinate their activities to achieve developmental goals effectively. As the modernizing state assumes more functions, there is a greater need for coordination and interagency cooperation. One might assume that centralized politics would be able to coordinate developmental policies, but this is not true in Latin America. Part of the reason, as we have just discussed, is that centralized political systems do not exert effective centralized control through the administrative systems. Thus the essential bureaucratic cooperation needed for state-directed development is lacking, and the more bureaucratized a political system, the more costly this lack becomes.

This lack of coordination is no secret in Latin America. An ECLA study of social services in the region found that "despite . . . centralization, there is no real unification of standards of service. Each institution, program and unit functions with the minimum of communication, and while there may be some written regulations and procedures, implementation is on the basis of personal relationships. The very rigidity and complexity of administrative procedures and personnel policies contribute to this 'compartmentalization.' It prohibits free communication and mobility and favors the formation of cliques."[38] The study also concludes that there are too few interagency coordinating or consultative bodies, but even the few that do exist do not function effectively. Cannon claims, "A committee meeting in Latin America is likely to turn into a monologue of some authority figure, or if it utilizes discussion, to evolve into a prolonged, somewhat random set of opportunities for individual expression rather than a serious and interrelated progressive elaboration of relevant data and analysis leading to a rational decision."[39] Sometimes a different type of problem prevails; in Colombia the minister of agriculture serves on sixty-three boards and commissions. Other studies refer to ministries and decentralized agencies as independent empires and feudalities in which consultation is kept to a minimum and collaboration is almost nonexistent.[40] Because of the lack of coordination, Latin American bureaucracies perform most poorly in administering distributive policies for the poor, agrarian reform, port facilities, and urban services.

The fourth problem plaguing Latin American bureaucracies is corruption. The state-directed strategy of development increases the possibilities of corruption, and expanding corruption seriously hampers the effectiveness of bureaucracies in bringing about modernization. There is some corruption in every society, but there is more of it in

Latin America than in the Western industrial countries, and Latin American societies can afford it less.

Corruption means that officials take advantage of their public offices and decision making to obtain private gain. That is, they take bribes; they hand out privileged information to business partners, friends, and relatives; they smuggle; they take advantage of disasters such as earthquakes and hurricanes; they speculate in currency and real estate; and they enforce the law in a particularistic manner to aid and/or punish friends and enemies. Such behavior is a continuation of the colonial legacy in which a large number of laws were honored only in the breach. In Latin America, law continues to be extensive in its scope and particularistic in its application and thus invites corruption. Because citizens cannot expect justice from public officials, those who can afford to do so attempt to buy special consideration and favors. The prevalence of corruption contributes to feelings of insecurity, since so many officials and citizens have broken the law and could be exposed by enemies. According to Joseph Nye, a significant level of corruption is likely in Latin America because of the following factors: "great inequality in distribution of wealth; political office as the primary means of gaining access to wealth; conflict between changing moral codes; the weakness of social and governmental enforcement mechanisms; and the absence of a strong sense of national community."[41] The dilemma for Latin America is that corruption has deep and constantly reinforced roots, the many who practice it do well, and the few who get caught are not punished severely. In the absence of a public service tradition, the prevailing attitude is that "a smart man helps himself when he has the opportunity." In brief, too many bureaucrats exploit their positions for private gain; they "privatize" public decision making.

The prevalence of corruption is reflected in anecdotes, language, and specific events. In Brazil, the publicized scandals of 1954 caused President Getúlio Vargas to complain that he was drowning "in a sea of mud." In Panama the joke is told concerning how the president makes his budget decisions: a third for the state and himself; a third for his friends and himself; a third for himself. In Ecuador, former Finance Minister Luis Gómez Izquierdo stated, "I understand why the business community does not want to pay taxes. . . . Aside from the obvious, we have always believed that the government was corrupt, irresponsible and squandered whatever it got its hands on."[42] In Argentina, President Juan Perón's minister of education in 1952 recalled twenty years later how he resigned when he saw that a man with legitimate business with the president had to bribe staff members to see him. "Look, Ivan," the minister remembered Perón as saying, "The British Empire was built by good men and pirates, and I'm going to build the Argentine empire with good men and pirates."[43] In Colombia, "The term *politiquería* refers to a type of selfish political maneuvering which tends to subordinate all policymaking goals to the personal rewards of the politician and his clique. Most of those who are involved in *politiquería* are individuals who participate in politics for no other reason than for the materialistic rewards which flow from the position obtained."[44] In Nicaragua, the corruption of the Somoza government significantly contributed to the eventual triumph of the Sandinistas in 1979. Many Nicaraguans were particularly outraged by how Somoza and his cronies took advantage of the 1972 earthquake that devastated Managua.

But the best-known corruption in Latin America occurs in Mexico. Decades ago General Alvaro Obregón announced that "there is no general that can resist a barrage of 50,000 pesos," and former President Emilio Portes Gil complained that administrative corruption at times "produced a climate of virtual asphyxiation." In 1976, presidential candidate López Portillo was proclaiming, "Corruption is the cancer of this country."[45] Six years later, López Portillo was building a multimillion dollar estate for himself and his family outside Mexico City while the new president, Miguel de la Madrid Hurtado, was calling for a "moral renovation" and arresting the former head of PEMEX for corruption. A certain level of corruption is a norm of administrative behavior in Mexico, from the customs official who accepts a routine bribe (the *mordida*) to President Miguel Alemán (1946–52) who became a millionaire developing Acapulco. (Bribes at the top are called commissions.) Corruption allows politicians and administrators to taste wealth, and allows business executives and labor union officials to buy favors. Mexicans tell each other the cynical joke that their country is one of the richest in the world; every six years it produces a new crop of millionaires. It is believed that corruption is particularly rampant during the last year of each administration because many officials cannot be sure they will have a job in the next regime. In Martin Greenberg's words, "The predicament of the bureaucrat, with no real union protection, no job security, and no guarantee of future income, causes him to turn to corrupt practices. Further, the life style expected of even middle-level bureaucrats demands an income well in excess of their formal salaries. The result is that these bureaucrats turn to extracting payments and kickbacks in order to attain a 'respectable level of living.' "[46] Controlling corruption is made difficult because two potential watchdogs of public morality—the press and the judiciary—are themselves part of the same system controlled by the PRI.

The style of state-directed development in Mexico provides too many tempting opportunities for bureaucrats to ignore. Agencies decide what can and cannot be imported and exported and which private firms will receive private loans for their expansion; they set price ceilings on a variety of products and services, and grant tax exemptions to individual plants. One well-known example of corruption is that many filling stations in Mexico are owned by politicians, and PEMEX (the government oil corporation) assures them of a near-monopoly in very profitable locations. Moreover, budgetary control of top officials is almost nonexistent. Antonio Ugalde examined the state budget in Baja California in 1967 and found under the heading "Personal Expenses of the Governor" an appropriation of a quarter million pesos (12.5 pesos equal one U.S. dollar) for social research, but there was no publicly available record of just what kind of research was being conducted. The governor's salary was 120,000 pesos, but over 700,000 pesos were earmarked for the governor's expenses, plus 100,000 pesos for maintaining his residence.[47] Raymond Vernon correctly notes, "In a setting such as this, only mortal fear or an extraordinary elan could restrain some public officials from developing their liaisons with the private sector and exploiting their information."[48] Such fear and elan do not predominate in Mexican public administration.

In brief, without a strong public service tradition, a free press, and a strong independent judiciary, the strategy of bureaucratic development provides numerous and enticing opportunities for graft.

Conclusion: Bureaucracy and Public Policy in Latin America

The stress on bureaucratically managed development takes the Weberian bureaucracy several steps beyond its normal function. Not only is the bureaucracy expected to implement the policies of the political elite in a rational and efficient manner, but it is also expected to play a major role in the formulation of policies and the regulation of interest groups and social sectors. The role of bureaucracy in Latin American development has steadily expanded. Progress depends upon many variables, but most Latin American nations have placed themselves in a situation where the quality of their public sector will be the chief determinant of their success or failure in the foreseeable future. In many countries the rationality of public decision making is the major determinant of the rationality of the economy and the political system. Many of the political, economic, and especially the military elites have decided that the kind of development they want requires "certainty," and that certainty can best be provided by subjecting major economic and political sectors of the society to bureaucratic control.

The problem in this strategy is that the growing bureaucratization of Latin America is not necessarily leading to the growing rationalization of these countries in terms of development. Latin America inherited a bureaucratic style from the 300-year colonial period, a style that was designed to maintain a stable and unchanging system. Grafted onto this traditional bureaucracy are modern kinds of agencies with a greater commitment toward and capability of implementing rational public policy. Hence the development of these countries is hindered by what Schmitter calls "structural overbureaucratization" and "behavioral underbureaucratization." Structurally, the bureaucracy is constantly subdividing itself as agencies proliferate, but major segments of the bureaucracy still fall short of Weber's ideal behavioral characteristics. Despite the efforts of administrative reformers, efficient bureaucratic agencies have frequently been isolated; great portions of the bureaucracy have been able to resist reform.

As the countries of Latin America increase in population, as their cities rapidly expand and require coordinated public services, as they nationalize important sectors of their economies, and as they fail to encourage local initiatives or mass mobilization, it becomes increasingly necessary for the public bureaucracies to improve their administrative skills. But, with major segments of their bureaucracies performing at low levels of efficiency, a serious drag is placed upon the pace of development. Moreover, the bureaucratic capabilities of many countries are often stretched beyond the breaking point because they are being asked to carry out the traditional burdens of government (maintaining internal order, controlling finance, public works, and foreign policy), as well as building and maintaining the infrastructure necessary for further modernization, administering an educational system necessary to supply future human resource needs, managing a host of public enterprises, and overseeing a whole set of welfare policies.

Just how suited the ideal Weberian bureaucracy is to developmental administration is a matter of debate. Some have argued that in Europe the Weberian bureaucracy was related to the transfer of power from the aristocracy to the bourgeoisie, and therefore it is inappropriate to Latin America where the bourgeoisie are already in power.[49] Critics claim that the Weberian bureaucracy is overly conservative with its emphasis on careerism, hierarchy, and routine functioning. They contrast the routinization and predictability of a Weberian bureaucracy with the innovativeness and the entrepreneurial spirit needed by the developmental administrator. Critics are also skeptical of the ideal, contending that bureaucrats overestimate their capacity for rationality and underestimate how much personal and class orientations affect their decision making. On the other hand, those who criticize the Weberian bureaucracy fail to see that it can be instrumental in changing the status quo under a reformist or revolutionary regime as well as maintaining it under a conservative regime. Critics underestimate how much constructive social change—as opposed to destructive change which relies on violence and mass mobilization—is dependent upon social predictability, rationality, and efficiency. Increased productivity and distributive justice are contingent upon laborers showing up for work, students being taught, trains and buses running on time, electric power being available, taxes being collected, major public enterprises such as a nationalized oil industry or a copper mine showing profits, rational engineering practices, and efficient urban services. A more rationalized bureaucracy could mobilize resources, coordinate policies, and display the wisdom required to predict and choose which investments will produce the optimum benefits for the economy and society. Limited administrative skills mean limited policy options in dealing with developmental problems. Increasing administrative skills means an increasing number of policy options and the opportunity to select more rational choices. Moreover, in the hands of an incompetent bureaucracy, rational and irrational policy may end up looking equally ineffective. For bureaucrats to be able to administer the development of their societies, the administrative instrument itself must be further developed. The blind cannot lead the blind. Traditional bureaucracies, where public jobs are viewed as sinecures and sources of employment, do not easily lend themselves to the innovative behavior needed to promote development.

The bureaucratic style of development chosen by the Latin American elites has a number of consequences for their societies. First, such a strategic choice is not compatible with a movement toward democracy in these nations. Neither traditional nor more modern bureaucrats seek to encourage mass political participation. Mass participation interferes with the personalistic style of the traditional bureaucrat and the technocratic style of the modern bureaucrat. Bureaucratic and technocratic means of resolving problems appear to be more compatible with the authoritarian traditions of Latin America than with democratic and participatory methods.

Second, the state-centered style of development has a strong tendency to concentrate bureaucrats in the capital cities. Provincial areas are thus deprived of the talented administrators they need for development. This situation contributes to warped and uneven national development. Moreover, decision making in the provinces has to be filtered through the clogged channels of government in the capital city, which is wasteful and time-consuming.

Third, the bureaucratic development of the state inevitably creates interests of its own that are partially separate from those of various social groups. The bureaucratic state does not merely reflect the interests of dominant social groups; neither does it have to ignore the weaker social sectors (although it usually does). The bureaucratic state aims to be the ultimate patron. From this perspective, "The state does not simply arbitrate among bickering factions; it proposes, disposes, and imposes its will."[50] The bureaucratic state is thus faced with a paradoxical task: it must have autonomy and it must sink roots. In Tony Smith's words, "It must have the autonomy of a unitary actor if it is to make long-term plans and to implement them despite some opposition. . . . Particularistic interests of every variety must be weaker than the state, which is competent to act on behalf of what it will call the collective good. At the same time, the state must sink roots, both as a precondition and as a result of this very effort at change. If some interests must be checked or broken, others must be mobilized and controlled if the state is to attain its ends."[51] This paradox is not likely to be overcome until a public service ethos is finally instilled in Latin American bureaucrats. The bureaucracy is both an instrument for goal accomplishment and a growing constituency that can devour enormous resources. On still too many occasions bureaucrats "privatize" the formulation and implementation of public policy.

Fourth, the growth of public bureaucracies has not yet sufficiently increased rationality in making of public policy. Presidents, ministers, and governors like to link their administrations with a distinctive social and economic program. Consequently, the policies of one administration are rarely pursued by the next. With the lack of social mobilization in Latin America, programs do not build up the clienteles as they do in the United States, which helps to account for zig-zag patterns in the former and the greater policy continuity in the latter. Such personalistic styles of adminstration also help to explain why so little attention is paid to the problem of adequate maintenance of buildings and infrastructure. Why use scarce resources to maintain what was created by a predecessor and for which you will receive no credit? Gary Wynia found, in his study of policymaking in the five Central American republics, that bureaucrats preferred to build longer roads with existing resources while outside consultants suggested shorter roads with higher standards that would require less maintenance work. Because highway maintenance does not bring the personal glory of highway construction, the former was seriously neglected with negative consequences for development.[52]

In Colombia, Lauchlin Currie has complained, there are no decision-making units concerned with insuring that public expenditures yield the highest possible return to the economy in terms of well-being; feasibility studies are almost always positive and original cost estimates are unrealistically low. In Currie's words, "Generally a large project seems to capture the imagination and receives preference over a number of smaller ones, regardless of their merits. . . . Slogans like 'opening up the country,' 'bringing new land into cultivation,' and 'eliminating the middlemen' are worth volumes of arguments and statistics."[53] Similarly, in post–World War II Venezuela, Levy concluded: "In the allocation of public resources, there was no concept of priorities or considerations of alternatives. A project was judged on its engineering or political merits; economic criteria rarely entered into consideration. Consequently, a project was often undertaken more as a monument to its engineer, to its minister, or to the regime than as a contribution to national progress."[54] In Mark Hanson's study of the educational bureaucracy in Venezuela, he found a typical Latin American bureaucratic problem:

Many of the administrative processes in Venezuela seem to be formulated for ideal conditions that do not exist in the real world. Under ideal conditions everything is predictable and controllable. The highly rule-oriented system guides the actors through their prepared steps. Unfortunately, there is little provision made for the unanticipated. Thus, when maps wear out, or windows are broken, or a typewriter stolen, or a teacher wants to introduce a new way to teach reading, the administrative system is not equipped to deal rapidly with these unanticipated developments. That is to say, if the administrative process does not go according to the plan, there is no built-in correction device (i.e., low level supervisor with authority) which can resolve the problem where it happens when it happens.[55]

In some ways, the Latin Americans have chosen a style of development that they are not culturally prepared to pursue—which is just another manifestation of the vicious circle of underdevelopment. Reforming their bureaucracies following Weberian principles is antithetical to the dominant social values in Latin America. But despite this problem and others we have discussed, the elites in Latin America appear committed to this strategy because they perceive it as the one most compatible with their interests. Nevertheless, they are also being confronted with increasing demands for political participation as new groups become socially mobilized. The responses to these new participatory pressures are the subject of chapter 5.

5

Political Participation and Public Policy

In making the strategic choice between emphasizing bureaucratic development versus social mobilization, most Latin American countries have opted for the former. It is part of the political culture of the region to fear the creation and operation of autonomous interest groups. That is to say, what is praised in a pluralist democracy like the United States is distrusted in the more authoritarian environment of Latin America. Nevertheless, there is political participation in even the most authoritarian political system. This study will attempt to identify the major groups that influence public policy because most students of politics assume that there is a relationship between who participates in politics and what public policies are decided. Because policymakers understand that those allowed to organize and articulate their demands influence public policy, each government feels compelled to evolve policies—either implicit or explicit—to control who will participate in the making of public policy.

The relationship between who is mobilized to participate and public policy has eluded definition and measurement in even the most open and fully studied political systems, such as the United States. The problem in understanding this relationship in Latin America is that so much of the policymaking process is hidden. Whereas in the United States there are hundreds of case studies that reveal the participatory roles of various groups, in Latin America there are very few. Under these conditions one is tempted to substitute ideological explanations for empirical explanations. However, it is more honest to concede that Latin American public policymaking "remains a rather amorphous, highly complex, and typically mysterious process in which it is often difficult, and sometimes impossible, to determine the extent of involvement of the key participants."[1]

In any case, the purpose of this chapter is to analyze political participation and its relationship to public policy in Latin America. To accomplish that goal, we will discuss: (1) modernization and political participation, (2) patterns of political participation, (3) the military and political participation, and (4) corporatism.

Modernization and Participation

As a society modernizes, the level of political participation increases. That is, as a society becomes more urban, industrialized, specialized, literate, educated, secularized, and subject to mass media influences, a growing number of citizens will attempt to influence public policy. The process of modernization erodes traditional, fatalistic orientations and encourages individuals and groups to develop a secular consciousness that the "good material life" is possible. The dissolving of traditional bonds frees individuals to be politically mobilized by either governmental or nongovernmental leaders.[2] Citizens are now "available" to be mobilized to make demands upon policymakers. Moreover, as a society modernizes, citizens make increasingly complex demands upon the state; these demands can be defined as "individual or collective activities aimed at extracting certain types of benefits from the political system by influencing the decisions of incumbent officials," in the words of Wayne Cornelius; "Demand making is thus differentiated from political participation aimed at influencing government resource allocation by replacing or retaining the incumbent authorities (i.e., electoral participation) or by overthrowing or restructuring the political system itself (e.g., through revolutionary violence). Political demands are defined as needs whose satisfactions are felt to depend upon governmental action, and which are asserted by individuals or groups as specific claims upon the government."[3] Citizens also become available to be mobilized to provide supportive participation, that is, citizen behavior that aids in the achievement of policy objectives. In the same way that demand participation is important for policy formation, supportive participation is vital for policy implementation. Regimes that lack legitimacy are often unable to mobilize supportive participation and thus have great difficulty in successfully implementing their public policies. Alienated citizens are less likely to comply with governmental objectives.

The modernizing state thus must deal with the modernizing society. As the state increases its capacity to extract, produce, and distribute resources in society, the stakes of citizen participation increase. As governments make decisions that affect all segments of the society, that is, as they fill the "policy space," they have to deal with groups who want to be included in the policymaking process. Groups who were originally subjects of public policies eventually try to become participants in the formulation of policies that affect their interests. It is quickly learned that those who do not participate in policymaking are not likely to have their interests seriously considered and will therefore often become the "victims" of public policy. Conversely, those who are organized and participate are more likely to be among the beneficiaries of public policy. Hence, the modernization of the state creates incentives for increasing numbers of groups to organize and attempt to influence public policy. The dilemma for modernizing regimes is that "having stimulated expectations, central governments become at the same time the focus of demands and the targets of grievances."[4]

The way a state responds to the increasing social complexity brought about by economic development determines its political classification (democratic, authoritarian, or totalitarian) and its pattern of political development. It is particularly important how a modernizing political system responds to the creation, needs, and demands of the working class. Howard Wiarda adds, "Labor relations provide one of the major anvils on which the structure of the modern state and society have been forged. The ways in which societies and nations have dealt with the rise of organized labor as a new aspiring or mass participant in the national life has a profound, even determining effect on the nature of these systems and their sociopolitical development. The manner in which different systems have tried to react to the rise of capitalism and its accompanying 'social question'—the 'revolt of the masses,' the class struggle—has been the most critical issue of the 20th century."[5] A government's policy toward freedom of association can vary from complete control (totalitarian political system) to complete permissiveness (ideal pluralist system). Between these extremes is some form of mixed pattern whereby rulers may sponsor some groups, encourage others, discourage others, and forbid some groups from organizing. Charles Anderson is correct when he asserts, "The intervention of organized interests is not simply a 'given' in the policymaking process. It is to some extent intentionally created, structured and institutionalized through state action. The political system is not merely a derivative from the configuration of group interests. It is also, at least in part, conscious contrivance of public policy."[6] Under these circumstances, policy outcomes should *not* be viewed as dependent variables solely determined by interest group politics.

A regime that is serious about modernization must become serious about the mobilization of different sectors of the society. The state in its interaction with society needs compliance, support, and information. The modernization of society requires the mobilization of people to perform an expanding number of tasks, which range from entrepreneurial functions to teaching peasants how to read and write. Groups must be mobilized to support the regime and to behave in a way that is compatible with the prescribed developmental strategy. Even conservative regimes that emphasize bureaucratic development find themselves forced to deal with the issue of participation. Increasing participation is not only an attribute of a modernizing society, but it is also one of the means for achieving further modernization. The participation necessary to promote modernization would include, for example, landowners growing enough crops to provide surpluses for exports and food for internal consumption; capitalists utilizing their entrepreneurial skills efficiently and investing high percentages of their profits; workers increasing their productivity; civil servants performing their functions efficiently and honestly. Conversely, policymakers should also be concerned with preventing types of behavior that would impede their developmental strategy such as capitalists transferring their wealth overseas; landowners smuggling their produce out of the country; workers engaging in costly strikes; students mounting violent demonstrations; and peasants supporting guerrilla movements. In brief, the participation problem of the Third World leader is to prevent those who are paying the highest social costs of development from mobilizing politically (or to persuade them of the legitimacy of their paying the costs) while encouraging those supportive of the chosen development strategy to demonstrate political support and to cooperate in economic matters so as to promote that development strategy.

Giovanni Sartori emphasizes that, as political participation increases, there is an expanding need for the development of political parties; political parties are intermediary structures between society and government. Parties provide a means whereby the people can express and channel their demands upon the state. The more politicized a society becomes, the greater the need for parties to articulate, aggregate, and channel demands. Without this crucial communications link between society and the state, rulers are more likely to engage in irrational policymaking and the regime is more likely to be considered illegitimate.[7]

The modernization of society and the increase in political participation present a number of problems for elites. As a society becomes more diversified, the number of prominent economic and political "families" increases and political participation can no longer be dominated by traditional interests. A modernizing society creates a more socially differentiated power structure. Added to the traditional social sectors—the large landowners, the old military, and the conservative clergy—are new "power-contenders" such as commercial farmers, a more professionalized military, a more liberal clergy, public bureaucracies, bankers, industrialists, merchants, professional groups, populist politicians, unions, and peasant organizations. The power structure becomes more complex; cooperation among its members will be more difficult to achieve; and new means will have to be developed to legitimize the elites' privileged position. Elites will now have to prove, in a situation where there are competitive values and interests, that their domination of the policymaking process serves the *national* interest and not just their own.

Modernization not only creates a more socially differentiated power structure, it is also likely to induce disagreement among elites concerning how to respond to the growing pressures for participation. Portions of the elite will try to continue ruling on the basis of traditional authority; others will urge the state to employ repression to destroy the subversion of rising peasant and/or working-class consciousness; others will advocate cooperation through accommodations; and there may even be some dissident members of the elite (traitors to their class) who attempt to mobilize the lower classes to further their own political ambitions at the expense of the old social order. The reliance on traditional authority is not likely to be successful. One major problem for the elite is that in the twentieth century the will of the people has become generally accepted as the source and legitimization of political authority, so even the most authoritarian dictators try to convince their population that they rule on the basis of popular consent. Selecting the option of severe repression increases the power of a rival elite—the military. Accommodation of new groups into a legitimate, highly institutionalized political system can reduce tensions and promote stability, but the participation of new groups in nonlegitimate and less institutionalized political systems is likely to result in increased tensions and political instability. Unfortunately, the latter situation—a condition that Samuel Huntington labels praetorianism—characterizes the situation in Latin America more than the former. In Samuel Huntington's words, "The expansion of political participation in Great Britain made

Disraeli's two nations into one. The expansion of participation in Argentina made the same two into mortal enemies."[8] The final option is also not pleasant for the elites, who can hardly be expected to take pride in the fact that members of their own social class have subverted the social order. Obviously, increasing political participation will severely test the political creativity and adaptability of elites.

Thus most political elites will encourage or discourage broader political participation based on how such participation affects their own ability to gain office, to remain in power, and to achieve those policy goals they see as desirable. Huntington and Nelson proclaim that "the attitude of the political elites towards political participation is, in any society, probably the single most decisive factor influencing the nature of participation in that society. Mobilized participation occurs only when political elites make efforts to involve masses of the population in politics. Autonomous participation can occur at reasonable costs only if political elites encourage it, permit it, or are unable or unwilling to suppress it."[9] In brief, in the short run the values of the political elites and their public policies will usually determine the patterns of political participation more than any other factor; but in the long run changes in the social and economic configurations of a society will alter these patterns.

Finally, increased political participation changes the nature of the policymaking process. That process is now more complex because it requires more information, expertise, bargaining, and compliance on the part of those involved. Politics can no longer be practiced within the confines of dialogue among traditional interests; it now entails the ability to mobilize a greater number of dispersed and diffuse forces. Policymakers will have to create communication links between the state and society to facilitate the cooperative efforts necessary in promoting development. However strong these links are, no set of policymakers is completely autonomous or completely dominated by major social sectors. While the major determinant of a government's policies is likely to be the power structure to which it owes its existence, the policymakers of each state may often develop interests of their own which can decisively affect the types of policies selected. One of those interests is survival, which creates incentives for policymakers to search for new bases of support; developmental policies inevitably change the relative power of various groups, sectors, and regions within a nation. Moreover, developmental policies change over time, and each change usually requires the creation of a new coalition of supporters.

Patterns of Political Participation in Latin America

Until recently, political participation in Latin America was a rather neglected subject of study because it was assumed that the authoritarian tradition of the region meant that public policy was essentially determined by either caudillos, presidents, or military juntas. The assumption was that only executives counted in answering the question, "Who influences public policy in Latin America?" Today there is greater awareness of the evolution of participatory patterns in the region. According to John Booth and Mitchell Seligson:

> Social forces connected with economic modernization and a revolution in communications have helped transform the Latin American masses from a state of relatively low political awareness and activity into much more politically conscious and active citizens. Among the processes described in the mobilization literature are the historical expansion of the politically active population from the tiny elite sectors of the colonial era to include the growing middle strata, the expansion of the electorate, the development of nationalism, the integration of increasing percentages of the population into the participant sector, the growth of the number and size of organizations making demands upon the political system, and the increasing activism and political significance of the urban and rural lower classes.[10]

The evolution of increased political participation has been hampered by a colonial legacy—what George Foster has labeled the "conquest culture"—which stressed the nonparticipation of Indians and peasants and their economic exploitation at the hands of large landowners (*latifundistas*).

Large Landowners

After independence, public policy during the nineteenth century was essentially a function of the interaction among *latifundistas,* the Catholic church, and the military. The large landowners controlled wealth, access to social prestige, local law enforcement, and peasants. As many Latin American nations began to industrialize in the twentieth century, the relative power of the large landowners declined; they lost their dominant position and had to adjust to being one of a larger set of groups contending for power. Yet in many countries they retained considerable influence at the local level. Frequently they could not stop the passage of agrarian reform legislation, but they could hinder its successful implementation. Their fear of agrarian reform and/or the quest for greater profits caused many of them to surrender the traditional manner of the hacendado and adapt the more modern management style of the commercial farmer. The elimination of hacendados as power contenders in the Mexican, Bolivian, and especially the Cuban revolutions provoked extreme reactions in other countries such as Guatemala. Guatemalan landowners have amassed great wealth in recent decades based upon cheap, labor-intensive agriculture (coffee, cotton, and sugar) provided by 500,000 Indians and peasants. These landowners have viewed any policy (agrarian reform, education) or group (the more liberalized Catholic church) that might increase the independent well-being of their work force as subversive and a threat to their economic existence. Such a threat is used to justify the most barbaric behavior. They have employed vigilante groups and the military to repress, torture, mutilate, and murder any persons who try to reform the system. Any Indian or peasant who displays any leadership qualities is identifying himself or herself as a target for repression. In this way the increased political participation of the Indian and peasants is prevented, but such repression may have the unanticipated result of increasing support for leftist guerrillas.

Commercial Farmers

In the latter half of the nineteenth century a new group, the commercial farmers, edged its way into the power structure and began to influence public policy. This group included the cattle raisers and grain producers of Argentina, Uruguay, and southern Brazil; the coffee producers of Colombia, Brazil, and Central America; the truck farmers surrounding most large cities; sugar plantation owners of Brazil and the Caribbean; the banana producers of Ecuador and Central America; and the cotton farmers throughout the region. As Latin American nations became more integrated into the world economy, the power of commercial farmers became strategically important because most of these nations relied heavily on the export of agricultural products for desperately needed foreign exchange. Their dominant influence has declined, but remained important, since the 1929 Depression and World War II, when many of these nations began to pursue import-substitution industrialization (ISI). Commercial farmers have used their power to obtain low taxes, easy credit, low tariffs, high support prices, adequate infrastructure (roads, railways, and storage facilities), and the government's aid in suppressing rural labor organizations. In Gary Wynia's words, "Like farmers elsewhere they want to be protected against adversity but allowed to take advantage of opportunity. And as in Europe and North America, they have created organizations to represent them before government officials. Commercial farmers covet membership on government boards and commissions as a means of gaining control over agricultural policy making. Though they do not eschew political parties, they prefer to deal directly with the officials who make policy, avoiding the broader political issues in favor of more narrow technical decisions."[11]

Business Elites

In the twentieth century, as the various Latin American states began to industrialize, the commercial entrepreneurs became an important component of the power structure. Aided by the strategy of ISI, the bourgeoisie has expanded in numbers and power. The ISI strategy has encouraged oligopolies to form in many industries, but in most countries the bulk of industrialists and merchants run small family firms, employing less than two dozen workers. In almost every country commercial, financial, and industrial sectors have organized pressure groups to represent their interests before policymakers. Individual firms also engage in private contacting with government officials in order to request favorable administrative decisions concerning import licenses, credit, tariff, subsidies, and so forth. For example, in Argentina, José Luis de Imaz found out that "entrepreneurs obtain benefits exclusively for their own enterprises, whether these benefits pertain to customs, tariffs, credit, or taxes. They negotiate, petition, and bring influence to bear until they get the favorable decision for themselves and their business, but not for the industry as a whole."[12] As we learned in chapter 2, these business elites have been major beneficiaries of public policy for decades; many of them have grown wealthy with the help of state aid and protection. They have used their power to demand low taxes, easy credit, subsidies, high tariffs, free market pricing, and the repression of militant labor unions. In other words, they have demanded public policies that socialize risks but allow profits to be privatized.

Despite its wealth, the Latin American bourgeoisie is a very insecure group. It is culturally insecure because capitalist values and skills are less revered and considered less nationalistic in the twentieth century than in the nineteenth.[13] Moreover, divisions and rivalries between domestic multinational corporations, large and small firms, and commerce, banking, and industry add to this sense of insecurity. For example, after interviewing a hundred Argentine businessmen, John Freels found general agreement among them that "there was little political unity in the industrial sector and that successful intervention in government affairs was thereby reduced."[14] Similarly, the bourgeoisie is targeted for destruction by radical ideologies that have come to power in the Soviet Union, China, and—closer to home—Cuba, and are popular in many Latin American universities. Second, there is an obvious contradiction between the rhetoric and actual behavior of the bourgeoisie. While the bourgeoisie espouses nineteenth-century laissez-faire ideology about governmental noninterference in the economy, business leaders have grown rich because of government interference in their favor. It is a paradoxical fact that business has become increasingly dependent upon the state to resolve its problems while becoming more mistrustful of the state. In Stanley Davis's study of Chilean business executives, for example, he found that senior managers claimed they spend between a third and a half of their working time in and around government offices. In the words of one of them, "For me to run my company successfully, I have to spend my time in places like the Ministry of Economics, the Central Bank, and the Chamber of Industry and Commerce, not in my office or in my factory."[15] When the state attempts to withdraw or reduce its probusiness policies, the bourgeoisie frequently retaliates quickly by reducing investment, transferring capital overseas, laying off workers, and accusing the offending politicians of being demagogues or communists. Such behavior does not increase the popularity or the nationalist credentials of the commercial sector. Thus the mistrust and insecurity felt by both business leaders and policymakers grows.

Labor Unions

As the various Latin American nations began to industrialize in the twentieth century, an urban working class was formed which struggled to become a part of the power structure. No preindustrial power structure finds it easy to accept the demands of a growing working class, but this has been especially true in Latin America. Many of the early labor organizers were immigrants who brought anarcho-syndicalist, socialist, and—after 1917—communist ideas from Italy, Portugal, and Spain. Labor leaders were condemned as alien and subversive by the traditional elites. However, the elites viewed the working class differently from the peasants. Judging by the European experience, Latin American leaders assumed that the process of industrialization would undoubtedly increase the proletariat and decrease the number of peasants. Labor was the target of ideologies and organizers who proclaimed that the future belonged to the working class, whereas no viable ideologies made such claims for the peasants. For the most part, a repressive regime could prevent the peasants from organizing. But industrialization, urbanization, and the example of the European experience made workers "available" for mobilization; political leaders concluded that either the state controlled this process or subversives would organize the working class.

Unions in Latin America evolved from (or replaced) nineteenth-century benefit societies (*mutualidades*) which collected monthly dues and provided subsidies in the event of sickness, and contributed toward funeral expenses. In the early part of this century labor unions began to develop among workers in the export sectors of the mining, petroleum, and meat-packing industries, and then spread to others. Given the "juridical culture" of Latin America and the fears created by Marxism, organized labor was not allowed to organize autonomously. From the beginning, therefore, the elites believed that labor's participation would have to be controlled through the bureaucratic system. Many Latin American nations first assigned the handling of labor affairs to their ministry of interior, which also served as the administrative agency for the national police. By 1930, however, Argentina, Brazil, and Chile had created national labor ministries. As the working class increased in numbers, nearly every Latin American country enacted labor codes designed to control almost every aspect of labor union organization and procedure. Wiarda explains the significance of these labor codes:

> Law in Iberia and Latin America, including the labor charters, derives from a Roman and code law tradition. The codes consist of a complete body of written law covering virtually all contingencies and issued by non-judicial authorities. In this context the chief aims of workers' organizations, and the means they use, are ordinarily directed toward inducing the state, particularly the labor ministry, to expand the provisions contained in the codes, effectively implement them, and enact new provisions that can be applied to specific cases at issue through the law and the state machinery. This helps explain why collective bargaining is so

weakly institutionalized, why the unions are so "political," and why they ultimately turn to government for satisfaction of demands and not to employers. Unlike labor organizations in the United States tradition, with its incremental collective bargaining, the Latin American unions, governed by the codes, have developed under state supervision where each wage increase and social advance must be sanctioned and ratified by the state.[16]

Wiarda stresses that these labor codes were created "from above" *before* there was any direct pressure from the proletariat. Typically, these codes were in advance of the real economic and social situation; they reflected visionary goals to be achieved instead of operating reality. In most cases, organized labor played almost no role in the drafting of the codes, which were eclectic combinations of corporatist, Catholic, liberal, positivist, International Labor Organization (ILO), and socialist influences. The elites feared the potential, not the present, power of labor; hence, Wiarda writes, "The purpose of these codes was to coopt and assimilate labor, . . . not to free labor or grant it increased power. . . . The labor laws and courts were given a paternalistic character, the granting of new benefits to labor was more an act of charity than of giving genuine independence and bargaining power to the unions. It was a means of keeping the unions from launching radical challenges to the system; it helped keep them conservative, dependent, and tied to the state."[17] In other words, these labor codes were meant to provide a framework by which the growing power of labor could be both accommodated and controlled. They combined concessions and controls—carrots and sticks—to reward workers when they behaved and punish them when they violated the rules.

Some Latin American countries pioneered in regulating working conditions by adopting progressive standards regarding maximum hours, minimum wages, child labor, and night work. Article 123 of the 1917 Mexican constitution was particularly progressive and subsequently influenced labor legislation in other Latin American countries. Later labor legislation dealt with such benefits as the payment of various forms of cash bonuses, long service and severance allowances, transport and housing facilities for workers, probationary periods, authorized absences from work with or without pay, breaks and rest periods, employer-supplied work clothes, and funeral expenses. But the rights and benefits conferred by progressive labor legislation, though liberal in some respects, were patrimonial in others, because they were selectively enforced and distributed, thus treated not as rights but as privileges.

Despite the growing power of labor, much of the existing social order has been maintained because the controls have fulfilled some of the goals of their framers. So far, the most important goal of the elites has been achieved: labor has not become a revolutionary force, nor even a unified movement. Labor law, according to Louis Wolf Goodman, has operated to divide the working class. First, the law makes it difficult to form a union, so that only 15 to 20 percent of the Latin American work force is unionized. Thus a division exists between the bulk of the workers who are not unionized and the minority who are. The second split separates blue-collar workers (*obreros*) from white-collar workers (*empleados*). In a situation that is analogous to the United States salary/wage distinction, white-collar workers are usually paid a monthly salary (*sueldo*) while blue-collar workers are paid an hourly or daily wage (*jornal*). The law reinforces the status divisions between these two types of workers and has contributed to the competition and lack of cooperation between them. A third divisive influence are laws that fragment the categories of white-collar and blue-collar workers. "In some countries this is achieved by prohibiting unions from national organizations along industrial or craft lines and restricting them to single workplaces. In other countries further fragmentation can be achieved by enforcing geographic or type-of-industry divisions. Another divisive practice is the common prohibition against public and private employees joining the same union."[18] Fourth, labor is made insecure by the fact that new decree laws may change the rules and classifications at any time. Goodman summarizes the consequences of these four factors:

> This complex fractionalization of the work force is especially effective given the low standards of living and constant monetary inflation which plague most Latin American countries, and the fact the government is the final arbiter for the wage and welfare demands of most workers. These conditions cause organized workers to compete against unorganized workers, *empleado* against *obrero,* and factory A against factory B in a war of all against all to extract the best conditions from the government. Thus workers' energies are often expended, not in making demands on employers, but in competing against other workers for scarce resources doled out by the state.[19]

Most Latin American economies, as described in chapter 2, are not conducive to the rapid expansion of labor power. Typically, the manufacturing sector is small and not expanding, when measured in terms of the proportion of the total work force employed in it. The sluggish growth of the manufacturing sector can be explained by the capital-intensive strategy of development encouraged by ISI and fears of the potential power of labor on the part of the bourgeoisie and policy-makers. The high unemployment and underemployment rates further weaken the labor movement. Finally, the continued predominance (in terms of numbers) of small family-owned firms and shops makes it extremely difficult to unionize many workers.

However, the framers of the labor codes and labor legislation were not successful in preventing the politicization of labor. Even in the most authoritarian political systems, a considerable amount of "politics" and bargaining is carried on between representatives of the state and labor organizations. Politics may be a forbidden activity, but labor relations have been structured in such a way that every worker understands that it is the results of the political process that determine the most vital issues concerning labor. Since the state controls so many of the benefits that labor seeks, workers obtain many of their goals only if they play the game of politics successfully. Playing that game frequently means threats, violence, demonstrations, and strikes. Inevitably, the unions that demonstrate the most power, rather than those that docilely obey the law, receive major distributive rewards.

What the traditional elites have not understood is that all economies are strategically vulnerable at certain stress points. As an economy grows more complex, the number of vulnerable points where labor can exert pressure through strikes or sabotage increases. Whereas in the past only those workers directly concerned with export trade posed a threat to national economic welfare, now the more urbanized societies are susceptible to threats of strikes from utility workers, transportation workers, teachers, and bank employees. Given this style of labor relations, it is not the working class as a whole that has benefited, but only those workers who could organize and exert pressure at vulnerable points. In brief, a "labor aristocracy" has been created. Strategically located workers use their power to obtain unusually high incomes (and benefits) in comparison to the general wage level, which is low.

In the early stages of this labor-bargaining game, policymakers could selectively dole out benefits to the few; in the later stages, spurred on by the populist leaders who appeared after World War II, the few have become many. Unless the economy is growing rapidly, the game may reach a threshold beyond which it can no longer be played politically— or should one say civilly. The military may be called in (they are always listening for the call) or decide on their own to end the game. This essentially occurred in Brazil in 1964 and Argentina in 1966.

In 1967 Henry Landsberger described Latin American labor's role in the policy process with these words: "Labor as a whole exerts tremendous influence on certain decisions without any of its leaders being close to the decision-making process, because those involved anticipate how 'labor'—and not necessarily its leaders alone—would react if one rather than another decison were made. It is in this sense that we have called labor's influence impersonal and 'faceless.' "[20] Even the few governments relatively friendly to labor often propose policies without consulting union representatives. The problem with this style of policymaking is that labor is likely to feel very insecure. What workers gain by this arrangement is paternalistically granted to them, but it can also be withdrawn. By being kept out of policymaking councils, union representatives do not become educated about and sensitive to the interests of other groups and the state. The whole process encourages labor to adopt a short-range, get-it-while-you-can attitude, which confirms the policy elite's predilection for keeping labor at arm's length.

These generalizations are supported by what has taken place in Argentina, which is generally believed to have the strongest labor movement in Latin America. Internal strife among communists, socialists, and syndicalists has contributed to a weak and divided labor movement. Before the army coup of 1943, there were some 400,000 union members. Under Perón's leadership, union membership soared to about 3 million by 1948, and the workers became his major base of support. Perón never permitted any trade union leader to emerge as an independent source of power. He provided the rank and file with so many social and economic benefits during his first term in office that no labor leader could successfully challenge his authority. Under Perón, "Industry-wide bargaining was instituted; labor courts were set up to enforce the rather progressive laws already on the books as well as new laws; social security coverage was greatly expanded; increased minimum wages were decreed; . . . the system of *aguinaldo* was introduced (one month's extra pay at Christmastime); and a controversial Law of Professional Associations was adopted in 1945, which provided for obligatory withholding of union dues by employers, recognition of only one union per branch of activity, and direct union participation in political action under supervision of the state."[21] As a consequence of these reforms, labor's share of the national income rose from about 45 percent in 1943 to 59 percent in 1949. A few years after the fall of Perón, labor's share of the national income dropped to less than 46 percent. By 1980, the military dictatorship, which overthrew Isabel Perón in 1976, had succeeded in reducing real wages by about 40 percent."[22]

The history of labor relations in Latin America confirms Wiarda's conclusion that "in the final analysis, regardless of the law, it makes a major difference, probably *the* major difference, if labor has a friend in the national palace or not."[23] Most labor movements have experienced a roller coaster of state policies toward them depending on who was in power. For example, in Argentina there were periods of relative indifference (pre-1930), active repression (1930–43), and paternalistic support (1943–55). In Peru, James Payne writes, "In 42 years of existence (1919–61), the labor movement has experienced 21 years of intense repression, 11 years of moderate repression, and only nine years of freedom. . . . Worker organizations in Peru have been rather like plants growing under a box, receiving sunlight only occasionally."[24] Epstein reports that in Chile labor's share of national income increased from 31 percent under President Alessandri (1958–64), to 37 percent under President Frei (1964–70), to 55 percent under President Allende (1970–73).[25] The Pinochet military dictatorship that has ruled since 1973 has severely repressed unions and reduced labor income.

In summary, labor has become an active participant but weak power contender in Latin American politics; its political activities can be temporarily stifled only by military coercion. Although rarely challenging the elites for direct control, the trade unions apply constant pressure upon policymakers to stay ahead of, or at least not fall behind, the inflation rate. Labor is also concerned that, by not being represented at the top levels of decision making, it will be required to bear the sacrifices of austerity policies designed to reduce inflation and improve the balance of payments. The Latin American style of bargaining has generally not been conducive to raising wages for the working class as a whole, but only for those organized workers who control some vital artery in the nation's economy. Nor is it compatible with institutionalizing a legal system of nonviolent bargaining in which both better working conditions and mutual trust are achieved.

Bureaucratic Elites

The top levels of government officialdom were important during the colonial era and they have become an even more important part of the power structure in the twentieth century. Since we dealt extensively with the bureaucracy in chapter 4, we need not add much here. Earlier we stressed that the bureaucratic elites of today have inherited the assumption that policy decisions should be made at the top with minimal political participation from the mass of the public. The latter are considered unqualified to provide constructive influence and are most likely, if autonomously mobilized, to cause violence and chaos. Bureaucratic elites believe that the less autonomous political participation there is in their country, the more secure the political system and social order will be. One factor in controlling the increased demands for political participation is the growth of the administrative state. Within that administrative state, mass participation conflicts with the personalistic style of the traditional bureaucrat and the technocratic perspective of the modern bureaucrat. Government officials believe that the state should control social pressures more than it should respond to them because citizens have a limited ability to know what is best for themselves. Conversely, bureaucrats place a high value on their own capacities to decide what is best for their subjects, themselves, and their nation.

Military Elites

The armed forces have maintained a major influence in the power structure of most Latin American countries throughout the region's history. After playing a critical role in the wars of independence, the military became a key component of the nineteenth-century power elite, allying itself with the landowners and the Catholic church to preserve the status quo. In the twentieth century, until the 1964 Brazilian military revolt, the military frequently played a "moderating role," in which the dissonant interests of the traditional elites and their competitors often were arbitrated by direct but temporary military intervention. Since 1964 the military has taken a more direct and long-term policy role in promoting development. To oversimplify, the military has tried to shift from a conserving, to a moderating, to a developmental role in politics, with varying amounts of success.

There is a cyclical element about the military's role in Latin American politics. There are periods when there are numerous military inter-

ventions and military governments; at other times, civilian governments predominate. In the early 1950s twelve of the twenty Latin
American republics were ruled by military officers, but by 1961 only
one of these—General Alfredo Stroessner of Paraguay—was still in
power. An epidemic of military interventions broke out in the 1960s
and 1970s, including revolts in Uruguay and Chile—two countries that
believed themselves immune to the disease because of their institutionalized, competitive, democratic political systems. The nations that
have been most successful in institutionalizing civilian authority are
Mexico, Colombia, Costa Rica, and Venezuela. Costa Rica went so far
as to eliminate its military in the early 1950s. Cuban and Nicaraguan
revolutionaries destroyed their traditional military establishments because of their ties to Batista and Somoza, but both have rebuilt even
stronger armed forces. In the mid-1980s, the military has withdrawn
from a direct role in Argentina, Peru, Ecuador, and Honduras, but
continues to rule Brazil, Chile, and most of Central America. It is still
a tragic standing joke in Latin America that the final promotion in the
military is the presidency.

The military continues to play an important role in Latin American
politics because of internal and external factors. Internally, the growing professionalization of the military has not, as some reformers predicted, inhibited its propensity for political intervention; indeed, the
opposite may be true. A major part of the armed forces' power is
derived from their ability to recruit a steady stream of adolescent
boys—who are attracted by the opportunities for social advancement
that military schools and careers provide—and imbue them with a
corporate identity. In Latin America, writes Gary Wynia, "The typical
military careers begin with a young man's admittance to a military
secondary school at age 13 or 14. After graduation come four years at
a service academy, then advanced training in specialty schools, and,
before promotion to the rank of general, additional training at a war
college of some kind. The result is an educational and professional
experience that occurs in relative isolation from civilian society and
gives military officers a strong corporate identity that separates them
psychologically and socially from civilian politicians."[26] That corporate
identity includes loyalty to the military; a belief in discipline, hierarchy, and nationalism; generous budgetary support; and autonomy in
administering internal military affairs. The socialization process associated with their training convinces officers in the army, navy, and air
force that in promoting their corporate interests they are simultane-

ously defending the national interest. Conversely, those who oppose the military's corporate interests are violating the national interest. Hence, military officers have few moral qualms about overthrowing a civilian government that they consider to be desecrating the nation's institutional concerns.

The external factors that lead to military intervention include: "The substantial growth in popular political demands; the apparent ineffectiveness of parliamentary and other liberal democratic forms of government when faced with the need to industrialize increasingly modernized societies; the growth of the military's concern about internal security threats, frequently identified as the result of an inefficient corrupt, and unjust middle-class and upper class parliamentary and social system."[27] It should also be remembered that virtually every social sector in Latin America has, on occasion, called upon the military to intervene as a political ally when they felt their policy interests needed help. Many of these external factors can be attributed to the notion of the failure of political parties to solve the problems of responding to higher levels of political participation and creating political legitimacy through effective policy performance. Civilian regimes that cannot establish their legitimacy become bankrupt in moral authority and overly dependent upon the military to establish internal order, whereupon armed forces that are used as police to maintain domestic order are likely to take advantage of the opportunity to play a far more extensive policy role. The military function of protecting national security has been extended from protecting the nation from external and internal enemies to promoting national development. In the mind of the new military officer, the lack of economic development is the most significant national weakness because it "invites" economic aggression by more developed states and subversion by leftist guerrillas. The conditions associated with underdevelopment are threats to national security and are therefore of increasing concern for military officers.

The military are emboldened to play a more dynamic role because the superior war colleges and advanced nonmilitary training have in the past thirty years created a pool of bureaucratic and technical specialists which, in their estimation, are better able to promote development than civilian politicians. Wynia argues, "Many officers blame underdevelopment on the politicians who have governed their countries. Steady economic growth cannot, they argue, withstand the rancor, conflict, and uncertainty characteristic of civilian politics. Continual disputes over the rules of the political game, legislative indecision and delay, demagogic incitement of the masses, and the disruptive activities of urban and rural guerrillas all impede the kind of economic development envisioned by many officers."[28] Perhaps the essence of the military's new role was summed up by a Peruvian colonel after the 1968 coup: "The masses in Latin America are starting to stampede. We the military are the only ones who are capable of leading them and us onto safe ground."[29]

However, the validity of the second half of the colonel's statement can be questioned. Military dictatorship can at least temporarily block the stampede, but generals frequently find the problems of governing to be much more difficult than they had imagined. The military is often more united about the regime they are against than they are about what policies they are for. Even after parties are abolished, newspapers censored, and unions repressed, the policy issues that had divided civilian politicians inevitably begin to splinter the military also. With its institutional unity threatened, and facing increasing hostility by civilian society, many military officers advocate a withdrawal from a direct policy role and a return to the barracks. Thus, one of the great paradoxes of Latin American politics is that, although the military is frequently the strongest power contender, no military has succeeded in militarizing its society. The military is not popular; no matter how long they are in office they cannot win a free election, which explains its contempt for that democratic institution. Indeed, the experiences of Arbenz in Guatemala and Perón in Argentina suggest that a military leader can only attain mass popularity at the cost of alienating himself from his fellow officers.

Changes in Political and Social Patterns

The evolution of Latin American politics and its present structure are nicely summarized by Howard Wiarda and Gary Wynia. Figure 3 symbolizes the changing structure of society and political power from the colonial period to the present. Table 21 portrays the composition, political objectives, and political resources of the participants in contemporary Latin American politics. As the elite structure has grown larger and more complex, the elites have had to adapt to each other *and* to a more complex and less docile citizenry. There was political instability in Latin America when the elites were much smaller and simpler, and so it is not surprising that the trend of instability has persisted. In the nineteenth century the elites divided over the issues of

FIGURE 3
The Changing Structure of Society and Power in Iberian and Latin American Development Patterns

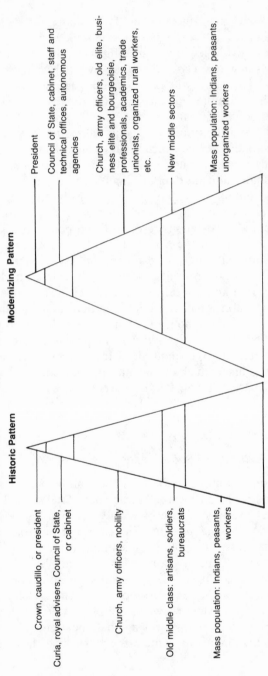

Historic Pattern

Crown, caudillo, or president

Curia, royal advisers, Council of State, or cabinet

Church, army officers, nobility

Old middle class: artisans, soldiers, bureaucrats

Mass population: Indians, peasants, workers

Modernizing Pattern

President

Council of State, cabinet, staff and technical offices, autonomous agencies

Church, army officers, old elite, business elite and bourgeoisie, professionals, academics, trade unionists, organized rural workers, etc.

New middle sectors

Mass population: Indians, peasants, unorganized workers

Source: Based on Howard Wiarda, "Critical Elections and Critical Coups: The Process of Sociopolitical Realignment in Latin American Development," in *The Continuing Struggle for Democracy in Latin America* (Boulder, Colo.: Westview Press, 1980), p. 33.

who was to rule, what church-state relations should be, and whether unitary or federal structures should prevail. As the nations developed, the limited consensus and mutually supportive role of the power elite toward the issues of the proper role of government and the scope of political participation were shattered. Today the elites struggle over who is to rule, how rulers are to be chosen, who is to be allowed to participate in politics, what are acceptable levels of repression, and what choices to make among a whole host of developmental alternatives. There are sectoral clashes among the military, the primary export sector, industrialists, labor unions, mining interests, and commercial farmers in regard to policies toward foreign investment, taxes, credit, exchange rates, and the direction of public expenditures. Developmental policies are particularly divisive once it is realized that they produce changes not only in the economy, but also in the power structure as well.

Elite Vulnerability

In brief, the elites are insecure because they mistrust one another, the lower classes, and the future. Their ability to cooperate is limited because "the prevalence of distrust in these societies limits individual loyalties to groups that are intimate and familiar. . . . Mutual distrust and truncated loyalties mean little organization."[30] The low levels of interpersonal trust are reflected in Enrique Baloyra's survey in Venezuela which concludes, "Most respondents in the 1973 sample (N=1521) believed that one should 'peel the eye' instead of trusting others (91%), that people mind their own business and are not helpful (82%), and that if one is careless, others take advantage (84%)."[31] Similarly, a study on Venezuelan elites concluded, "Plainly we are dealing with a heterogenous elite, some parts of which are given to a murderous and self-defeating competition."[32] In societies of greater social trust, one will find the concept of the extensive good, that is, the idea that bargaining can lead to outcomes which are mutually beneficial. In societies dominated by social mistrust, the concept of the limited good prevails; in other words, what one group gains is always at the expense of the other. Obviously, it is much more difficult to achieve compromise in the latter than in the former. It may be impossible to create mutual trust where you have groups attracted to Marxist ideologies that target the bourgeoisie, religion, and private property for destruction, and conservative governments that arrest, torture, and murder politicians, labor leaders, and priests.

TABLE 21
Major Power Groups in Latin America

	Description of Group	Political Resources	Political Objectives
Latifundistas	Large landowners with traditional socio-economic power and prestige	Wealth, prestige, control over local law enforcement, economic dependence of rural workers	Autonomy, minimal regulation by the state, minimal taxes, assistance of local law enforcement, repression of peasant organizations
Commercial farmers	Owners of large-scale productive farms using modern technology	Wealth, personal and economic ties with commerce and industry, control over production of essential cash crops and exports	Stable government, low taxes, high tariffs, high support prices, easy credit, repression of rural labor organizations
Business elites	Owners of large domestic industries, wholesale and retail firms, and financial institutions	Wealth, economic power and expertise, control over critical economic activities	Stable government, low taxes, high tariffs, subsidies, free market pricing, easy credit, repression of militant labor unions
Bureaucratic elites	High-ranking civil servants and government technocrats	Bureaucratic authority and expertise, control over provision of goods and services	Personal wealth and social status, political power, control over policy decisions
Military elites	Army, navy, and air force officers	Military power and expertise, hierarchical organization, managerial skills	Strong and orderly government, economic development, government support for the military, defeat of communism

Group	Composition	Power/Resources	Goals
Middle sectors	Middle-income professionals, teachers, owners of small businesses, white-collar workers in private and public sectors	Management of most urban economic institutions, skills in political organization, numbers as voters, consumers, and protesters	Government patronage, state-promoted industrial growth, public services, protection of economic gains
Organized labor	Labor union workers in industry, commerce, transport, food processing, banking, and the public sector	Influence over critical economic activities, organizational capability, numbers as voters and protesters	State support for collective bargaining, high wages and benefits, state social services
Campesinos	Mestizo, Indian, and black rural poor, tenant farmers, wage laborers, plantation workers, subsistence farmers	Numbers, capacity for violence at the local level, potential for mass electoral support	Economic security, increased income, liberation from dependence on landowners, access to credit and technology
Multinational corporations	Foreign-owned firms in manufacturing, mineral extraction, commerce, finance, and utilities	Wealth (investment capital), advanced technology, access to foreign markets, control over provision of jobs	Stable government and economy, minimal state regulation, access to raw materials, subordination of labor unions
U.S. government agencies	U.S. State Department, Defense Department, Central Intelligence Agency, Treasury	Military power, economic power, foreign assistance, capability for covert military action	Political and economic stability, defeat of communism, cooperation in mutual security effort, access to resources and markets, support in international organizations

Source: Gary W. Wynia, The Politics of Latin American Development (Cambridge: Cambridge University Press, 1978), pp. 46, 47, 74.

The elites also feel vulnerable because they cannot agree on a for-mula with which to legitimize their rule. In Jack Hopkins's words, "There appears to be a weak consensus, if any, among Latin American elites about the desirable form of government."[33] The increasingly di-versified elite groups cannot achieve any stable agreements concerning a preferred form of government and the scope of participation in poli-tics. Because the political culture is fragmented by the conflicting tradi-tions of liberalism, authoritarianism, Catholicism, corporatism, and so-cialism, it is terribly difficult to establish any political systems that are compatible with the societies they are trying to govern. As Levine suggests, "Different worlds rub elbows in the same nation, institution and individual consciousness. This intra-national cultural diversity im-plies profound differences in the meaning of processes and outcomes to political actors, and related variations in the identification of key problems and possible solutions. Combined with a fragmented distri-bution of power stemming from rapid economic change, cultural heter-ogeneity intensifies conflict by making the creation and use of common institutions very difficult."[34] The result of this situation is often political instability and cycles of failed attempts to establish either democratic or authoritarian political systems. The dilemma for Latin America is that neither the democratic nor the authoritarian form of government is compatible with the nature of the social forces which must now be dealt with. In Latin America development does not necessarily pro-duce democracy, as was believed during the 1950s; nor does develop-

FIGURE 4
The Liberal Model

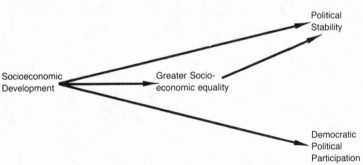

Source: Samuel P. Huntington and Joan M. Nelson, *No Easy Choice* (Cambridge Mass.: Harvard University Press, 1976), p. 19. Reprinted by permission.

ment necessarily produce bureaucratic-authoritarianism, which was asserted by O'Donnell during the 1960s, based upon the experience of Brazil and Argentina.

The conventional wisdom of the 1950s, derived from Western political experiences, believed in the compatibility of socioeconomic development, equality, political stability, and increasing political participation (see figure 4). Instead, however, the empirical investigations of the 1960s revealed that socioeconomic development frequently brought about more inequality and that greater political participation caused political instability. When the liberal model failed to predict events, it was replaced by the populist model displayed in figure 5. In terms of political participation, populist policies—and this has been illustrated by the examples of Perón's Argentina (twice!), Goulart's Brazil, and Allende's Chile—can lead to the following sequence: more political participation → more socioeconomic equality → less economic growth → increasing social conflict, inflation, and the polarization of society as more groups attempt to share in a stagnant, or only slowly growing, economic pie → leading to a "participation implosion," in which the military take power and repress political participation.[35] Alfred Stepan describes the breakdown of the 1961–64 populist government of Brazil under President Goulart as caused by the following forces: "(1) an

FIGURE 5
The Vicious Circle of the Populist Model

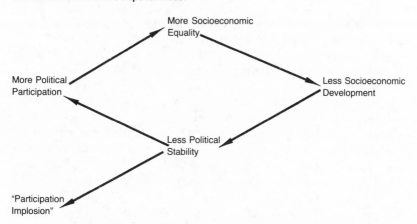

Source: Samuel P. Huntington and Joan M. Nelson, *No Easy Choice* (Cambridge, Mass.: Harvard University Press, 1976), p. 25. Reprinted by permission.

FIGURE 6
The Vicious Circle of the Technocratic Model

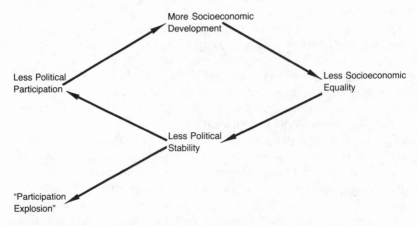

More Socioeconomic Development

Less Political Participation

Less Socioeconomic Equality

Less Political Stability

"Participation Explosion"

Source: Samuel P. Huntington and Joan M. Nelson, *No Easy Choice* (Cambridge, Mass.: Harvard University Press, 1976), p. 24. Reprinted by permission.

increasing rate of political and economic demands made on the government, (2) a decreasing extractive capability due to the decline in the growth of the economy, (3) a decreasing political capability to convert demands into concrete policy because of fragmentation of support, and (4) an increasing withdrawal of commitment to the political regime itself."[36]

In rejecting the populist model, some nations have been attracted to the technocratic model (see figure 5). In this model military and civilian bureaucrats try to substitute administration for politics by severely restricting the people's freedom to organize and articulate group interests. One possible weakness in this model is revealed by the following sequence: less political participation → more economic growth → less socioeconomic equality → less political stability → more repression → leading to a participation explosion. This sequence approximates what happened in 1969 to Onganía's regime in Argentina. Some have predicted a similar participation explosion in Brazil, but, as explained in chapter 6, Brazil's "decompression" policies have so far averted this phenomenon.

In any case, the elites in most Latin American political systems now recognize the need for political support. Their populations have become more urbanized, more literate, more educated, more in contact with the mass media, and more conscious that the state makes decisions that affect individual and group welfare. Under these conditions, regimes without significant support will be overthrown, as witnessed by the revolutions against Díaz in Mexico, Batista in Cuba, and Somoza in Nicaragua. The dilemma for most Latin American nations is that their political systems lack diffuse support—that is, they lack legitimacy—and they do not have the political will, resources, and administrative capability to play the politics of distributive justice efficiently enough to create a sufficient level of specific support. The low level of support accounts for the low level of compliance on the part of so many groups in the region. This lack of compliance can be seen in the behavior of bourgeois citizens failing to pay taxes and putting their capital in foreign banks; for workers, it can be observed in terms of strikes. Since the success of most government policies requires the coordinated activities of numerous social sectors, this lack of supportive compliance seriously weakens the impact of many strategies of development. The lack of compliance means that difficult developmental problems become insoluble problems.

Hence, most governments have become increasingly concerned about controlling political participation. In pursuit of this goal, the educated elites have an apparent advantage: because Latin American nations are a penetrated and peripheral region of the "West," following patterns already laid out in other nations, the more enlightened elites can anticipate what the various other social sectors will demand *before* they demand it. Thus, the more intelligent elites—in Mexico, Brazil, and Colombia, for example—have practiced a preemptive style of policymaking in which benefits have sometimes been granted to certain groups before there was any great pressure to do so.

The elites also fear that their national economies will not be able to provide an adequate standard of living for—depending on the particular country—20 to 60 percent of the population in the foreseeable future. The mobilization of the poor masses would be disastrous to the status quo. With the notable exception of Castro's Cuba, the elites in Latin America are generally committed to what Robert Dix has called "defensive modernization." The elites, understanding that the desire for modernization is irresistible, want to guide the transformation of their nations with a visible, bureaucratic hand while maintaining their own political and economic privileges. To paraphrase Barrington Moore, they want to rule and make money. Most policymakers are primarily in favor of economic growth because this provides the wherewithal for the good life for themselves; they favor select distributive policies because these are considered necessary for political stability, but they are desperately afraid of the autonomous mobilization of the working class, urban squatters, and peasants. The elites believe that group autonomy leads to diversity and diversity easily becomes anarchy. For many policymakers, "The idea that the existence of a plurality of competing interests could lead anywhere except to anarchy is almost beyond comprehension."[37] The elites' fear that their loss of control would lead to anarchy is validated by the Mexican Revolution in 1911, *la violencia* in Colombia in 1948, and the Bolivian Revolution in 1952. These fears are especially prevalent today in several Central American countries.

The elites desire controlled change from above. For example, in attempting to control the urban poor, "Governments often make policy concessions not on a broad basis that affects large segments of the urban poor, but rather distributively, as in the case of conceding lots and titles to squatters, greatly disaggregating benefits by dispensing them on an individual basis. Thus, rather than pursue costly redistributive policies such as government housing, the state acquires land relatively cheaply and doles it out piecemeal, maximizing control while minimizing the likelihood of serious challenges to the overall allocation of public resources."[38] Similarly, in his study of social security in Brazil, James Malloy writes, "The concept of political co-optation refers to a system of political participation which is weak, dependent, and hierarchically controlled. Specifically, it is a politics in which those who control the state have the means to incorporate emergent groups by linking group leaders into a dependent relationship with the state. The image that emerges is of an activist patrimonial state, operating through a bureaucratic-administrative elite, that seeks to control society by linking potentially powerful groups into dependency relationships that are controlled from the top down. From its inception social insurance policy was tied to such a political project of co-optation and control."[39]

However, no elite has the wisdom, the resources, the organization, and the ruthlessness to exclude popular influences of policymaking over the long run. And even reform from above, accompanied by mobilization of citizens engineered from above, may not be enough to forestall the snowballing effect of interest group demands. The attempt to promote acquiescence among potentially hostile social groups by predicting future demands and providing limited reforms before there is any great popular pressure to do so is not always successful. Albert Hirschman notes that Latin American policymakers frequently choose problems to deal with in a preemptive style rather than waiting for a problem to generate intense pressures. But, he observes, "a chosen problem can turn into a pressing one if tinkering with the problem has the usually unintended effect of mobilizing those who stand to benefit from the proposed or advertised solution. This is the 'sorcerer's apprentice' dynamic: timid or perfunctory reform moves lead to demands for far more vigorous policies than had been contemplated by the authorities who had initiated action without any visible outside pressures."[40]

The elites fear not only losing control over the popular sectors, but also losing control over themselves. The ruling elites are afraid that dissident leaders (traitors to their class) will split off from ruling coalitions and attempt to mobilize the lower classes for their own partisan and/or ideological advantages. Intraelite competition has encouraged certain members of the elite to seek lower-sector support which not only provides alternative channels for demand making but also encourages such demands. In Mexico, Cárdenas surprised Calles by organizing the peasants and workers. Similar unpleasant surprises for elites were lauched by Perón in Argentina and Castro in Cuba. In 1964, President Goulart of Brazil was deposed when he antagonized military officers by trying to mobilize enlisted soldiers against their superiors in support of leftist policies.

Populism

After World War I up until the early 1970s, many dissident leaders were attracted to the movement known as *populism*. A variety of political leaders were labeled populist; representatives would include Gaitán (Colombia), Cárdenas (Mexico), Perón (Argentina), Vargas, Kubitschek, Goulart, Julaio (Brazil), Velasco Ibarra (Ecuador), and Belaunde (Peru). One could hardly call populism an ideology; it could more accurately be called a movement led by dissident members of the elite who bid for the support of the lower classes through promises of benefits. Populist rhetoric was emotional, nationalist, antioligarchic, and economically unsophisticated; it emphasized distributive policies rather than growth policies. Populist leaders did weaken the rural conservatives' near-monopoly over political office and increased the concern of governments regarding nationalism, urban welfare, and political participation. Populist leaders tended to be excellent agitators but poor organizers (except of mass demonstrations), notorious opportunists, and inept administrators. Their personalistic leadership style hindered the development of viable political parties, effective development policies, rationalized bureaucracies, and autonomous labor and peasant organizations. Once elected, the populist leader rarely sought to institutionalize the means by which different social sectors could participate in policymaking. Instead, the populist believed in his own rhetoric that he embodied the aspirations of his countrymen (exemplified by Gaitán's statement, "I am not a man, I am a people!").

Because they could not organize effectively, most populist governments were not successful; their multiclass coalitions proved brittle in times of stress. Their ineptitude as evidenced by inflation, corruption, and lack of economic growth, sometimes led to their replacement by bureaucratic-authoritarian governments that promised to restore order and promote further industrialization through more orthodox economic policies. José Nun sees populist governments as "a reflection of the deep contradictions of the middle classes, with their ambiguities, their attempts to use the working class as a maneuvering tool against the oligarchy, and their need of the protection of this oligarchy when the masses seem to be out of control."[41] Wynia provides a more positive evaluation of populists: "They were imaginative and opportunistic leaders who skillfully mixed the new idea of mass electoral politics with such old Latin American practices as personalism and authoritarianism. In so doing they transformed political participation from a privilege exclusively of the elite and the middle sectors to a process that for the first time involved the urban masses as voters and emotionally committed followers of the country's political leadership."[42] In essence, the populists were often not able to reorganize the societies whose traditional patterns they had helped to undermine by their emotive appeals to the masses.

Unequal Participation

The populists could not overcome a chronic problem in Latin America, namely, the inability or unwillingness of policymakers and interest-group representatives to institutionalize communication and bargaining networks. The colonial period established a style of governing that emphasized the nonparticipation of the bulk of the population. Rulers were not expected to consult widely. Indeed, such behavior was a sign of weakness; the leader should know what to do. Traditional notions of the *caudillo muy macho,* who would not surrender to pressure, combined with the dictator's own fears of displaying weakness and thus inviting expulsion, caused leaders to emphasize their independence from social pressures. Today policymakers habitually underestimate their need for information and overestimate their ability to induce and/or command the behavior they seek from various social sectors. Military governments, as we shall examine later, are especially likely to overrate their ability to command compliance. Hence, a system of mistrust, uncertainty, and lack of cooperation is maintained which increases the probability of irrational and unsuccessful policymaking.

The lack of communication between social sectors and policymakers has been found even in the more developed countries with fairly extensive interest groups. Brazil provides an example. Roett concludes, "The policy of the patrimonial state is to identify its goals without consultation with the people, and to act independently of any expressed opinion of the people is a long-standing and venerable tradition in Brazil. This tradition, combined with little, if any, sustained political mobilization of a majority of the population, provides an uncomplicated and relatively efficient means for the political elite both to survive and to govern the nation."[43] Similarly, Schmitter's study of Brazil suggests that development had by 1970 brought about the predicted increase in interest group organizations and activities, but *not* in their ability to influence public policy. Partially because of the weaknesses of Brazilian interest groups and parties, many problems are ignored until they reach a crisis, and violence is frequently used as a signaling device. Schmitter concludes,

> In spite of the finding that associational activity has not come to dominate the process of public policy-making, the consequences of this corporate or limited pluralist form of interest expression have been crucial for the larger political system. The sense of dependency and helplessness, the lack of rational interest or class consciousness, the expressions of deference and timidity, and the sheer disorganization—all characteristic of Brazilian interest politics—are in fact major contributions (along with the absence of a nationally organized party system) to the outstanding characteristic of the political system as a whole: namely, the autonomy of the professional political and administrative class. Relatively free from dependence upon organized special interests or classes, authority groups have been able to control the developmental process and its political consequences.[44]

Clearly these conditions have allowed the Brazilian elites to be freer of social constraints in formulating public policies than the Argentine elites.

The lack of bargaining and communication networks manifests itself differently in Argentina. Here the state is viewed more as a partisan instrument in policymaking, but one that is less independent of social forces than is true in Brazil. In Argentina the state has appeared to be the temporary instrument of fragile coalitions that abruptly change policies but cannot resolve problems. O'Donnell claims that Argentine politics since the 1930s "were continually changing and hardly ever implemented, as the state danced to the tune of the dynamics of civil society."[45] Since the 1940s there has been an intense ideological conflict between a loose alliance of conservative, laissez-faire–oriented landowners, industrialists, and financiers (with the support of a significant proportion of the military), and a coalition of entrepreneurs, labor leaders, some segments of the urban middle class, and some military officers, who support a more nationalist and populist program. Each coalition governs for a period of time, fails, and then is replaced by the other. The social and economic dislocations caused by repeated changes in government have seriously weakened Argentina, like many other Latin countries. According to Wynia, "No promise of future reimbursement for current sacrifices [farmers getting lower prices for their products, higher labor costs, higher prices for consumer goods, and so forth] could reduce the effect such deprivations had in reinforcing perceptions of the state as a partisan instrument. Nor was it enough to argue that such policies were dictated by indisputable economic realities, since interpretations of these realities differed from sector to sector and from class to class."[46] In Emanuel Adler's words,

The economic programs of both groupings crumbled one after the other, and the economy zigzagged. Thus, the conservatives' free-trade programs that supported the rural or financial sectors were as futile and damaging to the economy as were the nationalists' industrialization programs aimed at reducing imports. Thus, because one grouping's policies ignored or injured the other's, political and economic stalemates resulted. The economy and political system, as well as the various interest groups, are far too developed to be served by only one idea of progress and by economic measures that favor only one grouping. Consequently, even if these arch-enemies do not perceive it, neither grouping can solve Argentina's problems by itself. These enemies are as interdependent as the nation's rural and industrial sectors.[47]

In short, policymaking in Argentina has tended to be centralized, insulated, and secretive. Power groups in Argentina believe they must control the policy process in order to influence and benefit from it; groups outside the governing coalition believe they cannot influence policy and will be victimized by it. The most discouraging aspect of Argentina's condition has been that so little seems to have been learned from the experience. Argentina is no closer to a solution to its economic and political problems in the early 1980s than it was in 1944. The opposing interests have not learned how to negotiate, compromise, and share power; nor have they been able to agree upon a set of policies that enable both rural and urban interests to prosper.

The lack of institutionalized channels of political participation in many countries increases the already high levels of uncertainty due to the overcentralization of formal authority. In highly centralized political systems where only members of the ruling coalition are allowed to influence public policy, the level of political conflict between the "ins" and "outs" is likely to be intense. To oversimplify, there are too few "ins" and too many "outs." In overly centralized political systems it is almost impossible for the president or military dictator to appear nonpartisan, for the top executive must decide too many conflictual issues. In such centralized systems political conflict is not deflected and dispersed as it is in more participatory and decentralized political systems. In systems with overcentralized authority, but lacking the ability to mobilize commensurate power and support, many groups that are excluded from access to central authority become alienated, noncompliant, and often attracted to behavior that precipitates coups. Such systems are characterized by violence, repression, and instability.

In another pattern of political participation, private interests literally capture a policy area. Traditionally in Latin America, certain groups have administered their own affairs (the Catholic church, the military, and large landowners). Today, more modern elites have attempted to extend that traditional pattern of policy formation and implementation by seeking to carve out their own slice of policy sovereignty. In some ways, this pattern seems to contradict an earlier point regarding the relative autonomy of political decision makers. Actually, the two patterns are related. Interest groups fear each other and government officials. To overcome their own insecurity, interest groups try to gain control of policy areas that are of strategic importance to themselves. Hence, the armed forces still control military policy in almost every country; the minister of defense is usually a military officer. Students and faculty have attempted to gain control over the university through the concept of the autonomous university. In Colombia, coffee policy is dominated by private coffee farmers through their "guild" known as the National Federation of Coffee Growers. The federation has been delegated complete responsibility by the Colombian government to aid and regulate the coffee economy. It handles price policies, taxation, international negotiations, quality control of exports, and other matters related to the coffee sector.[48] In pre-Castro Cuba, "Interest groups took over the direct conduct of those areas of government of most concern to them. Sugar mill owners and sugar farmers made sugar policy; labor unions made labor policy; bankers made banking policy. Cuban politics was highly organized, but fragmented. . . . Prerevolutionary Cuba produced strong interest-group institutions but no strong social class or national institutions."[49] The power struggles caused by this segmentation of policy areas add significantly to the difficulty of maintaining political stability.

This process has been documented in the field of social security policy. Comparative studies have indicated that the major role in the creation of these social security systems were not interest groups but reformist factions of established elite groups. Social security was often granted by governments in a preemptive manner not to the working class, but to specific groups of workers in amounts commensurate to their actual or potential power. Separate social security funds were set up for the military, civil servants, banking employees, railroad workers, industrial workers, and so forth. Rosenberg and Malloy describe the situation:

> The pattern of representation as well as the strategic location of these various groups meant that they could hold the state as a virtual prisoner in this policy domain, with the costs being shifted downward to those who had progressively less access. In effect, the multiple provision of social security benefits by groups has meant that, in countries like Brazil, Chile, Argentina, and Uruguay, there has been no generalized "public interest" or even "class interest" articulated by the state, but only a variety of variously competing state sanctioned group interests. . . . The

piecemeal cooptation from below of the social security funds has been part of a larger process evident in the region wherein particularized groups have 'colonized' large parts of the state apparatus leading to the . . . existence of large and formally powerful state structures which in practice are internally disarticulated and quite weak.[50]

Political Parties

Latin America's failure to respond successfully to the problems of increasing political participation by so many different power groups is partially a function of the inability of many of its member states to create viable political parties. Hundreds of parties have been created in Latin America, but most of them have not lasted long. Dissident members of the elite have formed many personalistic parties that have disintegrated after the party failed to win the presidency. The armed forces generally have been fiercely antiparty, and, upon coming to power, frequently abolish the old political parties, as they have done in Brazil, Argentina, Bolivia, Peru, Chile, and Uruguay. The 1973 military revolts in Uruguay and Chile eliminated two of the most highly institutionalized political party systems in Latin America. One can unlock many of the mysteries of Western political systems by analyzing their political parties, but this approach is less rewarding in Latin America. Party systems in Latin America have generally not provided a means for representing the people by expressing and channeling their demands from society to the state. Instead, parties frequently have been vehicles of personal ambition to obtain office. For partisans, the stakes of elections have been extremely high because control of the government was the major means.of social mobility in societies characterized by rigid and highly status-conscious social structures and uncertain economies made precarious by booms and busts but never able to provide enough jobs for the soaring population. These pressures have caused many parties to engage in fraudulent elections and corrupt practices, which, along with the populist and leftist-oriented parties, have contributed to the rise of military dictatorships. A 1980 study of parties concluded, "Today parties in Latin America are surely at their lowest ebb in three decades. There remain only two truly stable democracies (Costa Rica and Venezuela), three shaky ones (Colombia, the Dominican Republic, and now Ecuador [in 1984 one might add Argentina, Bolivia, and Peru]); and one which is actually semi-authoritarian (Mexico). Many of the more common characteristics of Latin American party systems are not generally prevalent in Western systems. Personalism, particularism, disinterest in grass roots organization, lack of a mass popular base, and the transient nature of both parties and their membership are typical of Latin American organizations."[51] The most significant recent development in Latin American parties is the withdrawal from power of the Argentine military and the victory of Raúl Alfonsín as the presidential candidate of the Radical Civic Union over Italo Luder, the Peronist candidate, in the Argentine elections of October 1983.

In 1980 the most institutionalized party systems in Latin America existed in Colombia, Costa Rica, Mexico, and Venezuela. The institutionalization of these party systems was aided by elite fears of continuing violence possibly resulting in mass uprisings and anarchy, by creative political leadership, by concern for patronage and by presidents who were not allowed to practice *continuismo*. Venezuela's principal parties, Acción Democratica and COPEI were aided by the creative leadership of Rómulo Betancourt and Rafael Caldera and by steadily rising oil revenues. In Mexico, Calles and Cárdenas created an official governmental party that practices a unique form of authoritarianism in which a presidential dictator is changed every six years. In Costa Rica, following the 1948 revolt, the military was abolished, and the parties—especially the National Liberation party—developed a social welfare system that produced a 90 percent literacy rate, an excellent health and social security system, and an urban middle class of government employees. Since 1948 Costa Rica has had eight successive free elections, and on all but one occasion, the ruling party has been put out of office in contests where the average voter turnout has exceeded 80 percent.

In Colombia, the Liberal and Conservative parties were both created in the 1850s. Both parties were elitist in origin (parties of notables) but have developed a very high level of party identification throughout the social structure on the basis of patronage and reactions to violence. The Colombian military has briefly seized power only three times—in 1830, 1854, and 1953. Robert Dix explains the absence of dictatorship in Colombia in terms of the elite's traditional commitment to elections: "What legitimacy does attach to the government of Colombia is a republican legitimacy, one of whose control tenets is popular choice of the nation's rulers."[52] Liberals and Conservatives in Colombia have killed each other more than have members of any other parties in Latin America, but, because they are two powerful, permanent organizations competing in a relatively poor, medium-sized country, they have been forced to try to reconcile their differences. Beginning in the nineteenth century, there developed a coalitional impulse among oligarchical politicians of both parties that resulted in political coalitions in 1904, 1910, 1930, and 1946. In 1948 the assassination of Jorge Eliécer Gaitán, combined with the long-smoldering "hereditary hatreds" between partisans of both parties, launched a period of civil strife known as *la violencia* (1948 to 1958) and a 1953 military coup led by Rojas Pinilla, an admirer and imitator of Perón. Dix stresses that this "violence threatened to burst the bonds of elite direction and control; it bore . . . the potential of mass mobilization by counterelites. Peasants in some instances assaulted landlords, and some guerrilla bands took on a Marxist coloration. At times it seemed possible that partisan warfare might be transformed into social revolution."[53] *La violencia* and the military dictatorship of Rojas Pinilla finally induced the creative leadership of Alberto Lleras Camargo of the Liberals and Laureano Gómez of the Conservatives into negotiating the National Front agreement. This agreement was accepted as part of the constitution by a plebiscite in 1957, went into effect in 1958, and with some future modifications, served as a guideline for party cooperation for the next sixteen years. The National Front was upheld by three pillars: first, parity within all legislative bodies and the bureaucracy at the national, departmental, and municipal levels; second, alternation of the presidency between Liberal and Conservative candidates every four years for sixteen years; and, third, a required two-thirds majority vote to pass legislation in all legislative bodies to ensure bipartisan cooperation. (The two-thirds majority rule was removed from most legislative subjects in 1968). In November 1967, the Liberal president, Carlos Lleras Restrepo, negotiated an agreement whereby parity would be maintained for the bureaucracy until 1978; after 1978 the minority party would be guaranteed "adequate" representation in government positions. These steps have been taken by the Colombian oligarchy out of fear of losing control, as it did in 1948. The bifurcated Colombian oligarchy has learned that it can continue its domination only through coalitions. These coalitions, which can be negotiated because each party is riddled with factions, have been forged by the fear that a breakdown in the relations between the parties would result in the toppling of the system, probably through a military coup as in 1953. But the oligarchy also fears that there is a potential mass opposition base in the millions of Colombians who are poor and who do not vote (the abstention rate is exceptionally high) which might be mobilized by another Jorge Eliécer Gaitán, Camilo Torres, or Rojas Pinilla should the Liberal and Conservative parties lose their unique capacity to cooperate and share power. Singly, neither party can keep the lid on the volcano; together, they believe they can.

Military Governments and Political Participation

When political parties fail to govern effectively they are replaced by the military. The military then tries to operate as a single ruling party. It claims to be the sole, legitimate expression of the national will in much the same mythical way that the Communist party claims to represent the objective interests of the proletariat. Whereas before the 1964 Brazilian military coup the military was content to act as a moderator or arbitrator in politics, today powerful factions within the armed forces are more likely to become exasperated with corrupt political parties, fearful of the internal security threat posed by rural and urban guerrillas, and confident that they possess the wisdom to play a permanent political role in producing more rapid development. The traditional raison d'être for military intervention, namely, taking temporary control in order to restore order and work for a speedy return of civilian rule, is clearly inadequate for the grandiose goals of national reconstruction that now are used as justifications for military intervention.

In attempting to create a new legitimizing formula, the military is hindered by its belief that "politics" has retarded national development and, therefore, it should rule without succumbing to the morally eroding game of politics. Since the military represents the national interest, there is no need to engage in elections, consult with interest group representatives, negotiate with dissenting groups, or provide incentives to ensure compliance. This style of governing requires the military government to isolate itself from society, to formulate the most rational decisions on the basis of technocratic criteria, and to substitute administration and repression for politics. In brief, the military wants to decree development. But the military cannot decree economic growth, higher farm production, honesty in administration, higher labor productivity, an end to capital flight abroad, and higher rates of private investment. Nor can order be simply decreed or maintained by high levels of repression. Military officers have not learned that "by isolating themselves from interest groups in order to make policy unhindered by private demands, they only increase distrust of the policy-making process and encourage resistance to their decisions."[54]

The military style of governing is not compatible with running a society and promoting economic development. What is desired is a political silence that can only be achieved temporarily and at the expense of a great deal of repression. Inevitably, many original civilian supporters become alienated. In Chile, for example, an irate business executive showed a friend the following order to attend a meeting of the parent-teacher association at his children's school: "Brig. Gen. Nilo Floody asks all parents to a reunion that will take place on Tuesday, September 3, at 20 hours sharp. Failure to comply with this citation will be more than sufficient cause for immediate detention."[55] In Argentina the military endlessly asserts its moral superiority over venal politicians. General Juan Carlos Onganía "was convinced that he could not allow interest groups to meddle freely in the policy-making process since he believed that government concessions to their narrow demands had undermined the economic programs of his predecessors. . . . Instead of reorganizing interest groups or bringing them under direct government control, he chose to isolate them as subjects who were expected to expend their energies executing government policy rather than debating or influencing its content. In this arrangement, communication flowed in only one direction because there was no need to receive and process the demands of subjects who existed primarily to carry out the will of the state."[56] But labor subjects in Córdoba, refusing to play their designated role, engaged in a "participation explosion" in 1969, and Onganía's military colleagues, seeing that his administration could no longer maintain order, forced him to resign.

The point is that the armed forces are frequently no better in governing than the party governments they replace. Their initial "panicked consensus," based on fears of populism, left-wing subversion, rampant inflation, corruption, and disorder, disintegrates when they encounter the hard choices and inevitable failures of governing. A reaction sets in. Chalmers and Robinson suggest that "considerable pressure for liberalization comes from the middle sectors heretofore content to remain passive 'acceptors' of the authoritarian regime, who are drawn into active involvement with the ramifying state activity because of their range of specialized interests and concerns. The many demands to participate on particular issue areas have built up to more general demands for liberalization."[57] Even if outside pressures are decreased by outlawing parties, strikes, and demonstrations, it is likely that similar pressures will be generated internally by military and bureaucratic factions that become increasingly divided over developmental issues. As the military government confronts policy failures, growing hostility from the civilian sector, and expanding internal problems concerning how to reward and promote officers for their military and/ or political activities, there will be expanding pressures from within the military to withdraw from the direct control of the government. Since governing inevitably conflicts with the maintenance of military unity, the military frequently retires to the sidelines. But it is never more than a whistle away from getting back into the game.

The Peruvian Example

One military government that was concerned with the issue of political participation was that of Peru, which ousted the civilian administration of Fernando Belaunde in October 1968. The armed forces were influenced by the Center for Higher Military Studies (a Peruvian war college) and the experiences of fighting and defeating leftist guerrillas in 1965. The military believed that Peru's underdevelopment was a threat to national security and its own institutional integrity. It blamed Peru's underdevelopment on the stifling power of the upper class (*la oligarquía*), the absence of national integration (especially of the Indian population), an "anemic" state (a phrase taken from an official speech), and international economic dependence, especially on the United States. The military felt that in defending the established order it was protecting the very causes of underdevelopment, which meant that when the inevitable revolution occurred the military would be destroyed along with the traditional elite. It also felt that the splintered, opportunistic, and corrupt political parties were incapable of correcting this situation. Hence, the only solution was for the armed forces to assume full power, eliminate the power of the oligarchy, end Peru's economic dependence, and promote national development and integration.

General Juan Velasco Alvarado and his colleagues claimed they were developing a third path to development for Peru that avoided the pitfalls of capitalism and communism. In President Velasco's words, the goal was to combine the best of the "libertarian, socialist, and Christian traditions" by "constructing in our country a democracy of full participation, that is to say, a system based on a moral order of solidarity, not of individualism; on an economy fundamentally self-managing (*autogestora*) in which the means of production are predominantly of social property, under the direct control of those who by their work generate the wealth; and a political order where the power of decision, far from being a monopoly of political or economic oligarchy, is diffused and rooted essentially in the social, economic, and political institutions and managed, without, or with a minimum of, intermediaries, by the men and women which form them."[58] Thus, the Peruvian third path would lessen class conflict and create "organic unity" by setting up agrarian collectives and cooperatives and granting both equity and managerial participation to the working class. Cooperation for national development would replace the divisions of class exploitation. Development would produce solidarity, not divisiveness. Moreover, the military wanted to create a social democracy with full participation, but not partisan participation. The government tried to eliminate the attractiveness of political parties (especially that of its historical enemy, the Apristas) by providing the people with mechanisms of participation that were more meaningful than those provided by the electoral and party system. Velasco's administration predicted that citizen support for the military government would be produced by its populist and redistributive reforms. The government's "conception of popular input into the revolutionary process was participation in productive units—unions, cooperatives, collectives, neighborhood councils—oriented toward national development," writes Sandra Woy. "The junta postulated that the emphasis on economic participation (e.g., profit sharing and self-management) or social participation (e.g., self-help and youth groups) would substitute for political participation in the partisan sense because the supposed objectives of these groups were collective not competitive."[59] In brief, the government tried to institutionalize new forms of political participation that would cause the political parties "to wither away."

The state agency designed to administer and encourage popular participation was the National System to Support Social Mobilization (SINAMOS). SINAMOS was formed in 1972 by combining eight agencies from several ministries into a political action organization. Stepan explains, "The basic law creating SINAMOS said it should 'promote the organization of the population into dynamic functional and territorial units of communal and cooperative nature' and 'foment and stimulate the dialogue between the government and the national population in order to orient the conscious participation of the people in the basic decisions that affect their environment, their interests and their communal objectives' as well as 'foment the systematic linkage between the coordinated actions and services of the government and those of the organized population.' "[60] Functionally, SINAMOS was a multi-purpose agency designed to replace parties, to serve the government as a propaganda unit to mobilize support, to serve the people at the local level as a public works department and as an approved mechanism through which citizens could articulate their sectoral (workers, peasants) and community needs. SINAMOS was supposed to provide a helping hand in the formation of grassroots units, regional units, and national confederations by informing the population of the available opportunities, by providing the administrative, financial, and legal support to create the units, and by training and assisting the leaders of the unit organizations.

By 1975 the Peruvian Revolution and SINAMOS were overwhelmed by problems and contradictions. The government had seriously weakened the traditional oligarchy and reduced economic dependence upon the United States by expropriating U.S. private investments, but the results were disappointing. Agriculture and fishmeal production declined and the price of copper exports fell, creating a serious balance of payments problem and increasing Peru's international economic dependence. Believing there were enormous reserves of oil in Peru's Amazon region, the government borrowed huge amounts of foreign capital, but not enough oil was discovered to justify the expense of the the pipeline that was built. Private capital fled the country because of fears of the government's industrial policy. The outcome of all this was a soaring foreign debt, a tenfold increase in inflation, rising unemployment, and the alienation of most sectors of society toward the military. The extent of public dissatisfaction was displayed in February 1975 when the Lima police went on strike and joined thousands of rioters who burned and looted and left over eighty dead. By August 1975, the physically ailing Juan Velasco was peaceably ousted by General Morales Bermúdez, who dismantled SINAMOS and later turned over the reins of power to Belaunde, the winner of the 1980 presidential election.

SINAMOS had obviously failed to mobilize the people in support of the military government as effectively as the Committee for the Defense of the Revolution had supported Castro when his economic policies were unsuccessful. The Peruvian Revolution was confronted with a greater problem of popular mobilization than the Cuban Revolution because Velasco was not a charismatic leader, and Peru has about twice the population of Cuba spread out over an area ten times as large, much of it either sparsely settled or inaccessible semidesert, jungle, or mountain areas. Moreover, because Peru has less than one-fifth as many television sets as Cuba, the problems of communicating the goals of the revolution were much greater. Moreover, SINAMOS was not able to overcome the fundamental contradiction that although they were mounting a revolution, the military wanted to control the population and not to allow it to mobilize autonomously. Conservative officers were apprehensive that the relatively open procedures of the lower-level units had permitted the partisans of the despised parties and unions to dominate these groups. In their view, SINAMOS was mobilizing mass elements that would not be loyal to the military. Such activity would only increase the level of demands on a political system that was already overburdened.

Another major contradiction was that General Velasco considered himself to be the "voice of the revolution," and he made his decisions in consultation with a small group of military advisors in the Council of Presidential Advisors (COAP). The new forms of interest representation had no direct access to presidential decision making. Furthermore, despite all of this emphasis on the issue of participation, the Peruvian military government had much less civilian participation at the cabinet level than the Brazilian government. Ironically, despite trying to appeal to a wider variety of people, the Peruvian government ended up with less support than the more conservative and repressive military government of Brazil.

Corporatism

Another Latin American response to the problem of controlling participation has been the trend toward a kind of authoritarianism called *corporatism*. The interest in corporatism has grown because most of the Latin American countries are not following either a democratic or totalitarian path toward modernization; rather they are pursuing routes that are influenced by their own unique historical and cultural heritage. One of these is corporatism. The term is derived from *corpus*, the Latin word for body, and is now used to refer to a perspective that views the political system as a kind of living organism. According to Erickson, "In the human body, the brain controls the hierarchy of organs and muscles and decides on actions which, in its view, will serve the interests and needs of the person as a whole. Similarly in a corporate state, the leader or leaders pursue policies designed so that their view of the general will prevails over particular interests. A corporate state, then, is one whose political culture, institutions, and processes reflect a hierarchical, organic view of society."[61] Put more simply, under corporatism, it is the state that legitimizes the participation of groups in politics.

There are a number of controversial questions surrounding corporatism. What are the historical and intellectual origins of corporatism? Is it a form of fascism? Can a school of thought that traces its origin back to medieval times promote modernization? Is it a natural or contrived arrangement? Which countries have a corporate-style regime? How many varieties of corporatism are there? Are all or only some groups subject to corporate controls? Which groups are included in, or excluded from, the formation of policy? Does a corporate regime practice a set of policies that can be distinguished from other types of regimes?

I agree with Stepan's view that Latin American corporatism is essentially "an elite response to crisis, a response that involves the attempt by elites who control the state apparatus to restructure the relationship between sectors of civil society and the state. . . . Corporatist patterns of interest representation are not so much a social input as a policy output, i.e., they are frequently the consequences of political structures consciously imposed by political elites on civil society."[62] Because Latin American societies are now more structurally differentiated than before and old forms of domination will no longer suffice in a situation where there are higher levels of participation and greater commitments to modernization, corporatism appeals to elites as a means of controlling change from above. Corporatism reflects the elites' fear of their own fragmentation due to the strains of modernization, and their desire to create new mechanisms to link and control new power contenders and the lower classes to the state. Moreover, corporatism offers a means whereby the elites can maintain their status, bureaucrats can make rational policy decisions, and the consumption demands of the lower classes can be subordinated to the needs of greater investment to promote more advanced industrialization. A corporatist regime can preserve much of the traditional social structure, but also adapt to change through the process of cooptation of new power structures. Corporatism assumes that rational administration can replace conflictual politics. Corporatism promises order, harmony, and progress because it avoids the group conflicts of democratic pluralism and the class conflict of socialism.

According to Linn Hammergren, "Corporatism presumes categorical groups with an exclusive, nonoverlapping membership. Hierarchy within these groups as well as within the society as a whole is also stressed. Contingent on the presence of hierarchies is the implication of exclusive channels to the center from the lowest levels up. Communication with the political center occurs vertically; horizontal communication between groups or segments of groups is rare."[63] By inhibiting horizontal communication, the elites hope to prevent autonomous social mobilization. Instead, the different social sectors are to be isolated from one another in particularist columns petitioning the state bureaucracy for distributive benefits such as subsidies, social security, and education. In granting some of these petitions, the state hopes to make these groups dependent and subservient. The moral role of the state in this system is to stand above these corporate columns and promote the general will. However, the "general will" generally reflects the interests of the elites.

A definition of corporatism that evokes the Weberian ideal is provided by Schmitter: "Corporatism can be defined as a system of interest representation in which the constituent units are organized into a limited number of singular, compulsory, noncompetitive, hierarchically ordered and functionally differentiated categories, recognized or licensed (if not created) by the state and granted a deliberate representational monopoly within their respective categories in exchange for observing certain controls on their selection of leaders and articulation of demands and supports."[64] A second definition by Ruth Collier and David Collier suggests that since there is no such entity as a pure and complete corporate regime, "One may define a system of state-group relations as corporative to the degree that there is (1) state structuring of groups that produces a system of officially sanctioned, non-competitive, compulsory interest associations; (2) state subsidy of these groups, and (3) state imposed constraints on demand-making, leadership, and internal governance."[65]

Although one could dispute the matter, Stepan claims that five Latin American countries have attempted to install corporatist regimes: Mexico after 1935; Brazil during the *Estado Novo* from 1937 to 1945 and after the military coup of 1964; Argentina after the military coup of 1966; Chile after the military coup of 1973; and Peru after the military coup of 1968. Stepan considers Mexico and Peru (1968–75) to be examples of inclusionary corporatism; the other three (except for the *Estado Novo*) he labels representatives of exclusionary corporatism. Both types of corporatism are elite responses to crises, and it should be understood that a particular regime may combine inclusionary and exclusionary policies depending upon changing conditions and the inclinations of different political leaders. Stepan believes that the elite response is likely to be inclusionary when oligarchical domination is beginning to disintegrate under the strains of early industrialization, and where political participation is increasing but is still relatively limited. Inclusionary corporatism is characterized by attempts to *incorporate* new social groups (the workers and peasants) into the ruling coalition primarily through cooptive, distributive, symbolic, and group-specific welfare policies. In inclusionary corporatism the political elites' characteristic partners will be the national bourgeoisie and (at the junior level) the newly encapsulated workers and peasants; its enemies will be the traditional oligarchy and foreign capital. The inclusionary regime attempts to legitimize itself by political populism and economic nationalism. On the other hand, the elite reaction is likely to be exclusionary when political mobilization is more intense and ideologically radicalized than that which precedes inclusionary responses. Hence, the state elites (the military, bureaucrats, and center-right politicians) emphasize the *exclusion* of autonomous organizations and most distributive demand-making that will obstruct the new priority on economic growth. The goal is to demobilize and gain control of the lower classes and students. State policies are primarily coercive and, secondarily, group-specific welfare policies, but there will be virtually no new distributive policies during the regime's initial stages. In exclusionary corporatism the ruling coalition will consist of the military, technocrats, some portions of the traditional oligarchy, and foreign capitalists. The exclusionary regime attempts to legitimize itself by stressing its commitment to Western Christian civilization, order, naturalism, and economic efficiency. Its characteristic enemies are subversion, populist and corrupt politicians, students, and the autonomously organized working class.[66]

With the exception of Mexico, which we will examine in the next section, most corporatist regimes have not been successful in institutionalizing their rule for several reasons. First, although there is a corporatist component in the political culture of Latin America, it is not dominant enough to legitimize a corporatist regime in the view of the bulk of the population. The idea that corporatism is a function of "cultural continuity" is undermined by the fact that such strongly Catholic countries as Colombia and Ecuador are not corporatist. In Stepan's words, "Explanations based on continuity are relatively weak where the phenomenon to be explained is not so much continuity but the emergence of stronger and novel forms of corporatism after a period of relative abeyance. The simple fact is that neo-corporatist institutions are more prominent in the Latin America of the 1970s than they were in the 1950s, or indeed than in the 'liberal' period in parts of Latin America from the late 19th century until the depression."[67] Moreover, it should be noted that corporatist regimes have failed as often as other types of political systems.

Second, corporatism is based on a false myth, namely, that it can eliminate politics. Corporatism's "avoidance of politics" turns out to be a highly secretive and devious brand of politics, hidden from public view by censorship and repression. According to Schmitter, corporatist politics consists of "shifting coalitions currying for special favor with their national leader; infighting between bureaucratic agencies for control over policy areas and within agencies for personal power and status; complex maneuvers in the hierarchy of military command; discrete devolutions of decisional authority from peripheral to central political institutions; defensive efforts by corporatized interest groups to protect existing privilege against further incursions of the state; preemptive co-optation of emergent class and sectoral leaders; unreported and unobserved acts of intimidation against individual opponents; prudent self-censorship by intellectuals and mass media; and the mobilization of legal violence through repressive police and judicial actions."[68] Moreover, the blurring of the distinction between the public and private sectors brought about by corporatism encourages the very corruption that has delegitimized other regimes.

Third, the actual operation of a corporate system reveals that the different social sectors are not equal in influence. Usually the interests of the military (again, Mexico may be an exception to this generalization), the technocrats, and the national bourgeoisie predominate. The working class and peasants are clearly in a subordinate position even if the regime claims to be inclusionary. In Erickson's phrase, "If the essence of corporative thought can be caustically summed up as, 'a place for everybody, and everybody in his place,' the place for workers is clearly a subordinate one."[69] The less powerful the sector, the more the corporate state can deal with it bureaucratically. The more powerful groups directly influence public policy and thereby enjoy much greater policy benefits. In brief, corporatism turns out to be selective, not comprehensive, in whom it incorporates in a subordinate fashion. Most of the elites and especially the military successfully resist being subject to corporate controls.

In summary, it is true that many Latin American leaders are attracted to corporatism, especially in terms of controlling the working class. But most corporatist experiments, such as Vargas's *Estado Novo* or Velasco's Peru, have ended in failure. The more powerful sectors resist being subject to corporate controls because they do not trust each other; they want both direct influence and privileged access to power. Nevertheless, the corporatist response to the problem of increasing political participation will sometimes be selected because corporatism is traditional in the region's fragmented political culture and it appeals to the military and technocrats as a mechanism for exerting state control over increasingly complex and rebellious societies.

Mexican Corporatism

The most successful Latin American example of corporatism is the Mexican political system. Mexican corporatism is different from other examples because it was not created in reaction to populist politicians and policies, but rather in response to Latin America's first social revolution, which expelled the ossified thirty-five-year dictatorship of Porfirio Díaz and destroyed the traditional oligarchy of the military, the landholders, and the Catholic church. After great turmoil, the creative political leadership of Plutarco Elias Calles and Lázaro Cárdenas launched a viable corporatist political system. Calles's major contribution was in not reassuming the presidency in 1929 when his first term as president had expired and the recently reelected Obregon (who had been president from 1920 to 1924 and was then succeeded by Calles) was assassinated. Instead, Calles ruled from behind the scenes and initiated the steps creating an official party. Cárdenas, after being elected president in 1934, exiled Calles, accelerated the land reform program, nationalized the oil industry, reorganized the party, and— despite his enormous popularity—voluntarily stepped down in 1940, a move which finally institutionalized the revolution's aspiration of "no reelection."

The Cárdenas regime established the legitimacy of the political system by nationalizing U.S.- and British-owned oil properties in 1938, and by distributing land to the peasants. Since 1940 the regime has generally proved capable of maintaining political stability, controlling the military, promoting economic growth, attracting foreign investment, and preventing hyperinflation. However, the regime has not been able to provide "effective suffrage" and social justice. A political system cannot be considered democratic when the official government party, the Institutional Revolutionary party (PRI), wins all major elections aided by repression and fraud. Nor can a regime be considered socially just when fifteen million peasants and Indians live below the poverty line; about 40 percent of the work force is estimated to earn less than the required minimum wage; the income spread between the top 5 and bottom 10 percent of the population is 1:39 as compared to 1:8.5 in the United States.[70] The Mexican business executive earns 50 percent more than the average Argentine business executive, while the Mexican worker receives only about half as much as the Argentine. According to Bizzarro, "Of the nearly 70 million Mexicans, less than 5 percent live in luxury; another 20 to 30 percent enjoy the relative ease and comfort of the middle class; and the majority . . . struggle for survival."[71]

What intrigues students of comparative politics is how the Mexican regime succeeds in resolving many of the problems that overwhelm other corporatist and Latin American political systems. How does the regime organize workers and peasants to support policies that benefit economic and political elites? How does it manage to be both authoritarian and adaptable, elitist and mass-based, corrupt and legitimate, nationalistic and attractive to foreign capital, revolutionary and conservative, bureaucratic and populist? The answers to these questions can be found in analyzng the presidency, the party, and the system.

The Mexican corporatist regime is a highly centralized bureaucratic system that is headed by an all-powerful president who controls the Congress, the governors, the courts, and the media. What is unique is that the president is a dictator with a six-year term who can command almost anything except reelection. During the fifth year in office the incumbent president consults with high-ranking officials of the government and the PRI and then selects the next president from among cabinet officials in a secretive process labeled *tapadismo*. Thus citizens have no say in the choice of the president, which is the single most crucial decision in the political system. The presidential candidate is then automatically nominated by the PRI and overwhelmingly elected in a ritualistic contest. During the year-long campaign the candidate, emulating the pattern set by Cárdenas in 1934, travels extensively throughout the country in order to mobilize support and meet with thousands of officials and interest group representatives. The new president then comes into office with a new team and usually initiates a different set of policies to overcome neglected problems from the previous administration. The new president is given great authority, shown great deference, and then retired. The Mexicans have succeeded in connecting charisma to the office of the presidency and not to a particular leader. Thus a change in the presidency every six years assures a circulation of elites and has prevented, so far, the rigidity that eventually destroyed Díaz.

During his *sexenio* (six-year presidential term), the president possesses the authority to steer public policy to the left or to the right. All presidents try to convey the image of a popular reformer by introducing and/or extending some distributive programs. Whether the president is championing a conservative model of stabilizing development (*desarrollo establizadora*) or a leftist model of shared development (*desarrollo compartido*), most politicians will echo and support the official view to a greater degree than in any other Latin American political system except Castro's Cuba. In the words of Susan Purcell and John Purcell, "The President sets the tone for the nation during his term of office, and all below him follow his lead. When the tone is radical and conflictual, as it was during Echevarria's *sexenio*, . . . the country teems with social revolutionaries. When the tone is more conservative and conciliatory, as it turned when José López Portillo became President in 1976, the same politicians demagogically denounce demagoguery, extol the virtues of increased efficiency and productivity."[72] Hence, losers in one administration can always hope their horizons will brighten under the next president, who is never more than six years away and who may turn out to be as leftist as Cárdenas or as rightist as Alemán. New presidents help legitimize the system by renewing hope.

The hopes of many ambitious individual Mexicans are encouraged and channeled by the official ruling party, the PRI. Whereas most Latin American corporatist regimes have been antiparty, Mexico has created an inclusive party structure that has provided a means for controlling political participation in a system-stabilizing manner. The PRI reflects its origins as a coalition of the different parties, factions, and ideologies that emerged from the 1910 revolution. It regards itself as the only legitimate heir to the revolution. Being adaptable and flexible, it can easily shift emphasis with each new president and still claim to be loyal to the revolution and to the eclectic contents of the 1917 constitution. It can accommodate the recruitment of leftists, rightists, idealists, and opportunists. Alan Riding stresses that the only crucial qualifications for membership are "loyalty, discipline, and discretion. The individual's opinions and beliefs are irrelevant; he must echo those of the political bureaucrat immediately above him on the pyramid. Only the President can, therefore, reveal himself in public, while every other mask is a mirror."[73] While coopting ambitious individuals, the PRI has divided the workers and peasants into separate sectors of the party through a skillful combination of repression and concession. "In this way," according to José Luis Reyna, "the state obtained popular support through interest representation, while preventing real political mobilization of these sectors."[74]

Cárdenas organized the official party into four sectors: peasants, workers, the popular sector (bureaucrats, professionals, teachers, and white-collar workers), and the military. In December 1942, the military was dropped out of the party structure. By the mid-1970s, the PRI claimed to have a membership of about nine million, or about 56 percent of the adult population. The popular sector (Confederación Nacional de Organizaciones Populares, CNOP) has done well within the PRI in terms of receiving beneficial public policies and holding public offices (since 1940 more than one-half of the seats in the Congress have been allocated to the popular sector although it makes up only 20 to 30 percent of the party membership). The agrarian and labor sectors have been less successful; they can be viewed as more controlled by the PRI leadership than as independent components of the revolutionary coalition. In the agrarian sector, all members of the *ejidos* (communal farms) must become members of the Confederación Nacional Campesino (CNC). Each *ejido* elects an executive committee, but these elections are presided over, and must be approved by, the government's agrarian department. At the state and local level, state governors usually choose the elected officials of the CNC. Most important, the CNC has not been successful in demanding and receiving policy benefits in the form of credit, transportation infrastructure, or irrigation.

With about 30 percent of its urban workers in unions, Mexico ranks second to Argentina as the most unionized nation in Latin America. The major national labor organization, the Confederación de Trabajadores de Mexico (CTM), was created in 1936 and later incorporated into the governing party. During the 1940s the government replaced the militant Vicente Lombardo Toledano with the more conservative Fidel Velásquez as head of the CTM, a position the latter has held for over forty years. Fidel Velásquez has kept the CTM loyal to the PRI even when, as was often the case, real wages were declining. When necessary, however, he has deflected the threat from rival unions by adapting more radical positions.

The PRI has created one of the major links between the political elite and the bulk of the Mexican people. This link is more efficient in conveying the commands of the government to the peasants and workers than it is in communicating the demands of the peasants and workers to the political elite. Nevertheless, enough social demands are communicated to maintain the legitimacy of the political system. The state apparatus is fairly autonomous, independent of the mainstream of Mexican society, but to sustain its legitimacy it must prove its nationalism against the United States and maintain certain commitments to social justice in terms of agrarian reform, minimum wages, subsidization of food staples, education, and social security. Thus, through politics and policy, the PRI monitors political participation. The PRI negotiates with dissidents and will usually offer and can deliver concessions, that is, seats in the Chamber of Deputies for legally recognized opposition parties. But the PRI retains the option of violent repression as the final solution to the problem of dissidents. In Mexico repression is usually used subtly, selectively, and sparingly; it is sometimes said that the government will use two carrots before it applies the stick. But the stick can occasionally be the enforcement terrorism of the 1968 "massacre of Tlatelolco" in which an estimated three hundred students were killed.

The PRI divides and rules the different social sectors; it intervenes in the national politics of different social groups to help one faction and destroy another. In such an environment, politics within the party is not so much a struggle among the three sectors of the PRI, but rather "the political process entails an increasing battle between factional *camarillas*, groups bound by loyalty to an individual leader (or *gallo*, cock) who is expected to award patronage in return for their support. Occasionally the *camarillas* possess a set of shared policy preferences that places them on the 'left' or 'right' of the political spectrum, but they consistently express fealty to the tenets of the Revolution—and their essential bond is more personalistic and instrumental than ideological. Thus, politicians acquire the labels of their leaders: this one is a *cardenista*, that one is an *alemanista*, the other one a *diazordicista*, and so on. In important (and revealing) ways, these attachments bear close resemblance to the *caudillismo* of years past."[75] In brief, by controlling elections, the press, the courts, the bureaucracy, and the police, the PRI constructs an environment in which the rational political actor concerned about having a successful career is most likely to accept the notion that there is no salvation outside of the party.

However, one has not explained the Mexican political system by describing the PRI. Business interests, for example, have benefited enormously since 1940 from public policy, but they are not represented within the formal structure of the PRI. All business firms must join either the National Confederation of Chambers of Commerce (CONCANACO) or the Confederation of Mexican Chambers of Industry (CONCAMIN). Businesses that refuse to enlist in these organizations can be prosecuted under tax evasion laws. These two business organizations are consulted by policymakers through a variety of agencies and commissions. According to Hansen, "Their influence is reflected in the content of all those special policies adopted to promote economic growth in Mexico: high tariffs, import licensing, tax rebates, special forms of governmental financial assistance, and so forth."[76] Furthermore, such pro-growth policies have encouraged the development of a dozen or so investment groups, generally recognized by the names of their leaders or dominant families, which control networks of interests in finance, industry, commerce, and real estate. Despite its revolutionary origins and continuing populist rhetoric, Mexico has one of the most effective pro-business governments in Latin America, perhaps surpassed only by the post-1964 Brazilian government.

While entrepreneurial activity has been richly rewarded, there is still a great deal of distrust between business and political elites. Peter Smith, in *Labyrinths of Power,* has demonstrated that business and political elites in Mexico are separate in social origins and career patterns; they are often in competition. The former recognize and resent the fact that they operate in an environment where politicians, who are often corrupt, have the option to reward or punish any private firm. While most public policies have benefited the business elite, there are provisions of the 1917 constitution and numerous statutory laws that, if implemented, could seriously injure the private sector. Smith claims that the complex relations between politicians and businessmen are based on three premises: "(1) The popular masses, especially labor, should be kept under, (2) the public and private sectors must often act in explicit coordination; and, given these conditions, (3) entrepreneurs and politicians can still compete for relative superiority."[77]

Obviously, the realities of the Mexican political system are subtle, complex, often secretive, and not fully explained by labeling it a corporative, bureaucratic-authoritarian, or tutelary democracy. It prefers to rely on inclusionary techniques, but it maintains the option of employing violence and illegal methods of repression. The regime has succeeded in developing the capability of regulating the flow of demands upon itself, which allows state policymakers considerable freedom in their decision making. The PRI "frees" the state by controlling the population. Smith stresses that "the primary task of all Mexican *políticos* . . . is to contain, control, and mediate conflict so as not to engage the attention or concern of their superiors, especially the president. By this criterion, an effective politician is one who does not let crises get out of control. . . . The function of politicians is to keep the lid on."[78]

Even here we should not lose sight of how flexible Mexican corporatism is. Because of the populist strain in the revolution, it is sometimes permissible for ambitious politicians to mobilize segments of the poor "as long as the goal is the incorporation of the disadvantaged group into the *existing* distribution framework rather than the destruction of the system. The rules of the game also require, however, that once an aspiring leader has become a member of the elite alliance and his followers have been rewarded, the leader is amenable to keeping his newfound constituents' demands under control."[79] This flexibility is obviously contingent upon the continuous expansion of the political elite and economic growth so that benefits to new groups will not be at the expense of the already incorporated sectors. Such flexibility will clearly be limited for several years because of the austerity program that Mexico has been forced to accept by the IMF in 1983 in order to repay its US$80 billion foreign debt.

The lid is kept on more effectively in Mexico than in most Latin American countries because Mexico has developed a petitioning pattern of political participation that maintains the loyalty of the bulk of the population. The system encourages individuals and small groups to solicit favors (distributive benefits) from a paternalistic bureaucracy and party. Officials satisfy some lower-class petitioners by merely granting them an interview. The government can respond to these unaggregated demands in a piecemeal and often protracted basis. More important, "This pattern of highly fragmented, non-threatening petitioning by the bulk of the population enables the regime to devote more time and resources to the satisfaction of demands by higher-status groups, which are seen as potentially more threatening to the political fortunes of incumbents and to the stability of the system itself."[80]

In summary, Mexico's corporate regime has devised a formula that reconciles many of the contradictions of the Latin American political culture in general and the Mexican political culture in particular. It has constructed a system that allows for controlled interaction among the following political ideas: individualism, machismo, continuismo, corruption, hierarchy, idealism, commitments to social justice, and nationalism. The system is authoritarian, but it is not rigid; it can change policy and personnel. To a great extent, it has reconciled political repression and developmental rationality. Despite its numerous shortcomings, the regime is considered to be legitimate by the bulk of its population and capable of improving conditions. However, even the most successful corporatist regime is not completely corporatist in structure; nor is it likely that Mexico's relative success with corporatism can be duplicated in other Latin American countries.

Summary and Conclusion

This chapter has attempted to describe who influences public policy in Latin America. A truly definitive answer is difficult to attain because so few directly participate in the policymaking process and because the process is usually so secretive. Such secrecy is, in some ways, an indicator of how elitist and authoritarian most Latin American political systems are. The more democratic the political system, the more is known about who influences policy.

However, we have learned that the process of social modernization is bringing about much greater pressure for political participation for more social groups than before. Whereas in the nineteenth century the major participants were the large landowners, the military, and the Catholic church, in the twentieth there is a far more numerous and complex set of contenders for power. These new groups, such as commercial farmers, the industrial bourgeoisie, the public bureaucracies, and the labor unions, not only make increasing demands upon the political system, but also their supportive participation is increasingly required for successful development. Since there was political instability in the nineteenth century even when the power structure was much simpler, it is not surprising that the legacy of instability has not been overcome in the twentieth century, when politics has become far more complex. The fundamental problem inherited from the colonial period is that it institutionalized a style of policymaking in which the overwhelming bulk of the population were nonparticipants. Policy decisions were made by executives who did not consult widely and often disregarded the will of the people. In the nineteenth century, the caudillo style of governing continued these procedures. It was part of the caudillo tradition for leaders to emphasize their independence from social pressures and to underestimate the importance of developing effective communication and bargaining networks with a wide variety of social groups. Such a legacy has handicapped Latin American political systems in developing political parties, legislatures, interest groups, and a free press. Although most Latin American political systems have been independent for over 150 years, they have not succeeded in legitimating their political systems; nor have they achieved self-sustaining economic development. Intractable political and economic problems have combined to cause governments to rely more on repression than on political bargaining and to drive frustrated segments of society to the extreme right or the extreme left. Such polarization reinforces the mistrust citizens have toward one another and toward the state. In Wynia's words, "Intense conflict over development policies . . . helps reinforce disagreements over the rules of the game, as each player comes to view particular sets of rules as giving unfair advantages to others in the contest for wealth, status, and power."[81]

For elites the rising outcry for political participation cannot be avoided, and they are forced to confront a number of problems. First, the record of instability and cycles of authoritarianism and democratic regimes suggests that the fragmented political culture of Latin America does not naturally support any particular type of regime. Lacking legitimacy, many political systems have attempted to increase their repressive capacity as a substitute for their political capacity to bargain. Today this is reflected in the creation of death squads, secretly led by state security forces, which engage in state terrorism to eliminate opponents in El Salvador and Guatemala. Second, elites find it increasingly difficult to convince the poorer members of their societies that an elitist hegemony serves *national* interests. Thus, the elites feel exceptionally insecure because: they are targeted for destruction by radical leftists who have come to power in at least one Latin American nation (Cuba); they find it increasingly difficult to cooperate among themselves; they fear that dissident members of their own social class will attempt to mobilize the lower classes; and they fear group autonomy because they believe that will lead to anarchy. Hence, elites are attracted to forms of bureaucratic-authoritarian and corporatist regimes as mechanisms to bring about economic growth, maintain their own privileged position, and tighten the controls over industrial and agrarian workers. Third, the elitist origins of the political systems have confronted a contradiction between, on the one hand, the need of a modernizing state to mobilize much greater levels of support, and, on the other, the lack of fundamental change in styles of policymaking and the fact that large numbers of citizens still do not benefit from public policies. It is likely that successful efforts to organize politically segments of the poorest 40 percent of the national population would be more effective than most distributive policies in reducing income differentials.

The kinds of political participation that are allowed in Latin America generally result in public policies that emphasize economic growth benefiting commercial farmers, the bourgeoisie, public bureaucrats, foreign capitalists, and strategically important labor unions. Political elites attempt to control the workers, peasants, and the poor through combinations of selectively distributive public policies, corporatism, and repression. The petitioning style of participation that is encouraged and which is compatible with the political culture results in a variety of policies that are often piecemeal, inconsistent, and personalistic.

Finally, this chapter suggests that there are no permanent solutions to the problems of increasing political participation. Modernization increasingly socially differentiates society, thus changing the relative power of different social groups. Any pattern of political participation can become rigid and inhibit the development of a new pattern that may be required for more progressive public policies. New strategies of development need new kinds of political participation. Each strategy must be socially supported; it cannot simply be decreed. In Latin America stable and/or democratic regimes appear to be the result of exceptionally skillful (and therefore not typical, nor easy to duplicate) political leadership. In brief, solutions to the problem of political participation in Latin America are likely to be temporary and require periodic political creativity.

Public Policy in Cuba
and Brazil Compared

If one could set up an experiment to evaluate two strategies of development, the antipodal examples might look like Castro's Cuba and the post-1964 military government of Brazil in that these two countries appear to have made calculatedly opposite strategic choices. The regimes symbolize two developmental models that are in competition with one another in Latin America but have never been systematically compared. Using Egil Fossum's categories, one can summarize their differences as follows: Cuba has stressed achieving an equitable distribution of wealth first and the accumulation of wealth second; the Brazilian government has emphasized the reverse set of policy priorities. However, no nation in the twentieth century is granted the luxury of prolonged, single-minded commitment toward either accumulation or distribution. Both are essential for development. Successful developmental policy requires a difficult-to-administer *shifting emphasis* between accumulation and distribution. The purpose of this chapter is to examine and evaluate the Cuban and Brazilian models of development in terms of how they contribute to economic growth and distributive justice.

The Cuban Model of Development

Castro's Cuba, led by its charismatic and self-righteous leader, is statist, authoritarian, nationalistic, and committed to social justice and the mobilization of all citizens. Consumerism is frowned upon, but the government places high priority on meeting the people's basic needs. In foreign policy it is hostile to the United States and dependent on the Soviet Union.[1] The Cuban model requires a swift transition from a private economy to a planned socialist economy since the latter is assumed to be capable of exercising a higher level of productive, distributive, and moral rationality. The regime, by emphasizing distribution over accumulation, succeeded in rapidly destroying Cuba's political enemies and later creating a system in which basic needs are met better than in any other Third World country. But Cuba has not been successful in shifting policy priorities in order to promote economic growth while maintaining social equity. Growth was supposed to be achieved by channeling investments into agriculture (especially sugar) and nickel production, but poor management, low labor productivity, and the continuing U.S. blockade have led to poor results. Since Cuba's capitalist economy was destroyed soon after Castro's rise, progress has been chiefly determined by the rationality of a few top policymakers and the efficiency of the bureaucracy. The quandary for Castro is that his policies keep increasing the very bureaucratization he personally detests. By the early 1960s, Castro had created a situation in which further progress was heavily dependent upon increases in administrative capabilities. To a great extent, Castro has made Cuban politics the administration of work, production, and distribution. The economic failures of the 1960s and the pressures from the Soviet Union have finally convinced Castro of the need to substitute technical and administrative cadres for social revolutionaries; technical qualifications in recruitment have become as important as ideological orientation. Castro has blamed a good share of Cuba's economic problems on the lack of administrative skills but has claimed that this was a transitory phenomenon that would shortly be corrected by the highly qualified students flowing from the educational system. However, Castro also publicly rejected the creation of a technocratic state which he believed would stifle the revolutionary process. This tension between Castro's commitment to mobilizational politics and the increasing bureaucratization of society in the Cuban model remains unresolved and is likely to remain so.

Castro has played too many roles in the revolution, including that of military strategist, administrator, diplomat, ombudsman, agricultural expert, judge, teacher, and leader of the only legal opposition when a policy change is required. Castro can be compared to an evangelist traveling from one part of the country to the other, exhorting the citizenry to "keep the faith." K. S. Karol claims that Castro's "achievements in the field are rather slim, especially compared with the tremendous effort he has put into them. The enthusiasm he kindles wherever he appears vanishes again soon after he leaves, and does not stand the test of the setbacks and hard realities of daily life. . . . Worse still, many of his own interventions and decisions made on the spur of the moment, show a great deal of confusion and do anything but alleviate the most pressing problems. A single person cannot be an infallible expert in all fields of technical endeavor."[2] During the 1960s a cycle emerged: secret discussions would be held among Castro and his advisors, followed by mass rallies, dramatic announcements, mobilization campaigns, and administrative changes; then problems would be discovered, Castro's speeches would become more and more critical, and Castro and his advisors would return to the drawing board. For those who believe that this situation changed fundamentally during the 1970s, it must be noted that Raúl Castro complained in 1979, "How long are we to go on allowing unsolved problems to reach crisis point and then ask Comrade Fidel to take over the situation and pull our chestnuts out of the fire?"[3] It is widely recognized that Castro is a socialist caudillo who believes and acts as if he is indispensable for the success of the revolution. Because Castro has made himself indispensable, he cannot fully institutionalize his own revolution.

The Cuban model also stresses mobilization. Castro's charismatic qualities, his adroit near-monopolization of nationalist symbols, and the regime's distributive performance have enabled the government to mobilize the Cuban people in support of public policy and against the enemies of Cuba. By the end of 1960, all political opposition to Castro and his activities was illegal. By the mid-1960s opportunities to oppose the government were minimal. In Cuba, people can be mobilized only *for*—never against—public policies. According to Jorge Dominguez, in the mobilization model, "hierarchical authority stifles criticism of the state's goals and policies. A sense of urgency and of planning in an atmosphere of crisis and attack is characteristic. Loyalty to proclaimed policies is crucial; a gradual and evolutionary approach to policy change is much more difficult to achieve. . . . Policy change often leads to scrapping an entire program rather than to a modification of only some of its aspects."[4] A mobilizational style of promoting and implementing public policy seriously inhibits criticism and information feedback that would alleviate or correct problems. Mobilization efforts appear to be an efficient means of attaining a specific, short-term goal (such as a vaccination drive), but much less so for achieving a more diffuse, long-term goal (such as higher labor productivity). So-called volunteer labor, induced by negative and/or positive sanctions, has been particularly inefficient. Nor has the creation of the "new communist man," devoid of all "bourgeois vices," been successful. Almost half the Cuban population of 9.7 million was born after Castro came to power early in 1959, but the "new" communist man appears to possess enough of the old vices to keep labor productivity low. Castro has legitimated this political system through personal appeal, constant reiteration of the theme that the nation has been freed from corrupt dictatorship and enslaving imperialism, emphasis on distribution performance, allowing malcontents to emigrate, and bureaucratic and mass organizational controls over the populace. His greatest problems are the absence of economic growth and lack of autonomy from the Soviet Union. In brief, Cuba represents an authoritarian state under charismatic leadership that has provided "socialism without abundance and mass mobilization without mass democracy."[5]

The Brazilian Model of Development

Brazil today takes its character from the corporatist legacy of Getúlio Vargas, the national security ideology of the Brazilian War College, the bourgeoisie's fears of populism and mass mobilization, and the skilled management of a growing number of technocrats. The Brazilian model of development assumes that initially public policy should be primarily concerned with promoting advanced industrialization. Growth is given preference because all agree that it is the fundamental prerequisite for future social development and, finally, democratic political development. In other words, only when the economic pie has expanded enormously can wealth be distributed to ensure everyone a decent standard of living, and only then will the country be ready for democracy. Thus, the model views development as a sequential unfolding of stages: from the economic, to the social, to the political stage. In President Médici's words of 1972: "The revolutionary state [read bureaucratic-authoritarian] will last as long as it takes to implant the political, administrative, judicial, social and economic structures capable of raising all Brazilians to a minimum level of well-being."[6] Evidently, the military intends to stay in power for a long time.

According to Mario Henrique Simonsen, democracy did not work before 1964 because "universal suffrage frequently rewards those candidates who promise to divide resources into parts whose sum is greater than the whole. This leads to an excessive emphasis on distribution policies whose consequences include rapid inflation, external indebtedness, the failure of growth, and social disorder."[7] Under conditions of mass poverty, say the technocrats, democracy becomes demagogery. Without the economic base and the necessary social conditions, the electorate can be manipulated by political demagogues into "premature welfarism" (which would reduce, if not eliminate, the capital necessary for investment), and xenophobic nationalism which fails to appreciate the potential benefits of foreign investment. To overcome these problems, the model calls for a policy deemphasizing popular mobilization and/or instituting corporate political controls over all politicians, intellectuals, and social sectors that might not agree with the government's priorities.

The combination of corporatist social controls, military authoritarianism, and limits on the mobilization of workers, peasants, and students has created a technocrats' dream: a situation where they could formulate public policy on the basis of their view of economic rationality with a minimum of political interference. Brazilian leaders were able to decrease the real wages of workers by about 30 percent between 1964 and 1967 and thus force the workers to bear the burden of slowing down inflation. Later, when wages were allowed to increase, they forced workers to contribute to the accumulation of capital through several compulsory mechanisms. The technocrats, especially Roberto Campos and Delfim Netto, were also able to create a hospitable climate for foreign private investment. By 1979 Brazil had attracted over $16 billion in foreign investment, one-fourth of which came from the United States. The administration of state enterprises was rationalized and expanded in scope and function. Material and market incentives were manipulated so that both domestic and foreign investors were encouraged to behave in a manner compatible with indicative national plans. Instead of relying on the market to induce allocative decisions, the technocrats used indicative planning to manipulate incentives to increase exports, to shift investments from coffee to soybean production, to invest in the Northeast and the Amazon, and to invest in consumer durables and capital goods, thus substituting the rationality of their own economic and political judgments for the rationality of the marketplace in the allocation of credit.

The Brazilian economy may be under tighter state control than any economy outside the Communist bloc. The military and the technocrats, having condemned the *unpredictability* of the previous political system, set out to create a more predictable situation by subjecting major economic and political sectors of society to bureaucratic control. By 1982, Brazil had 498 public corporations, employing 1.4 million people, and accounting for almost one-half of the nation's output of goods and services. These public corporations operate banks, gas and electric companies, oil related concerns from tankers to retailers, savings and loan institutions, airlines, armament factories, steel plants, an automobile company, shipping and shipbuilding firms, and food distributorships.[8]

Politically, the model is a coalition among the military, who supply the top leadership and maintain order, technocrats who provide expertise, and foreign and domestic investors, who supply capital and technology. Economically, it is a model that depends upon cooptation through consumption; it is based upon the bourgeois mentality in which individual hard work is rewarded by profits; however, profits are largely privatized, while risks are socialized.

The problem for the Brazilian model is that it lacks a legitimizing political formula. Poppino's point is still accurate: "The regime appears to suffer less from the actions of its enemies than from the absence of dedicated friends."[9] Even successful economic growth produces benefits for only a minority of the population; hence, growth does not "buy" legitimacy for the political system. Given the uneven distribution of income, cooptation through consumption can attract only a minority and may very well alienate the majority. On the one hand, policymakers have stressed that the more difficult stages of industrialization (the development of capital goods industries) require that the government demonstrate a political capability to maintain and create new but unpopular policies for an extended period; on the other hand, the military has searched for a political formula through which it could obtain popular support and legitimacy. That political formula is likely to be some form of democracy, with two or more political parties, a legislature, and elections. The commitment of Brazilian presidents to democracy waxes and wanes; it is never fulfilled, because the military cannot win authentically free elections; yet it is never extinguished because the military has no other formula that the population will accept. One must also see that democratization is not purely a political issue; it is also an economic issue and is evaluated by the elites in terms of its distributive consequences. Thus, there is probably an irreconcilable tension in the Brazilian model between the aspirations for democracy and the policy requirements of bureaucratic authoritarianism.

The issue now is whether the Brazilian regime can change its model of development. By 1974 some policymakers had decided that the model ought to be revised because of the following factors: the soaring foreign debt; the growing dependence on increasingly expensive foreign oil; the continuing concentration of income in the hands of a few, widely recognized as unjust; the unevenness of regional development; heightened mistrust among the military, the domestic bourgeoise, and the multinational corporations; and the lack of enthusiastic support from major social sectors. The Brazilian model is now being asked to adapt to a less expansive international economy, more distributive pressures to broaden the domestic market, and increasing demands for democratization. Presidents Ernesto Geisel (1974–79) and João Batista Figueiredo (1979–   ) have responded to demands for democratization by launching liberalization policies labeled, respectively, *distensão* (decompression) and *abertura* (opening). These programs were designed by General Golbery do Couto e Silva, the principal political advisor to both presidents, to restore gradually political rights taken away in the 1964 coup and to acquire more legitimacy for the Brazilian regime. Under these policies, political prisoners have been freed, most censorship has been lifted, an amnesty has been declared for thousands of Brazilians who were exiled or who lost their political rights, a variety of political parties have emerged, and relatively competitive elections were allowed in November 1982 for members of Congress, senators, governors, and local officials. However, the military government, under the complex and self-serving rules it has created, will still control the selection of the next president in January 1985 by an electoral college. A big question remains whether the hard-line faction within the military will accept any further steps toward democratization.

Economic Growth in Cuba

The major policy failure of the Castro regime is in the area of economic growth. Reasons offered to explain this failure include bad management, lack of spare parts, the U.S. blockade, absence of adequately trained technicians, excessive expenditures on social services, wage scales that do not provide sufficient incentives for productivity, and the ineptness of Castro and his policymaking elite in economic matters. Whatever the true set of causes, productivity, in both quantitative and qualitative terms, has been disappointing. Castro has been able to decree a distributive revolution; he has not been able to decree rises in productivity.

At first, Castro believed that it would be possible simultaneously to raise capital, elevate living standards, diversify the economy, and withstand the antagonism of the United States. This "humanist" stage of the revolution allowed Castro to avoid hard choices and seemed to work for the first eighteen months of the regime. During this period, living standards of the poor were raised and the economy grew. Economic and political problems then forced Castro to make harder choices; humanism was discarded and Marxism-Leninism was embraced. The latter offered Castro the means to gain Soviet aid and to promote rapid economic growth while maintaining strong central political controls over the course of the revolution. The plan was to discard the "immoral" and decentralized aspects of capitalism and replace them with a centrally planned and controlled socialist economy that would channel investments into sectors that would assure Cuba rapid economic growth. Cuban policy makers never doubted their ability to substitute their greater rationality for the lesser rationality of the market. With typical revolutionary utopianism, they believed that because the previous system was so corrupt and inefficient, their honesty, dedication, and wisdom would achieve rapid success. But the Cuban economy has not succeeded as they had hoped. Instead, rationing was introduced during the 1962 economic collapse and has become a permanent feature in Cuba.

Castro pledged to outperform the Batista regime in economic growth. For the period 1950 to 1958, the gross investment coefficient averaged about 18 percent of national income and resulted in an average annual growth of per capita national income of 2.1 percent.[10] Thus the prerevolutionary period was characterized by modest (most Cubans would say inadequate) growth, but not stagnation. In contrast, the Castro regime talked of rapid economic growth and of achieving Western European standards of living by 1970. In August 1961, Carlos Rafael Rodríguez proclaimed, "The Cuban Revolution is setting for itself minimum goals of 10 to 15 percent cumulative annual growth."[11] The actual achievements for the period 1960 to 1971 were a per capita GNP decline at an annual rate of 1.2 percent. Instead of rapid growth, there was economic chaos and stagnation as per capita income hovered near its 1962 level of $500. After the debacle of 1970, the Cuban economy grew at an average rate of almost 8 percent from 1970 to 1975 and then declined to an average of minus 1.4 percent between 1975 and 1979. By 1979 the economy was again stagnant, precipitating another wave of emigration (over 100,000 people) from Cuba in April and May 1980. In July 1982, Castro described a dismal short run economic situation, blaming the problem on declining sugar prices (down to six cents a pound), and conceding the possibility of negative growth rates for the next few years.[12]

This poor performance is not due to a lack of capital investment. While the coefficient of gross investment declined to 14 percent in 1959–60, it increased to 17.9 percent in 1961–1963, rose to 20.5 percent in 1964–66, and exceeded 30 percent in 1968. In the 1970s the rate of capital accumulation varied from 28 percent to 22 percent. Mesa-Lago concludes that "early in the Revolution, consumption was increased at the cost of investment restriction, but since 1961 the policy has been reversed."[13] These respectable rates of capital investment did not result in respectable rates of economic growth of the GNP (6 to 8 percent per year) because of poor planning, lack of proper maintenance, and low labor productivity. Like an enraged father scolding his children, Castro has complained that workers do not oil their machinery, that they use tractors to ride to baseball games, and that managers hoard spare parts (the Cuban index of consumption of spare parts may be the highest in the world). Despite impressive gross investment rates, the elimination of unemployment, the increased use of female labor, and the massive use of supposedly extra voluntary labor, the growth record remains poor.

Given Cuba's economic growth strategy, the lack of productivity was particularly painful in the sugar industry. Castro planned to increase sugar production from 6 million tons in 1965 to 10 million in 1970 with the latter figure serving as the ideological test of the revolution. Moreover, the continuation of the production level for the decade of the 1970s would earn the foreign exchange to develop the other sectors of the economy. Sugar production, thus designated as the leading sector of the economy, was supposed to stimulate the economy both by providing capital for modernizing agricultural production (fertilizers, pesticides, farm machinery, transport equipment) and in direct ways by providing molasses for cattle fodder and paper made of bagasse, the residue after the juice has been extracted from the cane. Castro also stressed, with his slogan of "the simultaneous battle," that Cuba would not have to sacrifice any other plan in order to fulfill the sugar target. Under these circumstances, efficiency in industrial yield—that is, the percentage of sugar obtained in the mills in relation to the weight of the cut cane—became of strategic importance. Normally, from eight to fifteen tons of raw sugar are obtained from every hundred tons of sugar cane cut. Variations in the yield can be caused by the weather, the type of sugar cane, when the cane is cut, how long it takes to process the cane, how the cane is cleaned of leaves and trash, and the efficiency of the industrial equipment used. During the 1950s, the average prerevolutionary yield was usually above 12.00—that is, 12.00 tons of sugar per hundred tons of sugar cane cut. Beginning in 1962, the yields began to decline; the average yield between 1964 and 1969 was 11.80. Castro planned to have an average yield of 12.30 for the 1970 harvest, but the actual figure was 10.71, which produced 8.5 million tons.[14] The productivity of the 350,000 workers mobilized for the sugar harvest was so low that the cost of the operation was perhaps three times higher than the sugar's value on the world market.[15] The simultaneous battle was lost on almost every front.

Since the weather was good, weather may be discounted as a reason for the failure. Three other factors help to explain it: the failure of mechanization, the shortage of professional cane cutters, and the low productivity of voluntary workers. Despite great efforts, the Russians and Cubans had not succeeded by 1970 in solving the complex technical problems of mechanizing the sugar harvest. The most successful technological innovation was to introduce mechanical lifters which handled 83 percent of production, but harvesting machines cut only 1.1 percent of the cane crop, whereas the plan called for them to cut 30 percent.[16] Wassily Leontief explained in 1971, "Persistent, albeit unsuccessful, experimentation with mechanical cane cutters seems to have been prompted by the belief that the low efficiency of labor could be compensated for by large-scale use of sophisticated automatic equipment. . . . Such hope is hardly justified. Careless handling and poor maintenance of machinery, buildings and all other kinds of fixed capital goods is one of the surest signs of an insufficiently motivated labor force. So long as moral incentives continue to work as badly as they apparently have up to now, large-scale introduction of costly new equipment might aggravate the economic difficulties of Cuba instead of alleviating them."[17] Paradoxically, in this case modernization came into conflict with the goal of higher productivity.

The dilemma for Cuban policymakers striving to bring about economic growth is twofold: (1) agricultural development is inhibited by the inherent weaknesses of communist systems in dealing with this sector, and (2) rapid industrialization is blocked by the bottleneck of a negative balance of payments. The Soviet record in agricultural development is hardly a model of economic efficiency. Even Castro conceded that, "the problems of the countryside are the most serious problems that revolutionary processes anywhere in the world have encountered."[18] As for the balance of payments, virtually all of Cuba's energy, most of its technology and capital goods, and a great deal of its raw materials have to be imported, which means that Cuba must have sufficient exports to finance this large volume of imports. This constraint appears to have bound Cuba, both before and after 1958, into producing and exporting sugar, the one major product the nation can sell overseas. Sugar usually accounts for 75 to 85 percent of Cuba's export earnings, with much smaller amounts coming from tobacco and nickel. In terms of growth the weakness of the Cuban model is displayed by the fact that since 1959 the nation has not experienced a single year with a positive balance of trade. The tragedy for Cuba is that it failed to take advantage of the expansion of international trade during the 1960s by increasing its exports. Despite the fact that Castro's decision to emphasize agriculture requires less imports than a policy of rapid industrialization would have, the expanding debt indicates that the present development strategy still demands levels of imports beyond the economy's capacity to finance them.

The collapse of the Cuban economy is forestalled only by the outright grants, subsidies, and technical and military aid provided by the Soviet Union. Almost every internal failure has caused Castro to become more dependent upon Moscow. In 1979, the Russians sold their oil to Cuba at about half the market price and bought Cuban sugar at the price of 44 cents a pound as compared to the world market price of about 10 cents. The Russian subsidy has steadily increased, and in 1983 it stood at about $4 billion a year or $11 million a day. These figures represent about 25 percent of Cuba's gross national product and do not include military aid, which the Soviets give Cuba without cost. While Cuba's foreign debt was $45.5 million in 1959, in 1983 it stood at over $12 billion, with $9 billion owed to Moscow and more than $3 billion (in hard currency) owed to Western governments.[19] The total debt to Russia is interest free until 1986. However, such aid severely limits Cuba's ability to expand and diversify its hard currency trade inasmuch as nonsocialist nations have no political or economic incentives to subsidize Cuban deficits. Havana's second five-year plan (1981–85) calls for Cuba to be the major socialist sugar supplier by producing 10 million tons by 1985. Cuba is now as locked into the Soviet trade orbit as it was locked into the United States' sphere before 1959.

After the failure of the 1970 sugar harvest, Cuba became increasingly dependent on the Soviet Union and introduced a new Economic Management and Planning System. This new administrative arrangement stressed the entrepreneurial functions in the management of state farms, factories, and other institutions. Administrators were now under pressure to generate a surplus of earnings over costs and were given some freedom in utilizing some of their profits. Managers were admonished to demand discipline from the workers to overcome absenteeism, loafing, and poor maintenance practices, and to insure that workers conformed to quantity and quality work norms. In 1971 the government enacted a law against loafing, which required all physically and mentally capable men from ages seventeen through sixty to work. According to Mesa-Lago, "One of the main purposes of the law was to incorporate idle men into production, and more than 100,000 were indeed recruited even before the law went into force. Another objective was to curtail the increasing absenteeism of the labor force which reached some 20 percent by late 1970."[20] The regime also upgraded the importance of material incentives. The new thinking was that wages would have to be connected to output in order to increase the latter. In September 1971, Castro proclaimed, "Society must do the most for those who do the most for society."[21] The rationing system was then altered to serve as a new individual material incentive to produce. Local labor assemblies were used to decide which high production workers should be rewarded with television sets, refrigerators, electrical appliances, and a week's vacation at a government beach resort. Labor union leaders, technicians, and physicians were granted preferential access to new cars imported from Argentina. Dominguez points out, "The rationing, which had once been an instrument for equality, now becomes a method to benefit the elite with the goods provided by new trading partners."[22]

In the pursuit of economic growth, Castro has been forced to accept policies that are not in harmony with his preferences. Although he has always preferred moral incentives, he had to acknowledge in 1970 that they were not only ineffective, but also counterproductive, as evidenced by absenteeism, loafing, and the decline in the number of professional cane cutters. He has reluctantly accepted the fact that material rewards will be important as long as scarcity exists, and scarcity will persist in Cuba for the forseeable future. Castro dislikes bureaucracy and mistrusts technicians, but has created an increasingly bureaucratic state. Castro has reflected a similar change in his attitude toward tourism. In his words, "We don't like tourism, we really don't like it, but tourism is simply an economic necessity for the Revolution."[23] Consequently, despite a housing shortage for its own citizens, Cuba is building new hotels for tourists and allowing refugees to return for visits. Castro is also now in favor of trade with the United States.

Before the revolution, Castro claimed the Cuban economy was stifled by its trade with the United States; now he recognizes that the Cuban economy is being damaged by the U.S. blockade. Finally, Castro has accepted a role in the "socialist division of labor," that of producing sugar, tobacco, cattle and nickel and of promoting tourism, while importing manufactured and capital goods—a role that closely resembles the one so despised before 1959.[24]

Economic Growth in Brazil

Since 1967, the battle cry for Brazil has been "Growth is the solution." More effectively than any other Latin American country, Brazil has utilized a variety of policy instruments to achieve rapid economic growth. This single-minded determination has sometimes been diluted, however, by fears of inflation, increasing foreign debt, and Brazil's incapacity to finance the importation of capital goods and oil. Until recently, this strategy avoided any direct concern for income equality and the redistribution of wealth. In 1974 Finance Minister Mario Henrique Simonsen argued, "Economic growth itself, by increasing the value of manpower, is one of the most effective automatic instruments of distribution."[25]

Since the stabilization efforts of the Castelo Branco administration (1964–67), the Brazilian economy has shown a remarkable ability to grow. Between 1968 and 1978, the gross domestic product expanded by 142 percent; per capita income grew from $893 to $1,639; industrial production increased by 169 percent; agricultural production expanded by 58 percent; and exports soared 572.5 percent. (But imports soared also, by 635 percent.) From 1968 to 1974 there was more economic growth than had been achieved since the creation of Brazil in 1822. This rapid growth broadened and deepened Brazil's basic infrastructure and productive base. Though it remains the largest coffee producer in the world, Brazil now manufactures a higher proportion of its capital goods and consumer durables than any other Latin American country.[26] Brazil is also the second largest food exporter and the third largest shipbuilder in the world. However, by 1974–75, the oil crisis, the increased prices of other imports and the mounting burden of external indebtedness had decelerated economic growth and had accelerated domestic inflation.

Much of the credit for Brazil's successful economic growth strategy belongs to Antonio Delfim Netto, who served as minister of finance under both Presidents Costa e Silva (1967–69) and Emilio Garrasatazú Médici (1969–74). Delfim believed that the stabilization policies of Roberto Campos in the Branco administration had stifled economic growth. Being less frightened by inflation than Campos, Delfim allowed minimum wages to increase and liberalized credit policy for business. He continued his predecessor's policies of attracting foreign private investment and of strengthening upper and middle-class demand for consumer durables, but he also worked to stimulate and diversify exports through subsidies and trade liberalization. Fortunately for Delfim, these policies were compatible with international conditions, since they coincided with a major expansion of both world trade and Eurodollar investment capital.

In 1975 Delfim stated, "No one can achieve rapid development without concentrating wealth. You've got to make the cake bigger before you can start slicing it up."[27] The problem with this notion is that Brazil, like most Latin American countries, has had its wealth concentrated in the hands of a small portion of its citizens since colonial days. By adapting to this skewed income distribution—instead of trying to alter it with distributive policies—Brazil's growth strategy has been socially conservative and economically limited in its impact. In initiating a strategy of growth geared to a consumer demand of less than 20 percent of the population, Delfim selected a method that did not change the marginality of the majority of the Brazilian population.

For example, there has been no emphasis on land distribution despite the fact that there are 9.5 million landless peasants. Most of the land that has been distributed has been for largely ill-fated colonization projects in the Amazon region. The government has generally chosen agrarian policies (high food prices, subsidies, cheap credit) which not only benefit the large commercial farmers, but have often encouraged them to extend their holdings. Thus the steady increase in agricultural production, occasionally thwarted by the weather, has been due mainly to increased acreages devoted to farming rather than to increased productivity. As is true in most of Latin America, agricultural productivity is low in Brazil. For instance, corn production over the 1965–71 period averaged 1,290 kg/hectare, compared with 4,740 for Canada, 4,100 for the United States, and 3,280 for Italy.[28] These figures suggest that the possibilities for the expansion of agricultural production in Brazil are great, but they also indicate that Brazil's strategy has had only moderate success in agriculture (with the notable exception of soybean production).

The socially conservative nature of Brazil's growth strategy is also reflected in its efforts to mobilize capital, which have created opportunities for those with money to make more money. For example, the Capital Markets Law of 1965 provided for (a) a substantial reduction in the withholding tax on dividends, (b) a personal income tax exemption on approximately $400 in dividends, and (c) a deduction from gross taxable income of 30 percent of amounts invested in newly issued shares of "open capital" companies, government bonds, and housing bonds, and of 15 percent for investment in mutual funds and saving deposits. Ness reports, "Fiscal incentives allow corporations to apply up to 50 percent of their income tax liabilities to approved individual projects in the impoverished northeast region of the country and in the largely unutilized Amazon and midwest regions and in certain sectors such as tourism, fisheries, and forestry, in which Brazilian potential for development was not being achieved. Rather than pay these amounts to the government as income tax, the company would use the funds to make these types of investment in approved projects. Liberal debt finance is also available for these projects through government banks."[29] In 1967 Delfim Netto created a new tax incentive, which permitted exporters to receive rebates for both taxes paid on exported goods and on a specified portion of products sold in the national market. This incentive gave the exporting company a competitive advantage in the domestic market, since similar firms that did not export would not receive a tax rebate on their domestic sales. To further stimulate an export mentality, the government has encouraged the creation of Japanese-style trading companies, which usually include a bank, a manufacturing organization, and an international marketing system. These integrated companies finance both required imports and sales of finished products. They are often involved in transport, advertising, and even consumer financing in the receiving countries.

Through the use of indexing and a compulsory mechanism for capital accumulation, the Brazilian government has overcome one of the major obstacles to promoting economic growth in an inflationary economy—the low propensity to save. Whereas there were only about 300,000 savings accounts in 1969 (the first year indexed savings accounts were offered), there were 7 million by 1975. The government allows holders of indexed savings accounts to make deductions from their gross income for tax purposes based on the average balance in the account during the year, and it waives federal income taxes on the first $330 of actual interest earned. There is no tax on the indexing payment.[30] In addition, the government has used the Employee Guarantee Fund (FGTS), created in 1966, to channel funds to the National Housing Bank (BNH); the Program for Social Integration (PIS), established in 1971, has been used to channel funds to the National Savings Bank; and the Program for Capital Formation for Civil Servants (PASEP), also launched in 1971, channels funds to the National Economic Development Bank (BNDE). Consequently, Brazil has been able to significantly increase its gross fixed capital formation as a percentage of the GDP from 19.8 percent in 1969 to over 25 percent in 1975.[31] Through its control and regulation of the banking system and its programs of compulsory savings, the government determines, directly or indirectly, the course of 65 to 75 percent of total investments in Brazil. In brief, as is true in most of Latin America, Brazil does not have an independent, self-reliant bourgeoisie; it has a bourgeoisie that is highly dependent upon subsidization by the state. What the Brazilian model has given its bourgeoisie is the most effective system of state aid in all of Latin America.

However, even this impressive system was unable to adjust to the effects of the second oil shock in 1979. In 1979 and 1980, expansion in real gross domestic product accelerated to a 7.3 percent rate, but severe problems emerged that caused growth to stop, or even to become negative, in 1981, 1982, and 1983. First, the price of many of Brazil's exports (coffee, sugar) dropped while the cost of oil imports jumped from $4.1 billion in 1978 to $9.4 billion in 1980. Second, inflation accelerated from a relatively stable (for Brazil) 41 percent growth rate in 1975–78 to 77 percent in 1979 and to an historic high of 110 percent in 1980. Third, foreign debt skyrocketed to unbelievable heights. In 1964, the foreign debt stood at $3 billion; by 1974, it reached $17 billion; by 1983, it had zoomed to a world-high figure of $90 billion. This borrowing, much of it from Western commercial banks, was used to finance growth, especially for the state enterprises. Fourth, interest rates on these debts rose from 4.4 to 5.0 percent in the early 1970s to 15 to 19 percent in 1981 and 1982. The possibilities of growth were strangled by the ratio of debt service payments to exports, which reached about 97 percent in 1982.[32]

Consequently, President Figueiredo's minister of planning, Delfim Netto, was forced to jettison his plans for growth and to negotiate an austerity package with the International Monetary Fund (IMF) to stabilize the economy, reschedule loan payments, and acquire new loans.

In 1983, this austerity package included: reducing the public sector deficit by severely cutting investment by the state enterprises; gradually eliminating many of the large interest rate subsidies; expanding exports and reducing imports; modifying exchange rate policy to ensure that the rate of minidevaluations in relation to the dollar would accelerate to a pace equal to that of domestic inflation; and a new wage law, which would limit salary increases in both public and private sectors to 80 percent of the official inflation index. These measures are supposed to stabilize the economy so that the nation can begin to grow again by the second half of the 1980s. However, there are fears that this humiliating austerity package will destabilize the political system since it will bring about declines in the standard of living and rises in unemployment. Politically, negative growth rates, soaring inflation, and the foreign debt crises are potentially lethal threats to the limited legitimacy of the regime and the "myth of technocratic omniscience" of leaders like Delfim Netto in that they constitute policy defeats for the elites on their own chosen field of battle.[33]

Distribution in Cuba

Cuba's most impressive policy achievement has been in raising the general standard of living through distribution. Except for the lack of political freedom, there is more social justice in Cuba than in any other Latin American country. In Cuba there is less unemployment, underemployment, illiteracy, malnutrition, disease, and there are fewer slums than in any other Latin American nation. Moreover, there are more jobs, educational opportunities, and social services. While a classless society has not been achieved, Cuba has become more egalitarian. The commitment to egalitarianism is hampered, however, by the inherent inequality brought about by the bureaucratization of the society and the special privileges granted to members of the Communist party.

Castro has stressed distribution over accumulation for a number of reasons. First, Castro is a humanist who believes the peasants and workers were exploited in pre-1959 Cuba and therefore deserved special consideration under the new political order. Second, because of his inexperience and ignorance of economics, he was not aware he was indeed making a choice between distribution and accumulation. That is, before 1962, Castro believed that distributive policies would automatically result in future economic growth: freed from alienation, the peasant and laborer who benefited from the new social policies would work harder. Third, distributive policies allowed Castro to reward his friends and punish his enemies, thus helping to legitimize the regime with the popular classes and to destroy the power of landholders, urban landlords, and domestic and foreign capitalists. Finally, because all distributive policies are directed by the state, they provide a comprehensive (some might say totalitarian) set of political controls. The political criterion of loyalty to the state is used to determine who has access to jobs, higher education, housing, vacations, and material goods.

During Castro's first few years in power, he reduced rural electricity rates, telephone charges, and urban rents; in addition, he eliminated rents for tenant farmers in the first agrarian reform bill (1959), raised the minimum salary for government employees, and encouraged the renegotiation of labor contracts to significantly elevate wages. By 1968 the regime was providing free education, social security, medical services, local telephone calls, water service, sporting events, and burials. Many workers were given free meals at their place of employment, and rent payments were regulated so as not to exceed 10 percent of family income. Ritter observes, "As a result of the redistributive reforms, higher wages and public expenditures, the share of the total before-tax income in the form of wages and salaries increased possibly by 13 percent (from 65 to 85 percent) of total national income."[34] By 1970 there was a minimum wage of $85 per month and a maximum of $450, while pensions were $60 a month. The rationing system assured that adequate food was available for all children, the old, and the lowest-paid workers. These distributive policies initially helped the poorest 40 percent of the population, increasing their income from an estimated 6 percent of national income to 20 percent by the mid-1970s. Most of these gains were made by 1962; after that, persons in the 50 to 70 percentile group whose incomes ranged from average to well above average, experienced the principal income gains. Gains were also made in diluting regional disparities.[35]

These distributive reforms, plus the ideology of a socialist revolution that aspires to grant all citizens equal rights to consumption, had the effect of multiplying demand and placing impossible pressures on supply. While economists are aware of soaring consumer pressures in countries like Brazil, Kahl points out that "it is not always recognized that expectations rise even faster in a successful socialist revolution, not for cars and foreign travel, but for equal access to beaches, milk, schools, and hospitals. The new morality gives all citizens a right to participate immediately instead of after they have painfully climbed the social hierarchy into a new middle class, a process which often takes a generation or two in other societies and disciplines desires in the meantime."[36] It was to overcome this situation that rationing was introduced in 1962. But because of the lack of economic growth, Cuban daily life is still dominated by the distribution of scarcity, with no relief in sight. The constant criticism of the evils of the consumer society in the press suggest that unsatisfied consumer pressures remain a frustrating element in Cuba.

In addition, economic errors in policymaking created a situation of socialist inflation, that is, a scarcity of goods on the one hand and an excessive supply of money on the other. Because of the free public services and rationing, most families received more money than they could spend each month. For example, a typical family in Havana might spend 10 percent of its income in rent, 25 percent on food and necessities, and save the rest. Mesa-Lago reports that in 1970 the excess of money over the available supply of goods meant that "the population could have lived one year without working. As a result of this situation, the black market (where goods were sold from 5 to 10 times the official price) flourished in spite of government restrictions."[37] Consequently, the new stress on economic growth after the sugar harvest failure of 1970 included policies to increase prices so as to reduce the money in circulation. Demand was decreased by raising the prices of cigarettes, beer, rum, water, electricity, long-distance transportation, and restaurant meals. Castro's promise made in 1968 to eliminate house rents in 1971 was reneged. The practice of bestowing 100 percent salaries to sick or retired workers in designated vanguard factories was terminated. Many workers who had previously received free lunches now had to pay 10 pesos monthly for lunch. In 1976 free calls from public phones were ended and a charge of 5 cents instituted. In 1977, day care centers began to charge enrollment fees according to the family's ability to pay. In brief, the amount of money in circulation was reduced by about one-third, the value of the remaining currency was increased, and the wage share of the gross product declined after 1969. In Dominguez's words, "The higher prices for goods and services allowed the government to rely on material incentives to increase individual productivity. Prices for everything except food, medicine, and essential clothing were decontrolled by the mid-seventies, a move that was made possible by increased production."[38]

Distribution in Brazil

As the Cubans were shifting their policy concerns from distribution to accumulation, the opposite was occurring in Brazil. The technocrats had hoped that successful economic growth would postpone any need for tackling the problems of social justice. But the post-1964 Brazilian experience suggests that even the most rapid economic growth does not automatically reduce social problems; indeed, such growth may increase them. Periods of economic growth always leave certain individuals, social sectors, and regions behind. Even in a conservative bureaucratic-authoritarian regime such as Brazil, pressures for distributive public policies have grown because of the rising urban population, the awareness among educated people of welfare-state policies in the West, the fact that welfare policies were championed and often initiated by populist politicians in the past, a commitment to social justice among some policymakers, bureaucratic aggrandizement (the minister of education wanting to build more schools), and the needs of political survival (buying off some potentially threatening group such as urban squatters by giving them access to public housing).

By 1974, the concern for distributive policies, which had been a continuing but lower priority for policymakers, gradually began to compete more energetically with growth policies. By then, the oil crisis had slowed down growth, and the distributive results of the "economic miracle" could be seen. One of those results was described as the "Belgium in India" situation, that is, a segment of the population numbering about 22 million with an average per capita income of about $1,000 in the midst of 85 million with incomes below $300.[39] Economic growth had worsened the already troublesome disparities among regions and social classes. In 1960 the wealthiest 5 percent earned an income equal to 20 times the average income of the poorest 40 percent; this proportion increased to 32 times in 1970.[40] Similarly, the ratio of the mean income of the top 20 percent to the bottom 40 percent of the income-earning labor force went from 9:1 in 1960 to 12:1 in 1970. These gross inequalities in income help to explain why life expectancy and infant mortality rates in Brazil are similar to those in nations with much lower average incomes. The World Bank estimates that a 10 percent increase in the income share of the bottom 40 percent of the Brazilian labor force is accompanied by an 11 percent decline in infant mortality. In short, raising the level of income of the poor in a country like Brazil is not merely a means of introducing the lower classes to the consumer society; it is a life and death issue.

A second result of the economic miracle weakened the argument of those who claimed that the economic growth of a modern sector (statistically and loosely defined as jobs paying at least the minimum wage) would automatically absorb all low-skilled labor from the traditional sector (defined as jobs paying less than the minimum wage). During the 1960s, employment in the modern sector grew at 3.7 percent per year, while total employment expanded at 2.7 percent. By 1970 the modern sector included 45 percent of total employment. A continuation of these rates would imply that the modern sector would require an additional 78 years to absorb the total labor force.[41]

The problem with the original Brazilian strategy of development was captured by President Médici in 1974 when he said, "The economy is doing well, but the people are doing poorly." Even a technocrat like Mario Henrique Simonsen, who earlier had crudely criticized policies designed to distribute income as being detrimental because they would increase the demand for food while decreasing the demand for automobiles, was now saying (as minister of finance), "We cannot ignore the problem. . . . It will catch up with us eventually, and the sooner we tackle it or begin to chip away at it, the better."[42] These heightened distributive concerns, tempered by the conservative components of the Brazilian model, were well summarized in a speech by President Geisel to Rio businessmen in November 1977:

> We will persevere in the market regime, in accordance with an economic perspective of a democratic and pluralistic society. No other model is compatible with our country's economic, social and political institutions. This model can function in Brazil, since the neocapitalism we subscribe to is capable of effecting national development, in a continuous process, without resource to radical experiments. This model has been pliant in the face of violent blows such as the oil crisis and offers today all the advantages of continuity. Its social feasibility depends on whether we continue to implement income distribution while keeping up growth and on whether we are not afraid of bringing about the necessary social changes. Its economic feasibility depends on our ability to avoid the increase of state-controlled areas and of denationalization, on the one hand, and, on the other, on our ability effectively to decentralize development, particularly industrial development.[43]

Since 1974, the Brazilian government has given distributive policies greater emphasis by both expanding old programs and creating new ones. For example, the government has expanded the number of social security beneficiaries from 5.7 million in 1964 to 20.7 million in 1978.[44] In addition, investment in water supply and sewage under the National Sanitation Plan (PLANASA) has been accelerated; an urban sites and services program and a construction materials loan program have been initiated to encourage low-cost, self-help housing construction; and a new program has been established to provide basic health care in the poverty-stricken rural Northeast. However, in 1979 and 1980 there were an increasing number of strikes by workers emboldened by the country's return to free speech and free assembly. In response, the government passed a bill in late 1979 providing for half-yearly cost-of-living increases, to be set by the government; these grant proportionally higher wage increases to those earning less than three times the minimum wage (about three-fourths of the labor force) than to those earning more. However, as we noted above, this program was ended in 1983 as part of the austerity package.

Cuban and Brazilian Policies Compared

To get a better understanding of distributive policies in Cuba and Brazil, let us now compare a variety of such policies, beginning with education. A basic overview of the two educational systems is provided in table 22. Some of the data underestimate the Brazilian commitment to education because about 8 percent of primary students, 40 percent of secondary students, and more than half of university students attend private (mainly Catholic) schools. Nevertheless, Cuba has clearly achieved more in education than Brazil. Cuba has a better (lower) teacher-student ratio and a significantly higher proportion of its school-age children in school than does Brazil. Between 1958 and 1978, the number of Cuban students at the primary level increased from 717,417 to 1,759,671, at the secondary level from about 150,000 to 1,700,000, and at the university level from about 15,000 to 140,000. In 1960, 21,310 primary-level students, 6,378 secondary students and 1,331 college-level students were graduated, compared with the 1981–82 academic year when 203,967 primary students and 314,803 secondary students were graduated, and there were 21,009 college graduates. From 1958 to 1982 the number of teachers increased from 22,798 to 247,479; the number of colleges increased from three to forty; and the number

TABLE 22
Education in Cuba and Brazil, 1960–75

	Cuba	Brazil
Public expenditures per capita on education (in US dollars)[a]	32	32
School-age population per teacher[a]	39	48
Percent of school-age population in school[a]	70	50
Percent literate[a]	85	68
Percent of population age 7–13 enrolled in school[b]		
1960	95.0	58.0
1970	111.9	74.0
1975	108.7	81.7
Percent of population enrolled in secondary school[c]		
1960	14.4	3.7
1970	29.6	9.8
1975	50.4	15.6

Sources: Ruth Leger Sivard, *World Military and Social Expenditures, 1980* (Leesburg, Va.: World Priorities, 1980); James Wilkie, *Statistical Abstract of Latin America,* vol. 2l, Latin American Center, University of California, Los Angeles, 1981; World Bank, *Brazil: Human Resources Special Report* (Washington, D.C.: World Bank, 1979).

Note: Of students beginning first grade in Brazil between 1964 and 1971, 41 percent completed second grade, 24 percent completed fourth grade, 28 percent completed fifth grade, 11 percent completed eighth grade, and 10 percent finished all grades.

a. Figures are for 1974.

b. Percentages exceeding 100 indicate inclusion of "over-age" pupils.

c. Secondary school enrollment figures for Cuba are for students age 14–19; for Brazil, age 15–19, grades 9–12.

of university major fields of study expanded from twenty-eight to ninety-eight.[45] When Castro assumed power, only Argentina (88 percent), Chile (85 percent), and Uruguay (89 percent) were more literate than Cuba; only about 23 percent of Cubans were illiterate, although almost half the school-age population was not attending school. Despite the emigration of many teachers, the literacy rate and the proportion of school age children have steadily increased. Because access to at least primary education has been universalized in Cuba, the current literacy rate probably stands at over 90 percent.

The areas of Cuban education that require future improvement are: reducing the dropout rates for fourteen-to-sixteen-year-olds (almost half the sixteen-year-olds are not enrolled in school); improving the quality of teachers; reducing the rate of failure in primary grades (79 percent of those who entered the class of 1965 did not finish in 1971); and reducing the gap between the quality of education in rural and urban areas.

The Brazilians have also made progress in reducing illiteracy, but it has been less rapid than in Cuba. Less than 40 percent of the Brazilians were illiterate in 1960; by 1980 that figure had been reduced only to about 30 percent. Whereas the Cubans launched a nationwide effort to eradicate illiteracy in 1961, not until 1970 did the Brazilians start the Movement for Brazilian Literacy (MOBRAL), partially financed by the state-run football lottery. The five month MOBRAL course, aimed at the fifteen-to thirty-five age group, has had only moderate success.

Despite lagging behind Cuba's educational commitments, Brazil has made significant progress. Roett observes, "In 1965, educational expenditures accounted for 11.9 percent of all public expenditures or 2.9 percent of GNP; by 1974 the figures had risen to 21.2 and 3.5 percent respectively."[46] During the period 1960–73, the student population increased from 8.7 million to 18.9 million, with the average annual growth rate of students (5 percent) exceeding the accompanying growth of the population base (3.4 percent).[47] In terms of school enrollments, progress was made in all regions, but the southeastern region maintained the advantage over the less developed northeast and the frontier region.

While educational opportunities are improving in Brazil, there are still enormous problems to overcome. For example, enrollment rates for grades one through eight in rural areas for the year 1974 were about half the level found in urban areas in all three regions. Perhaps even more depressing are the figures in the standardized cohort flow profiles which show that only 24 percent of all entrants into the first grade made it to the fourth grade by their fourth year in school. If one considers four years of schooling as being necessary for functional literacy, then these figures suggest that literacy is not being attained by roughly two-thirds of the school-age population. Many of these problems can be explained by the fact that in 1972 seven out of ten of the 165,000 school buildings in Brazil were one-room, one-teacher schoolhouses, and nine out of ten rural students attended this type of school. In these schools about 12 percent of the students drop out during the school year, an even greater proportion drop out between grades, and an additional 25 percent fail the course at the end of the year. Only 50 percent of pupils in the first grade are promoted at the end of the year. A typical rural school is described in a World Bank report:

> The school is a one-room house where groups of students (officially in different grades) sit and stare. The instructor is unlikely to have advanced beyond basic level education and is paid less than the minimum wage. She is supposed to teach the entire program of studies in all grades, but her knowledge of the subject is, at best, a product of sheer repetition. The room is overcrowded. There are no textbooks: some volumes were produced but have not been distributed; they are too expensive. Unquestioning repetition of the teacher's words is equated with learning. When this is achieved, the reward is moving to the intermediate or back rows in the classroom (a sign of grade promotion). The price of failure is to stay in the same row or drop out.[48]

There is also debate in Brazil concerning the priority given to the different levels of education. The cost per student for secondary students is four times that of primary students, while the unit costs in higher education are forty times higher than the unit costs at primary levels. From 1960 to 1980 the number of university students increased from about 100,000 to 1.5 million. The issue arises whether the rate of growth of higher education—more than four times that of primary education—is appropriate when only one-third of the school-age population is completing the four years of schooling considered necessary to achieve functional literacy.

As for their health policies, both regimes have shown improvements, but Cuba has clearly made more progress than Brazil (see table 23).

TABLE 23
Health Care in Cuba and Brazil, 1974

	Cuba	Brazil
Population per physician	1,122	1,600
Population per hospital bed	235	260
Infant mortality rate		
per thousand live births	29	82
Life expectancy	71	61

Source: Ruth Leger Sivard, *World Military and Social Expenditures, 1980* (Leesburg, Va.: World Priorities, 1980).

Before the revolution in Cuba, most doctors were in private practice. Medical care is now free and controlled by the Ministry of Public Health. All medical students must take a oath that they will not engage in private practice. In 1955, most doctors practiced in urban areas, with 62 percent of all doctors practicing in Havana Province; by 1972 this proportion had dropped to 42 percent (Havana Province's share of the population in the 1970 census was 27 percent). In 1958 Cuba had 6,000 doctors, providing Cuba with considerably better than average health care in comparison to other Latin American countries. In 1958 the death rate per thousand population was 6.4, and the death rate under age one per thousand live births was 33.4. About one-third of the doctors emigrated between 1959 and 1965, and Cuba was thus forced to train new doctors quickly and often inadequately. Health statistics declined during this period. During the 1960s, the infant mortality rate remained around 40 per thousand. However, because of the requirement that every new medical graduate had to serve two years in a rural area, and the increase in the ratio of hospital beds to population by 50 percent in all the provinces outside Havana, health conditions improved considerably in the latter part of the 1960s and into the 1970s. In 1982 Cuba had 16,836 doctors, 3,986 dentists, and 31,855 nurses. In 1959 there was one medical school with 300 graduates a year; today there are seventeen schools graduating 2,000 physicians a year. There are now 256 hospitals, 397 polyclinics, and 75 homes for the elderly.[49] Each polyclinic provides a full range of preventive and treatment services. The Cuban health care delivery system has been able to raise life expectancy to seventy-three years and lower the infant mortality rate to 18 per thousand. The leading causes of death in Cuba today are heart disease, malignant tumors, diseases of the central nervous system, and early childhood diseases; in this respect Cuba is similar to the developed rather than the underdeveloped nations. That is, most preventable diseases and deaths are avoided.

In Brazil public expenditures on health have increased fifteenfold in real terms since 1949 and in 1976 equaled about 2.5 percent of the GDP. In 1964, Brazil had seventy-one medical schools, producing 2,810 doctors per year; it had 34,251 doctors and a ratio of inhabitants per doctor of over 1,900:1. The death rate per thousand inhabitants was 13.0; the infant mortality rate was 93.3; and life expectancy at birth was fifty-seven years. By 1978, Brazil had over a hundred medical schools, producing 9,000 doctors per year, 70,000 doctors, and a ratio of inhabitants per doctor of about 1,600. The death rate per thousand inhabitants was 7.9; the infant mortality rate was 82; and life expectancy was about 63 years. The distribution of doctors remains a problem; while Rio has one doctor for every 240 Cariocas (residents of Rio), many cities and rural areas in the northeast and interior have no doctor at all. Few doctors can afford to establish their own private clinics, so most work for the National Medical Care and Social Welfare Institute (INAMPS), the health care branch of the National Social Welfare Institute. In 1960 INAMPS provided medical care for 32 million urban workers and their dependents; by 1975 it served over 64 million. By 1975 the social security system was financing and providing health care for 80 percent of the urban population and 40 to 60 percent of the rural population.[50]

Despite Brazil's economic growth, the nation is still plagued by the health problems of an underdeveloped society. Although life expectancy is improving in all regions, there remains a fifteen-year gap between the Northeast and the Southeast. The infant mortality rate in the Northeast is two-thirds higher than that prevailing in the Southeast. Forty percent of the Brazilian population is suffering from malnutrition. In the Northeast, with only a minority of homes possessing running water and sewage facilities, infections and parasitic diseases are extensive, accounting for almost half the deaths among children under five years of age. According to a World Bank study,

> The Northeast and Frontier exhibit the classical characteristics of underdevelopment: a high proportion of total deaths occurring in children under five years of age, and a high mortality due to infections and parasitic diseases and perinatal causes. Mortality patterns in the Southeast, in contrast, are closer to those observed in developed nations, where a relatively large proportion of deaths occur after 55 years of age, and the leading causes of death are diseases of the circulatory system and neoplasms (tumors). Further data on proportional mortality rates attributable to infections and parasitic diseases—when disaggregated into those reducible through immunizations (e.g., tuberculosis, diptheria, polio, small pox, measles, whooping cough), and through improved sanitation (e.g., typhoid, dysentery, enteritis, plague, malaria)—indicate that about 80 percent of all deaths from infections and parasitic diseases could be prevented by appropriate intervention.[51]

In brief, thousands of preventable deaths occur each year in Brazil. This is the area where the Brazilian model is weakest and the Cuban model strongest.

Conclusion

Whereas in Europe and Asia, the two largest nations (Russia and China) went communist, in Latin America a small island developed its own form of communism, while the largest nation (Brazil) developed its own style of capitalism. Cuba aspires to play a world role through its ideological leadership; Brazil wishes to be a traditional great power. The Cuban model first made the strategic choice of emphasizing distribution over accumulation but has shifted its priorities to economic growth since the early 1960s. The Brazilian model has stressed accumulation over distribution but has become more concerned with distributive policies since 1974. The Cuban and Brazilian experiences illustrate that, even when decisive strategic choices have been made, the political system will still be confronted with divisive political and economic debates. Both developmental experiences suggest that success in either a policy of accumulation or one of distribution does not necessarily lead to success in the other. Brazil has achieved a rapid economic growth and Cuba has achieved an impressive degree of social justice. Thousands of socially preventable deaths occur each year in Brazil; this is not true in Cuba. With a higher per capita income than Cuba, millions of Brazilians suffer from malnutrition and live an average of twelve years less than Cubans. The Physical Quality of Life Index (PQLI) is based on an average of its index ratings for life expectancy, infant mortality, and literacy. In the mid-1970s Cuba received a score of 86 on this index, Brazil 68. Obviously, Brazil should—and has the resources to—improve the quality of life of its citizens through distributive policies. But, as we have learned, the Cubans have been as inept in their growth policies as the Brazilians have been socially unjust in their policymaking.

The two models are compared in table 24. Differences between them are manifest. Instead of stressing their differences, however, a more useful and iconoclastic view might point out their similarities. Both nations have had great difficulties in institutionalizing a political party system. Both require enemies; for Cuba, those are Batista, the United States, *gusanos* (a pejorative term for Cubans who wish to migrate to the United States), and underdevelopment; for Brazil, subversion and

TABLE 24
The Cuban and Brazilian Models of Development Compared

	Cuba	Brazil
Original policy emphasis	Distribution emphasized over accumulation	Accumulation emphasized over distribution
Later policy emphasis	Economic growth	Distribution
Benefits of model	Social justice	Outstanding economic growth; rising standard of living for middle classes
Drawbacks of model	Lack of political freedom; loss of citizens through emigration	Lack of social justice
Mobilization of citizens	Strong encouragement to citizen political participation	Little encouragement to citizen political participation
Incentives to productivity	Moral incentives, then more emphasis on material incentives	Material incentives, cooptation through consumerism
Policy toward consumerism	Deemphasis on consumerism	Emphasis on consumerism
Encouraged personality	Heroic guerrilla and worker	Wealth-producing entrepreneur
Styles of decision making	Charismatic, elitist, bureaucratic, authoritarian, skeptical of market rationality, increasingly technocratic	Technocratic, elitist, bureaucratic, authoritarian, skeptical of market rationality
Unresolved tensions	Charismatic leadership versus technocratic decision making, bureaucratization versus popular mobilization, nationalism versus reliance on the Soviet Union	Democracy versus authoritarianism, nationalism versus foreign, private investment, social inequality versus challenges from the labor unions
National problems	Administrative inexperience and ineptitude, low productivity of labor, increasing foreign debt, scarcity of energy, overdependence on sugar exports	Conflicts among the military, the bourgeoisie, and multinational corporations, increasing foreign debt, regional disparities, inflation, scarcity of energy, lack of popular support, lack of legitimizing political formula

Source: Compiled by the author.

corruption. The two systems are authoritarian and fear autonomous political participation. Both models lack faith in the rationality of free markets and are attracted toward technocratic decision making (Carlos Rafael Rodríguez and Delfim Netto seem equally enamored of the value of technocratic planning). The two systems share a weakness in that, while Castro exhorts his people to be heroic workers and

Delfim urges Brazilians to be wealth-producing entrepreneurs, only a minority in each nation is capable of responding. The two models rely heavily on their military. All Brazilian presidents since 1964 have been recruited by and from the military. Castro's heir apparent, Raúl Castro, heads the Cuban military. In 1979 per capita military expenditures in Brazil were US$18; in Cuba, US$118. Should Castro die, there is likely to be a struggle between the military and the Communist party for control over the government. Horowitz and Trimberger argue as follows:

> In Cuba . . . the same kind of relationship is established between the military and the proletariat as that between the military and the bourgeoisie in the capitalist countries of Latin America. There is no denying the socialist character of Cuba or the capitalist nature of Brazil, . . . but the definition of the economy of these countries in no way precludes the military contol of the system of state authority. That is to say, as the Cuban military increasingly shows preeminence over the party, the kind of devil's bargain in which the military guaranteed the positive tranquility in exchange for high economic productivity becomes the enshrined pattern. In other words, the same structural arrangements and economic consequences obtain under "socialism" as under "capitalism."[52]

Finally, neither model is self-reliant; both spend beyond their domestic means. The 1977 per capita foreign debt for Brazil was $254; for Cuba it was $526. Both models need outside help, which offends national pride. In Brazil, nationalist military officers like General Albuquerque Lima accuse Delfim Netto of being an *entreguista*—that is, one who has delivered the national patrimony over to foreigners. In Cuba, which has fulfilled the dependence theorists' policy prescriptions of breaking ties with the United States, nothing magical happened except some Cubans found themselves fighting in Angola and Ethiopia. Even the great strides that Cuba has made in distributive policy have been matched by Costa Rica. The latter had a PQLI of 87 in 1975 and has preserved political freedom.

In short, the two models have proven capable of achieving economic growth and distributive justice, but not simultaneously. They have both recognized the need to shift gears to provide what is lacking for future development—growth for Cuba and distributive justice for

Brazil—but they have not displayed the ability to overcome their deficiencies. Although both models have achieved more success than most other strategies competing in the Third World, each needs considerable improvement. The tendency of some social scientists to become apologists and not provide critical evaluations of both the positive and the negative features of the two models does not help either regime make the necessary improvements.

7

Conclusion

This book has described and compared the policy behavior of Latin American governments. I have stressed that public policymaking is choice-taking, and each choice involves tradeoffs and opportunity costs. Policymakers must choose among competing goals and among competing means of achieving them. The ultimate skill of policymaking is to reconcile seemingly incompatible economic and political interests to create viable solutions. Nowhere are workable solutions more difficult to achieve than in making the policy choices involved with promoting development. Living in what is considered a peripheral region of the West, Latin Americans desperately want to modernize. Modernization is believed to be the result of public policy. To study Latin America's developmental policies, I have used Egil Fossum's set of critical developmental policy choices. These include two sets of variables: accumulation/distribution and bureaucracy/mobilization. Fossum's set of strategic choices were selected because they are sufficiently abstract to cover a wide assortment of cases and sufficiently real to be familiar to actual policymakers. These choices suggest that development policy is essentially an attempt to provide the nation with a balance between economic growth and distributive justice, and between the requirements of bureaucratization and the aspirations for political participation. Each chapter examines policies designed to fulfill one of these choices—that is, policies created to influence economic growth, distributive justice, bureaucratic development, or political participation. Although treated separately, each set of policies affects the other three. Policies designed to promote economic growth affect the distribution of income, different parts of the bureaucracy, and which groups are allowed (and not allowed) to mobilize. Distributive policies affect the rate of economic growth, bureaucratic proliferation, and levels of political participation. To emphasize bureaucratic development increases the probability of socially conservative policies. And to limit political participation maintains the power of those who are already socially mobilized and increases the probability that growth and distributive policies will benefit the already privileged sectors of society.

In the typical Latin American context, these policy choices must be made under conditions of insecurity because of population growth, urbanization, inflation, balance of payments difficulties, unemployment, and political instability (see chapter 1). The lack of political stability gives birth to either the illusion, the hope, or the fear that all choices are possible. Such a wide variety of possible choices, from Castro's Cuba to Pinochet's Chile, creates a very insecure, unpredictable, and competitive environment. This insecurity partially accounts for one of the pathologies in policymaking, what Raúl Prebisch labels "Immediatism, that is, the desire (very understandable from the political standpoint) to show quick results."[1] Such efforts frequently sacrifice long-range developmental goals.

Chapter 2 deals with the "politics of accumulation," which refers to the choices and policies government officials have made to promote economic growth. Since World War II, many Latin American countries have tried to accelerate their economic growth through a set of policies collectively known as import-substitution industrialization (ISI). The ISI strategy worked to industrialize significant portions of many Latin countries and produced economic growth, but in a frustrating, sporadic, stop-go pattern. I have criticized the ISI strategy because: it neglected agriculture and population control; it did not provide enough vertical specialization; it did not encourage nations to develop their own technology; it overprotected entrepreneurs; it led to an overemphasis on consumerism; it failed to alter the skewed income distribution; it did not reduce the unemployment rate; and it did not free the member-states from balance of payment difficulties. I was especially critical of the fact that the politics of accumulation encourages a self-indulgent consumerism that stifles the development of a social conscience, which is an important component in support of distributive policies. The minority in each country who have benefited from ISI have joined the traditional oligarchy in the pursuit of a truly luxurious life style. This life style, encouraged by the diffusion of consumption tastes modeled on those of the United States and Western Europe, stimulated especially by representatives of the multinational corporations and the influence of the mass media, helps to create a politics of envy that is stirred up by radicals, populists, and demogogues. Since participation in the consumer society under present income distributions can only be available to a minority of the population, political repression is inevitable. To overcome some of these problems, several nations have altered their economic growth strategy from ISI to neoliberal policies implemented by bureaucratic-authoritarian regimes. These governments have tried to combine political repression with economic rationality. However, by the early 1980s, no growth strategy was working well because of the foreign debt crisis and the sluggish nature of the international economy.

Chapter 2 also stresses that such economic growth policies, without previous distributive reforms, end up granting privileges to the already privileged, thus reinforcing too many of the elitist characteristics of Latin American societies. One noted anthropologist, Richard Adams, emphasizes that the increasing wealth of the upper sector serves as a brake on the development of society as a whole because the rich use their wealth to maintain their power "rather than to increase capital and achieve economic development."[2] Because of fears of political instability, radical ideologies, and the working class, this concentrated economic power is used in a very socially conservative manner. The central dilemma of economic growth policies in Latin America is how to soothe the uncertainties of entrepreneurs and encourage productive investment without at the same time reinforcing the concentration of wealth in the hands of a few people and buttressing the social conservatism that is at present inhibiting the achievement of greater distributive justice. In brief, ISI policies changed most of the economies in Latin America, but also concentrated economic and political power, thus making the capacity for continuous change more difficult. And it is this incapacity for continuous adaptation to the changing necessities of the international economy and to increasing political participation that is so notoriously problematic in many Latin American political systems.

Chapter 3 deals with the politics of distribution. I have stressed that the distributional patterns established by tradition or the market are no longer considered sacrosanct: modernization spreads the word that they can be changed by public policy. To a greater extent than in Western democracies and to a lesser extent than in Communist countries, Latin American governments decide who will get what, when, and how. Most policymakers believe that just as economic growth requires governmental intervention, so does distributive justice. What is particularly discouraging is the realization that even rapid economic growth by itself—as evidenced by the experiences of Brazil and Mexico—will not solve the problem of poverty within any politically acceptable period. The debate in most countries is not over the necessity for distributive policies, but over *who* should receive the benefits therefrom and *how much* such groups should receive. Latin American countries have dabbled with distributive policies for select groups (the military, the bureaucracy, the labor aristocracy) for some time. When one looks at the history of Uruguay, Argentina, Brazil, and Chile, at the social welfare provisions of constitutions since the 1917 Mexican constitution, and at the pronouncements of most political parties and populists since the 1930s, it is obvious that the political culture of the region is compatible with the welfare state. Whether the welfare state is compatible with rapid growth in Latin America is a more difficult question.

The distributive policy style in Latin America is analogous to everyone in a community being invited to a feast, but upon arriving, discovering that only those with power, luck, or personal connections will be served. For the most part, those who do not get served compete with one another to obtain the land, education, social security, health care, and housing promised them, but only a select few receive what they have been promised. When the distributive policies of the Western industrialized nations, which assure universal application, are adopted by the paternalistic nations of Latin America, they are applied in a highly selective manner. Given their paternalistic policy style, most Latin American states want to maintain discretionary control over their favors in order to reward the faithful, punish the disloyal, and maintain political stability. However, governmental and opposition rhetoric have contributed to demands to universalize and equalize social services, that is, to an ever expanding consciousness of social rights. The demonstration effect of progressive policies in the West has meant that these ideas have spread to Latin America, and now many of these countries have progressive labor legislation, social security programs, and mass education. But often these "progressive" policies do not produce a progressive society because they are concentrated in the modern sectors, which constitute a minority of the economically active population in most Latin American countries. Whereas in the West social policies often are oriented toward helping the needy, in Latin America they are primarily supplements to the already privileged. In Latin America, according to a United Nations study, distributive services "have evolved within social security systems, housing programs, modern industrial enterprises and special programs for public employees, the armed forces, etc. . . . . They have thus dealt mainly with groups having relatively secure incomes and jobs rather than with the marginal population. Even in the programs aimed at the latter, limited resources have made selectivity among potential beneficiaries unavoidable, and the better educated and more socially integrated potential beneficiaries have had a natural advantage in learning about and claiming the benefits."[3] Thus a paradox; distributive policies in Latin America have helped to reinforce social stratification rather than to overcome it. A Mexican economist makes the same point by stating that "what distinguishes the poor is precisely their incapacity to benefit from public expenditures."[4]

Another negative consequence of Latin American distributive policies emerges here. The fact that the better-off sectors of the economically active population are receiving the bulk of the benefits of distributive policies does not mean that they are satisfied. On the contrary, they want—and are politically mobilized to demand—more. It is a standing joke in Latin America that the middle sectors wish "to be born with a scholarship, live on a salaried job, and die on a pension." Hence, the governing elites have several tigers by the tail, a situation that some believe only the military is equipped to handle. First, the privileged sectors (the military, the public employees, the labor aristocracy) want more and better services, but it is difficult enough to keep them abreast of the inflation rate; second, the poor want social services to be universalized—a proposition that, if fulfilled, would cost astronomical amounts of money; and, third, there are large public bureaucracies administering each of these social services and committed to the expansion of these programs while devouring large chunks of their appropriations through administrative costs and corruption. The ability of the government to control this volatile situation is further reduced by the low degree of legitimacy commanded by so many Latin American political systems. Because of this lack of legitimacy, and the political instability that inevitably follows, each social sector demands special protection, special administrative representation, special funds, earmarked taxes, constitutional provisions, and so forth, to assure that, whatever happens politically or economically, their particular social sector will maintain its benefits and security. No group has faith in the honesty, impartiality, and efficiency of the government. These attitudes then contribute to the inability of the state to rationalize distributive policies in some overall development plan.

Chapter 4 emphasizes that most Latin American political elites advocate giving priority to the bureaucracy over social mobilization in order to promote an orderly process of modernization. Whatever the political orientation of a regime, state intervention has been an expanding part of public policy since the Depression. Whereas in the past it was the function of the state to protect and conserve society, today the relationship between the two has become more complex; parts of the state are trying to conserve the old society while other parts are intervening to change it through development. By emphasizing the bureaucratic state-centered approach to development, the Latin Americans have become dependent upon the rationality of their administrators in making public investment decisions, managing public enterprises, providing services to the ever expanding cities, and administering a complex variety of social services.

The success of this strategy is dependent upon the speed by which a Weberian bureaucracy can be constructed and implemented to rationalize selected aspects of government and the economy. Such bureaucratization involves both structural and behavioral changes. The problem for Latin America is that it has experienced what Schmitter labels "structural overbureaucratization" and "behavioral underbureaucratization." Structurally, the bureaucracy has differentiated itself into an ever expanding number of departments, agencies, boards, and especially autonomous agencies. Latin American bureaucracies are characterized by *personalismo,* nepotism, job insecurity, high turnover, lack of expertise, inadequate use of expertise when it exists, overcentralization of authority, formalism, stultifying legalism, lack of coordination, and corruption. Hence, the bureaucracy does not contribute what it should to increase the probability of creating rational developmental policies. The dilemma reflected here is that many of Latin America's political elites have selected a style of development that they are not culturally prepared to pursue.

Chapter 5 discusses how 300 years of Iberian colonialism institutionalized a style of governing in which only a few had great power and wealth, while the many were nonparticipants, docile subjects of a political economy that exploited them. This style of governing has had enormous difficulty in adjusting to the changes wrought by modernization: the elite is now larger, more complex, and can no longer rely solely on personal connections to maintain its power and privilege; the class and group structure of society is now more complex, less docile, and anxious to participate and influence public policies. By not resolving the legitimacy question in the nineteenth century, many Latin American nations are now confronted with illegitimate governments trying to promote economic growth and distributive justice while simultaneously handling the challenge of those demanding increased political participation. The fragmented political cultures of the region have meant a lack of consensus on both the type of regime and the set of policies best suited to promote the development of the nation. Because the stakes of winning or losing power are so high, the governing elite in each country has felt the need to develop and substitute the repressive capabilities of the state (in the form of bureaucratic authoritarianism or corporatism or death squads) for the political capabilities necessary to allow a more complex society to influence policy and reconcile group conflict. One can hypothesize that the more a country develops its repressive capabilties the less it will develop its political capabilities in setting up communication and bargaining networks between government and society. The tragic consequences of traditional elites emphasizing repressive capabilities, under the influence of a back-against-the-wall mentality, can now be seen in El Salvador and Guatemala.

Chapter 6 compares the Cuban and Brazilian models of development. Castro's Cuba initially made the strategic choice of stressing distribution over economic growth, but has shifted its emphasis since the early 1960s. The post-1964 Brazilian military governments have emphasized accumulation over distribution, but have become more concerned with distributive policies since 1974. Their developmental experiences suggest that, first, in today's world, a strategy of development cannot simultaneously achieve economic growth and distributive justice, and, second, that even rare and significant success with either a policy of accumulation or a policy of distribution, does not necessarily guarantee success with the other. Successful developmental policy requires a nation to make a continuing series of strategic choices, none of which can provide a permanent solution to the problem of achieving modernization. A nation must develop the capacity to shift gears in policy emphasis every five to ten years. The Cuban and Brazilian experiences demonstrate how necessary and difficult it is to shift gears.

Viable development requires some measure of success in each of these four policy areas. Experience suggests, however, that policy-makers cannot progress in all four areas at the same time; in fact, success in one area may cause problems in the other. Rapid economic growth, for instance, may cause warped, uneven development in which certain groups and regions prosper while others decline. Successful distributive policies may retard economic growth and be the cause of inflation, balance of payments difficulties, and "investment strikes" on the part of private entrepreneurs. Bureaucratic development, even in the Weberian sense, may cause political elites to lose touch with the people they are governing and thus result in "participation explosions." Increasing political participation beyond the capacity of what Huntington calls political institutionalization may result in political instability and reactionary backlashes. The paradox of successful development may be that, although it requires balance along these four dimensions, harmony is never achieved, but only continually striven for. Thus the issue of development can never be settled because there are always inadequately met needs and painful choices to be made. There is no final solution to the problem of development except for utopians.

In reviewing the policy behavior of Latin American political systems, one sees that policymakers often have less power than is realized (but more power than is acknowledged by the dependence theorists). Much of the nations' resources belong to foreigners, a great deal cannot be touched for fear of violent revolt (land, taxes), and much of what is available must be used to play the politics of survival instead of the politics of development. The public policymakers in Latin America can be likened to the captain of a ship trying to steer his vessel to a distant port (modernization). The captain of this ship is burdened by a potentially mutinous crew and passengers; indeed, the crew divides its loyalty among several alternate leaders, all of whom would like to take over. The captain, therefore, is at least as concerned with remaining captain as with reaching the destination. The captain, the crew, and the passengers are consuming so many of the provisions that their consumption is seriously impeding the ability of the ship to reach its destination. First and second-class passengers are especially consumption-conscious; if their consumption were reduced—and if the second-class passengers and the crew were not so intent on emulating the consumption of first-class passengers—third-class passengers would have a greater share. The captain is confronted with a bewildering array of choices in navigating through hazardous waters. His maps are inaccurate, his steering instruments do not respond, he has trouble receiving and communicating information from and to the crew and the passengers, and his crew sometimes does not obey. Thus the course of the ship sometimes appears to be irrational to segments of the crew, to the passengers, and to outside observers. Nevertheless, despite these problems, some captains (Cárdenas and Betancourt, for example) have managed to steer a progressive course. However, steering a progressive course requires such skill and luck that the probabilities of failure are, unfortunately, far greater than the chances for success.

Notes

Chapter 1. Introduction

1. Argentina, Bolivia, Brazil, Chile, Colombia, Costa Rica, Cuba, Dominican Republic, Ecuador, El Salvador, Guatemala, Haiti, Honduras, Mexico, Nicaragua, Panama, Paraguay, Peru, Uruguay, and Venezuela.

2. John J. Johnson, *Political Change in Latin America: The Emergence of the Middle Sectors* (Stanford, Calif.: Stanford University Press, 1958); Karl M. Schmitt and David D. Burks, *Evolution or Chaos* (New York: Praeger, 1963); Kalman H. Silvert, *The Conflict Society: Reaction and Revolution in Latin America* (New Orleans, La.: Hauser Press, 1961); James Petras and Maurice Zeitlin, eds., *Latin America: Reform or Revolution* (Greenwich, Conn.: Fawcett, 1968).

3. Claudio Veliz, ed., *Obstacles to Change in Latin America* (London: Oxford University Press, 1965); Claudio Veliz, ed., *The Politics of Conformity in Latin America* (London: Oxford University Press, 1967); John Mander, *The Unrevolutionary Society* (New York: Harper Colophon, 1969); Robert F. Adie and Guy E. Poitras, *Latin America: The Politics of Immobility* (Englewood Cliffs, N.J.: Prentice-Hall, 1974); James M. Malloy, ed., *Authoritarianism and Corporatism in Latin America* (Pittsburgh, Pa.: University of Pittsburgh Press, 1977); David Collier, ed., *The New Authoritarianism in Latin America* (Princeton, N.J.: Princeton University Press, 1979); James D. Cockcroft, André Gunder Frank, and Dale L. Johnson, eds., *Dependence and Underdevelopment: Latin America's Political Economy* (Garden City, N.Y.: Anchor, 1972).

4. Howard Leichter, *A Comparative Approach to Public Policy* (Cambridge: Cambridge University Press, 1979), pp. 91, 6.

5. Charles W. Anderson, *Politics and Economic Change in Latin America* (Princeton, N.J.: Van Nostrand, 1967), p. 116.

6. Marshall Wolfe, "Approaches to Development: Who is Approaching What?" *CEPAL Review* (first half 1976), ECLA, Santiago, Chile, United Nations, p. 171.

7. Egil Fossum, "Political Development and Strategies for Change," *Journal of Peace Studies* 1 (Summer 1970), 19–31. Fossum used a third set of choices, namely, *cooperation* with the international economic order, and *autonomy* from the international economic order. Although this choice is important, for reasons of space I concentrate on the first two.

8. Ibid., p. 27.

9. Terry McCoy, introduction to *The Dynamics of Population Policy in Latin America,* ed. Terry McCoy (Cambridge, Mass: Ballinger, 1974), p. xviii.

10. Ibid., p. xxi.

11. Lauchlin Currie, "Economics and Population," *Population Bulletin* 23 (Apr. 1967), 28.

12. *New York Times,* 5 Nov. 1979, sec. 1, p. 3; 31 Mar. 1980, sec. 1, p. 9.

13. Inter-American Development Bank, *Economic and Social Progress in Latin America, 1979 Report* (Washington, D.C.: IADB, 1979) p. 127; Jorge E. Hardoy, ed., *Urbanization in Latin America* (Garden City, N.Y.: Anchor, 1975), p. vii.

14. Thomas Skidmore, "The Politics of Economic Stabilization in Postwar Latin America," in *Authoritarianism and Corporatism,* ed. Malloy, p. 149.

15. Irving Louis Horowitz, "Introduction: The Norm of Illegitimacy," in *Latin American Radicalism,* ed. Irving Louis Horowitz, Josué de Castro, and John Gerassi (New York: Vintage, 1969), pp. 3–29.

16. Barry Ames, "The Politics of Public Spending in Latin America," *American Journal of Political Science* 21 (Feb. 1977), 153.

17. Howard J. Wiarda, "Latin American Development Process and The New Developmental Alternatives: Military Nasserism and Dictatorship With Popular Support," *Western Political Quarterly* 25 (Sept. 1972), 471.

18. Anderson, *Politics and Economic Change,* p. 87.

19. Richard M. Bird, *Taxation and Development: Lessons From Colombian Experience* (Cambridge, Mass.: Harvard University Press, 1970), p. 190.

20. Pedro Vuskovic, "The Economic Policy of the Popular Unity Government," in *The Chilean Road to Socialism,* ed. J. Ann Zammit (Austin: University of Texas Press, 1973), p. 50.

21. Albert O. Hirschman, "The Turn to Authoritarianism in Latin America and the Search for Its Economic Determinants," in *The New Authoritarianism,* ed. Collier, pp. 83, 85; Albert O. Hirschman, *Journeys Toward Progress: Studies of Economic Policy-Making in Latin America* (Garden City, N.Y.; Anchor, 1965), p. 237.

Chapter 2. The Politics of Accumulation: Economic Growth Policies

1. Rawle Farley, *The Economics of Latin America: Development Problems in Perspective* (New York: Harper and Row, 1972), p. 226.

2. Simon Kuznets, *Modern Economic Growth: Rate Structure and Spread* (New Haven, Conn.: Yale University Press, 1966), p. 427.

3. Raúl Prebisch, "A Critique of Peripheral Capitalism," *CEPAL Review* (first half of 1976), ECLA, Santiago, Chile, United Nations, p. 13.

4. Roger D. Hansen, *The Politics of Mexican Development* (Baltimore: Johns Hopkins Press, 1971), p. 3.

5. Farley, *The Economics of Latin America,* p. 210.

6. Robert J. Alexander, "The Import Substitution Strategy of Economic Development," *Journal of Economic Issues* 1 (Dec. 1967), 298. See also Celso Furtado, *Economic Development of Latin America* (Cambridge: Cambridge University Press, 1970), p. 125.

7. Aldo Ferrer, *The Argentine Economy* (Berkeley and Los Angeles: University of California Press, 1967), p. 151.

8. Inter-American Development Bank, *Economic and Social Progress in Latin America, 1976 Report* (Washington, D.C.: IADB, 1977), p. 63.

9. Osvaldo Sunkel, "National Development Policy and External Dependence in Latin America," *Journal of Development Studies* 6 (Oct. 1969), 24.

10. Inter-American Development Bank, *Economic and Social Progress in Latin America, 1980–81 Report* (Washington, D.C.: IADB, 1981), p. 10.

11. *New York Times,* 13 Dec. 1977, sec. 1, p. 12.

12. R. D. Mallon and J. V. Sourrouille, *Economic Policymaking in a Conflict Society: The Argentine Case* (Cambridge, Mass.: Harvard University Press, 1975), p. 64.

13. Victor Alba, *The Latin Americans* (New York: Praeger, 1969), p. 47.

14. Willian P. Glade, *The Latin American Economies: A Study of Their Institutional Evolution* (New York: Van Nostrand, 1969), p. 459.

15. Carlos Díaz-Alejandro, *Essays on the Economic History of the Argentine Republic* (New Haven, Conn.: Yale University Press, 1970), p. 113.

16. Gary W. Wynia, "Economic Policymaking Under Stress: Conflict and Exchange in Argentina," *LADAC Occasional Papers,* ser. 2, no. 11, University of Texas, 1974, p. 28.

17. Albert O. Hirschman, "The Political Economy of Import-Substituting Industrialization in Latin America," *Quarterly Journal of Economics* 82 (Feb. 1968), 7.

18. See comparative price data in ECLA, *The Process of Industrial Development in Latin America* (New York: United Nations, 1966), pp. 22–154.

19. Bela Balassa, "Regional Integration and Trade Liberalization in Latin America." *Journal of Common Market Studies* 10 (Sept. 1971), 61.

20. ECLA, *The Process of Industrial Development,* pp. 145, 87.

21. Albert Lauterbach, *Enterprise in Latin America: Business Attitudes in a Developing Economy* (Ithaca, N.Y.: Cornell University Press, 1966), p. 76.

22. Stanley M. Davis, "The Politics of Organizational Underdevelopment: Chile," in *Workers and Managers in Latin America,* ed. Stanley M. Davis and Louis W. Goodman (Lexington, Mass.: D.C. Heath, 1972), p. 287.

23. John P. Powelson, *Latin America: Today's Economic and Social Revolution* (New York: McGraw-Hill, 1964), p. 205.

24. ECLA, "Some Conclusions on Integration, Industrialization and Economic Development in Latin America," *Economic Bulletin for Latin America* 19, nos. 1, 2 (1974), 74.

25. D. M. Schydlowsky, "Latin American Trade Policies in the 1970s: A Prospective Appraisal," *Quarterly Journal of Economics* 86 (May 1972), 279.

26. Carlos Díaz-Alejandro, "Latin America: Toward 2000 A.D.," in *Economics and World Order,* ed. Jagdish N. Bhagwati (New York: Free Press, 1972), p. 234.

27. Raúl Prebisch, *Change and Development: Latin America's Great Task* (Washington, D.C.: Inter-American Development Bank, 1970), p. 27.

28. Claudio Veliz, "Centralism and Nationalism in Latin America," *Foreign Affairs* 47 (Oct. 1968), 71.

29. Clark W. Reynolds, *The Mexican Economy* (New Haven, Conn.: Yale University Press, 1970), p. 6.

30. Ignacz Sachs, "Selection of Techniques and Policies for Latin America," *Economic Bulletin for Latin America* 15 (first half of 1970), p. 23.

31. Alan Gilbert, *Latin American Development: A Geographical Perspective* (Baltimore: Penguin Books, 1974), p. 92.

32. ECLA, *The Process of Industrial Development*, p. 89.

33. *New York Times*, 30 Jan. 1978.

34. John M. Hunter and James W. Foley, *Economic Problems of Latin America* (Boston: Houghton Mifflin, 1975), p. 112.

35. David Collier, ed., *The New Authoritarianism in Latin America* (Princeton, N.J.: Princeton University Press, 1979); James M. Malloy, ed., *Authoritarianism and Corporation in Latin America* (Pittsburgh, Pa.: University of Pittsburgh Press, 1977).

36. Schydlowsky, "Latin American Trade Policies," p. 271.

37. ECLA, "Some Conclusions," p. 73.

Chapter 3. The Politics of Distribution

1. Gabriel Almond and G. Bingham Powell, Jr., *Comparative Politics: System, Process and Policy,* 2d ed. (Boston: Little, Brown, 1978), p. 323.

2. Harold L. Wilensky, *The Welfare State and Equality: Structural and Ideological Roots of Public Expenditures* (Berkeley and Los Angeles: University of California Press, 1975), p. 1.

3. Asa Briggs, "The Welfare State in Historical Perspective," *European Journal of Sociology* 2, no. 2 (1961), 225.

4. Richard R. Fagen, "Studying Latin American Politics: Some Implications of a *Dependencia* Approach," *Latin American Research Review* 12, no. 2 (1977), 90.

5. Republic of Colombia, National Planning Department, *Guidelines for a New Strategy* (Bogotá, 1972), p. 90.

6. *New York Times*, 2 Dec. 1970, sec. 1, p. 2.

7. David Felix, "Consumption Dynamic and the Future of Economic Growth," presented at the annual meeting of the International Studies Association, Washington, D.C., 1978, p.4

8. Raúl Prebisch, *Change and Development: Latin America's Great Task* (Washington, D.C.: Inter-American Development Bank, 1970), p. 16.

9. W. Arthur Lewis, *The Theory of Economic Growth* (Homewood, Ill.: Richard D. Irwin, 1955). p. 379.

10. Markos J. Mamilakis, *The Growth and Structure of the Chilean Economy* (New Haven, Conn.: Yale University Press, 1974), p. 358.

11. Anibal Pinto and Armando Di Filippo, "Notes on Income Distribution and Redistribution Strategy in Latin America," in *Income Distribution in Latin America,* ed. Alejandro Foxley (Cambridge: Cambridge University Press, 1976), p. 103.

12. Alejandro Foxley, Introduction to *Income Distribution in Latin America* (Cambridge: Cambridge University Press, 1976), p. 8.

13. Richard Weisskoff and Adolfo Figueroa, "Traversing the Social Pyramid: A Comparative Review of Income Distribution in Latin America," *Latin American Research Review* 11, no. 2 (Summer 1976), 71.
14. Ricardo Ffrench-Davis, "Policy Tools and Objectives of Redistribution," in *Income Distribution,* ed. Foxley, p. 197.
15. David Felix, "Income Inequality in Mexico," *Current History* 67 (March 1977), 111.
16. Pinto and Di Filippo, "Notes on Income Distribution," p. 92.
17. Hugh Heclo, "Frontiers of Social Policy in Europe and America," *Policy Sciences* 6 (1975), 406.
18. ECLA, *Income Distribution in Latin America* (New York: United Nations, 1971), p. 20.
19. Ibid., p. 21.
20. Ibid., p. 13.
21. Carlos Díaz-Alejandro, "Latin America: Toward 2000 A.D.," in *Economics and World Order,* ed. Jagdish N. Bhagwati (New York: Free Press, 1972), p. 244.
22. ECLA, *Income Distribution,* p. 49.
23. Gary W. Wynia, *Argentina in the Postwar Era* (Albuquerque: University of New Mexico Press, 1978), pp. 211–12.
24. Albert Berry and Miguel Urrutia, *Income Distribution in Colombia* (New Haven, Conn.: Yale University Press, 1976), pp. 29, 31.
25. International Labour Office, *Towards Full Employment a Program for Colombia* (Geneva: ILO 1970), p. 14.
26. Felix, "Income Inequality in Mexico," p. 112.
27. ECLA, *Income Distribution,* p. 101.
28. Richard C. Webb, "The Distribution of Income in Peru," in *Income Distribution,* ed. Foxley, p. 24.
29. Weisskoff and Figueroa, "Traversing the Social Pyramid," p. 87.
30. Berry and Urrutia, *Income Distribution in Colombia,* p. 89.
31. Jacques Lambert, *Latin America: Social Structure and Political Institutions* (Berkeley and Los Angeles: University of California Press, 1967), p. 77.
32. *Visión* (Mexico City), 15 June, 1976, p. 53.
33. *New York Times,* 23 Mar. 1977.
34. Gerrit Huizer, *The Revolutionary Potential of Peasants in Latin America* (Lexington, Mass.: D.C. Heath, 1972), p. 7.
35. Edmundo Flores, "Financing Land Reform in Mexico: A Mexican Casebook," in *Masses in Latin America,* ed. Irving Louis Horowitz (New York: Oxford University Press, 1970), p. 332.
36. Ernest Feder, *The Rape of the Peasantry: Latin America's Landholding System* (Garden City, N.Y.: Doubleday, 1971), p. 194.
37. Ibid., p. 221.
38. Ibid., p. 205.
39. Ibid., p. 242.
40. Inter-American Development Bank, *Socio-Economic Progress in Latin America, 1972,* (Washington, D.C.: IADB, 1971), p. 80.

41. Rawle Farley, *The Economics of Latin America: Development Problems in Perspective* (New York: Harper and Row, 1972), p. 184.

42. Edmundo Flores, "Issues of Land Reform," *Journal of Political Economy* 78 (July/Aug. 1970), 903.

43. *New York Times,* 26 Nov. 1976, sec. 1, p. 3.

44. Keith Griffin, *The Political Economy of Agrarian Change: An Essay on the Green Revolution* (London: Macmillan, 1974), p. 117.

45. Clark W. Reynolds, *The Mexican Economy* (New Haven, Conn.: Yale University Press, 1970), p. 142.

46. William E. Carter, "Revolution and the Agrarian Sector," in *Beyond the Revolution: Bolivia since 1952,* ed. James M. Malloy and Richard S. Thorn (Pittsburgh, Pa.: University of Pittsburgh Press, 1971), p. 248.

47. Feder, *The Rape of the Peasantry,* p. 196.

48. Enrigque Santos Calderon, *El Tiempo* (Bogotá), 22 Dec. 1974.

49. John Strasma, "Agrarian Reform," in *Peruvian Nationalism: A Corporatist Revolution,* ed. David Chaplin (New Brunswick, N.J.: Transaction Books, 1976), p. 299.

50. Ibid.

51. Colin Harding, "Land Reform and Social Conflict in Peru," in *The Peruvian Experiment: Continuity and Change Under Military Rule,* ed. Abraham Lowenthal (Princeton, N.J.: Princeton University Press, 1975), p. 237.

52. Strasma, "Agrarian Reform," p. 301.

53. Harding, "Land Reform and Social Conflict," p. 220. For definitions and illustration of these new rural structures see Susan C. Bourque and David Scott Palmer, "Transforming the Rural Sector: Government Policy and Peasant Response," *The Peruvian Experiment: Continuity and Change Under Military Rule,* ed. Abraham Lowenthal (Princeton, N.J.: Princeton University Press, 1975), pp. 179–220.

54. Peter S. Cleaves, "Implementation of the Agrarian and Educational Reform in Peru," presented at the conference on Implementation in Latin America's Public Sector, University of Texas, 1976.

55. Bourque and Palmer, "Transforming the Rural Sector," p. 203.

56. Harding, "Land Reform and Social Conflict," p. 242. For further evidence of peasant exploiting peasant, see Strasma, "Agrarian Reform," p. 317.

57. *New York Times,* 23 July, 1980.

58. Ibid., 3 Aug. 1981, sec. 1, p. 3; *Wall Street Journal,* 6 Feb. 1981, sec. 1, p. 1.

59. Feder, *The Rape of the Peasantry p. 201.*

60. Ibid., p. 207.

61. Frances M. Foland, "Agrarian Reform in Latin America," *Foreign Affairs* 48 (Oct. 1968), 98.

62. John P. Harrison, "The University versus National Development in Spanish America," 1968 Hackett Memorial Lecture, Institute of Latin American Studies, University of Texas, Austin, p. 8.

63. Oscar Vera, "The Education Situation and Requirements in Latin America," in *Social Aspects of Economic Development,* ed. Egbert De Vries and José Medina Echavarría, (Brussels: UNESCO, 1963), p. 298.

64. Robert F. Arnove, "Education and Political Participation in Rural Areas of Latin America," *Comparative Education Review* 17 (June 1973), 203.

65. David Felix, "Income Inequality in Mexico," *Current History* 67 (March 1977), 114; World Bank, *Economic Growth of Colombia: Problems and Prospects* (Baltimore: Johns Hopkins University Press, 1972), p. 408.

66. Vera, "The Education Situation," p. 280.

67. Roberto Moreira, "Education and Development in Latin America," in *Social Aspects of Economic Development*, ed. Egbert De Vries and José Medina Echavarría (Brussels: UNESCO, 1963), p. 308.

68. Vera, "The Education Situation," p. 293; Inter-American Development Bank, *Socio-Economic Progress in Latin America, Annual Report 1971* (Washington, D.C.: IADB, 1972), p. 100.

69. Ruth Verdejo de Northland, "Atlas de los deficite educativos en America Latina," *La Educacíon: Revista Interamericana de Desarrollo Educativo* 82 (Jan.–Apr. 1980), 51.

70. Kenneth N. Walker, "A Comparison of the University Reform Movements in Argentina and Colombia," *Comparative Education Review* 10 (June 1966), 259.

71. Larissa Lomnitz, "Conflict and Mediation in a Latin American University," *Journal of Inter-American Studies* 19 (Aug. 1977), 320.

72. Nicholas K. Bruck, "Higher Education and Economic Development in Central America," *Review of Social Economy* 27 (Sept. 1969), 163.

73. Orlando Albornoz, "Higher Education and the Politics of Development in Venezuela," *Journal of Inter-American Studies* 19 (Aug. 1977), 310.

74. Arthur Liebman, Kenneth Walker, and Myron Glazer, *Latin American University Students: A Six-Nation Study* (Cambridge, Mass.: Harvard University Press, 1972), p. 75.

75. Richard R. Renner, *Education for a New Colombia* (Washington, D.C., Office of Education, U.S. Department of Health, Education, and Welfare, 1969), p. 116.

76. Orlando Albornoz, "Academic Freedom and Higher Education in Latin America," *Comparative Education Review* 10 (June 1966), 252, 255.

77. Liebman et al., *Latin American University Students*, pp. 171–73.

78. Harrison, "The University versus National Development," p. 19.

79. Richard S. Pelczar, "University Reform in Latin America: The Case of Colombia," *Comparative Education Review* 16 (Jan. 1972), 241.

80. Robert Halpern, "Early Childhood Programs in Latin America," *Harvard Educational Review* 50 (Nov. 1980), 482.

81. German W. Rama and Juan Carlos Tedesco, "Education and Development in Latin America," *International Review of Education* 25 (1979), 192.

82. Ibid., p. 195.

83. Vera, "The Education Situation," p. 287.

84. *Visión* (Mexico City), Jan. 12, 1980, p. 8.

85. Pablo Latapi, "Trends in Latin American Universities: Selected Problems and Perspectives," in *New Trends and New Responsibilities for Universities in Latin America* (Paris: UNESCO, 1980), p. 14.

86. Bill Stewart, *Change and Bureaucracy: Public Administration in Venezuela* (Chapel Hill: University of North Carolina Press, 1978), p. 6.

87. Lecturas Dominicales, *El Tiempo* (Bogotá), 13 July 1975, p. 11.

88. ECLA, "Social Development and Social Planning: A Survey of Conceptual and Practical Problems in Latin America," *Economic Bulletin for Latin America* 11 (Apr. 1966), 50.

89. Aldo Solari, "Development and Educational Policy in Latin America," *CEPAL Review* (1977), p. 67.

90. ECLA, "Social Security and Development: The Latin American Experience," *Economic Bulletin for Latin America* 13 (Nov. 1968), 35.

91. Mark Rosenberg and James M. Malloy, "Indirect Participation Versus Social Equity in the Evolution of Latin American Social Security Policy," in *Political Participation in Latin America: Citizen and State*, vol. 1, ed. John A. Booth and Mitchell A. Seligson (New York: Holmes and Meier, 1978), p. 60.

92. Carmelo Mesa-Lago, *Social Security in Latin America: Pressure Groups, Stratification, and Inequality* (Pittsburgh, Pa.: University of Pittsburgh Press, 1978), p. 6.

93. Ibid., pp. 10, 14.

94. Quoted in James M. Malloy, *The Politics of Social Security in Brazil* (Pittsburgh, Pa.: University of Pittsburgh Press, 1979), p. 47.

95. Malloy, *The Politics of Social Security*, p. 41.

96. Ibid., p. l33.

97. Ibid., pp. 138–39.

98. Celso Barroso Leite, "Social Security in Brazil: Characteristics and Prospects of the SINPAS," *International Social Security Review* 31, no. 3 (1978), 318–29.

99. Carlos A. Paillas, "Pensions in Latin America: The Present Situation," *International Social Security Review* 32, no. 3 (1979), 289.

100. ECLA, "Social Security and Development," p. 33.

101. Mesa-Lago, *Social Security in Latin America*, p. 14

102. Ibid., p.33.

103. George E. Berkley, *The Craft of Public Administration*, 2d ed. (Boston: Allyn and Bacon, 1978), p. 20; Malloy, *The Politics of Social Security*, p. 135; Mesa-Lago, *Social Security in Latin America*, p. 244.

104. Mesa-Lago, *Social Security in Latin America*, p. 16.

105. Ibid., p. 3.

106. Milton I. Roemer, *Health Care Systems in World Perspective* (Ann Arbor, Mich.: Health Administration Press, 1976), p. 68.

107. Ibid., p. 236.

108. Ibid., p. 245; T. L. Hall and S. Díaz P., "Social Security and Health Care Patterns in Chile," *International Journal of Health Services* 1 (Nov. 1971), 362–77.

109. Dieter K. Zschock, "Health Planning in Latin America: Review and Evaluation," *Latin American Research Reviev* 5 (Fall 1970), 39.

110. Inter-American Development Bank, *Socio-Economic Progress in Latin America, 1969 Report* (Washington, D.C.: IADB, 1970), p. 115.

111. Robert Maguire, "Bottom-up Development in Haiti," Washington, D.C.: Inter-American Foundation, 1979), p. 9.

112. *Statistical Abstract of Latin America* 19 (Los Angeles: UCLA Latin American Center, 1978), 97–99.

113. World Bank, *Economic Growth of Colombia: Problems and Prospects* (Baltimore: Johns Hopkins University Press, 1972), p. 448.

114. Milton I. Roemer, *Comparative National Policies on Health Care* (New York: Marcel Dekker, 1977), p. 82.

115. Roemer, *Health Care Systems,* p. 246.

116. *New York Times,* 11 Dec. 1979.

117. *Inter-American Development Bank News* 6 (July 1979), 2.

118. Roemer, *Comparative National Politices,* p. 217.

119. Hall and Diaz, "Social Security and Health Care Patterns," p. 369; Howard Waitzkin and Hilary Modell, "Medicine, Socialism, and Totalitarianism: Lessons from Chile," *New England Journal of Medicine* 291 (25 July 1974), 176.

120. *Visión* (Mexico City), 17 Nov. 1978, p. 45; *New York Times,* 9 March 1979, sec. 1, p. 2.

121. Dieter K. Zschock, "Inequality in Colombia," *Current History* 67 (Feb. 1977), 72.

122. World Bank, *Economic Growth of Colombia,* p. 46.

123. Ibid., p. 437.

Chapter 4. Bureaucracy and Public Policy

1. Bill Stewart, *Change and Bureaucracy: Public Administration in Venezuela* (Chapel Hill: University of North Carolina Press, 1978), p. 11.

2. Solon L. Barraclough, "Agricultural Policy and Strategies of Land Reform," in *Masses in Latin America,* ed. Irving Louis Horowitz (New York: Oxford University Press, 1970), p. 109. See also John Leddy Phelan, "Authority and Flexibility in the Spanish Imperial Bureaucracy," *Administrative Science Quarterly* 5 (June 1960), 51.

3. Guy Poitras, "Welfare Bureaucracy and Clientele Politics in Mexico," *Administrative Science Quarterly* 18 (Mar. 1973), 19.

4. Quoted in James M. Malloy, "Social Security Policy and the Working Class in Twentieth-Century Brazil," *Journal of Inter-American Studies and World Affairs* 19 (Feb. 1977), 45.

5. Marcos Kaplan, "El Estado Empresarial en la Argentina," *El Trimestre Económico* 36 (Jan.–Mar. 1969), 74.

6. Milton J. Esman, *Administration and Development in Malaysia* (Ithaca, N.Y.: Cornell University Press, 1972), p. 62.

7. Merilee S. Grindle, *Bureaucrats, Politicians, and Peasants in Mexico: A Case Study in Public Policy* (Berkeley and Los Angeles: University of California Press, 1977), p. 4.

8. John M. Hunter and James W. Foley, *Economic Problems of Latin America* (Boston: Houghton Mifflin, 1975), pp. 236–37.

9. Guillermo O'Donnell, "Reflections on the Patterns of Change in the

Bureaucratic-Authoritarian State," *Latin American Research Review* 13, no. 1 (1978), 12.

10. Ibid., p. 6.

11. Grindle, *Bureaucrats, Politics, and Peasants*, p. 3.

12. Gary W. Wynia, *The Politics of Latin American Development* (Cambridge: Cambridge University Press, 1978), p. 293.

13. Arturo Valenzuela, "Political Constraints to the Establishment of Socialism in Chile," in *Chile: Politics and Society,* ed. Arturo Valenzuela and J. Samuel Valenzuela (New Brunswick, N.J.: Transaction Books, 1976), p. 18; see also Charles J. Parrish, "Bureaucracy, Democracy, and Development: Some Considerations Based on the Chilean Case," in *Development Administration in Latin America,* ed. Clarence E. Thurber and Lawrence S. Graham (Durham, N.C.: Duke University Press, 1973), p. 241.

14. Philippe C. Schmitter, *Interest Conflict and Political Change in Brazil* (Stanford, Calif.: Stanford University Press, 1971), p. 247.

15. Alan Gilbert, *Latin American Development: A Geographical Perspective* (Baltimore: Penguin Books, 1974), p. 265.

16. Gilbert B. Siegel, "Brazil: Diffusion and Centralization of Power," in *Development Administration,* ed. Thurber and Graham, p. 373.

17. Gilbert B. Siegel, *Vicissitudes of Governmental Reform in Brazil: A Study of the DASP* (Washington, D.C.: University Press of America, 1978), p. 29.

18. Schmitter, *Interest Conflict,* p. 34.

19. Lauchlin Currie, *Accelerating Development: The Necessity and the Means* (New York: McGraw-Hill, 1966), p. 236.

20. Charles J. Parrish and Jorge I. Tapia-Videla, "Welfare Policy and Administration in Chile," *Journal of Comparative Administration* 1 (Feb. 1970), 455–76.

21. Martin Weinstein, *Uruguay: The Politics of Failure* (Westport, Conn.: Greenwood Press, 1975), p. 109.

22. For examples, see Gilbert B. Siegel, "The Politics of Administrative Reform: The Case of Brazil," *Public Administration Review* 26 (Mar. 1966), 45–55; Lawrence S. Graham, *Civil Service Reform in Brazil* (Austin: University of Texas Press, 1968); Robert T. Groves, "Administrative Reform and the Politics of Reform: The Case of Venezuela," *Public Administration Review* 27 (Dec. 1967) 436–45; Robert T. Groves, "The Colombian National Front and Administrative Reform," *Administration and Society* 6 (Nov. 1974), 316–37; Thurber and Graham, eds., *Development Administration.*

23. Victor A. Thompson, "Bureaucracy and Innovation," *Administrative Science Quarterly* 10 (Mar. 1965), 10.

24. Grindle, *Bureaucrats, Politicians, and Peasants*, p. 43.

25. Roger D. Hansen, *The Politics of Mexican Development* (Baltimore: Johns Hopkins Press, 1971), p. 178.

26. Grindle, *Bureaucrats, Politicians, and Peasants*, p. 57.

27. Richard R. Fagen and William S. Tuohy, *Politics and Privilege in a Mexican City* (Stanford, Calif.: Stanford University Press, 1972), pp. 28–29.

28. Grindle, *Bureaucrats, Politicians, and Peasants*, p. 167.

29. *El Tiempo* (Bogotá), 28 July 1974, p. 1.

30. Republic of Ecuador, Junta Nacional de Planificacion, *Plan inmediata de desarrollo* (Quito: mimeographed, 1961), pp.79–80; my translation.

31. Stewart, *Change and Bureaucracy,* p. 9.

32. Jerry L. Weaver, "Bureaucracy During a Period of Social Change: The Case of Guatemala," in *Development Administration,* ed. Thurber and Graham, p. 329.

33. Ibid., p. 335.

34. William S. Tuohy, "Centralism and Political Elite Behavior in Mexico," in *Development Administration,* ed. Thurber and Graham, p. 279; see also Antonio Ugalde, *Power and Conflict in a Mexican Community: A Study of Political Integration* (Albuquerque: University of New Mexico Press, 1970), p. 122.

35. Mark W. Cannon, "Interactive Training Techniques for Improving Public Service in Latin America," in *Development Administration,* ed. Thurber and Graham, p. 173.

36. Kenneth L. Karst and Keith S. Rosenn, *Law and Development in Latin America: A Case Book* (Berkeley and Los Angeles: University of California Press, 1975), p. 65.

37. Richard M. Morse, "The Heritage of Latin America," in *The Founding of New Societies,* ed. Louis Hartz (New York: Harcourt, Brace, and World, 1964), p. 174.

38. Virginia A. Paraiso, "Social Service in Latin America: Functions and Relationships to Development," *Economic Bulletin for Latin America* 11 (Apr. 1966), 84.

39. Cannon, "Interactive Training Techniques," in *Development Administration,* ed. Thurber and Graham, p. 159.

40. Fred Lerry, "Economic Planning in Venezuela," in *Development Administration,* ed. Thurber and Graham, p. 83; Herbert Emmerick, "Administrative Roadblocks to Co-Ordinated Development," in *Social Aspects of Economic Development in Latin America,* ed. Egbert De Vries and José Medina Echavarria (Brussels: UNESCO, 1963), p. 350; Leopoldo Solia, *La realidad económica mexicana; retrovision y perspectivas* (Mexico City: Siglo Veintiuno Editores, 1970), p. 227.

41. Joseph S. Nye, "Corruption and Political Development: A Cost Analysis," *American Political Science Review* 61 (1967), 418.

42. *New York Times,* June 29, 1970, sec. 1, p. 1.

43. Ibid., Nov. 18, 1972.

44. David W. Dent, "Urban Development and Governmental Response: The Case of Medellín," in *Metropolitan Latin America: The Challenge and the Response,* ed. Wayne Cornelius and Robert V. Kemper (Beverly Hills, Calif.: Sage, 1978), p. 138.

45. Hansen, *The Politics of Mexican Development,* p. 125; *New York Times,* 29 June 1976.

46. Martin H. Greenberg, *Bureaucracy and Development: A Mexican Case Study* (Lexington, Mass.: D. C. Heath, 1970), p. 71.

47. Ugalde, *Power and Conflict,* pp. 120–21.

48. Raymond Vernon, *The Dilemma of Mexico's Development* (Cambridge, Mass.: Harvard University Press, 1963), p. 150.

49. Alberto Guereiro-Ramos, "The New Ignorance and the Future of Public Administration in Latin America," in *Development Administration,* ed. Thurber and Graham, p. 399.

50. Peter S. Cleaves, "Policymaking in Peru since 1968," presented at the annual meeting of the Latin American Studies Association, Houston, Texas, 1977, p. 2.

51. Tony Smith, "The Underdevelopment of Development Literature: The Case of Dependency Theory," *World Politics* 31 (Jan. 1979), 280.

52. Gary W. Wynia, *Politics and Planners: Economic Development Policy in Central America* (Madison: University of Wisconsin Press, 1972), pp. 150, 173.

53. Currie, *Accelerating Development,* p. 201.

54. Daniel Levy, *Economic Planning in Venezuela* (New York: Praeger, 1968) p. 83.

55. Mark Hanson, "Characteristics of Centralized Education in Latin America: The Case of Venezuela," *Comparative Education* 6 (Mar. 1970), 56.

Chapter 5. Political Participation and Public Policy

1. Jack W. Hopkins, "Democracy and Elites in Latin America," in *The Continuing Struggle for Democracy in Latin America* ed. Howard J. Wiarda (Boulder, Colo.: Westview , 1980), p. 150.

2. Karl W. Deutsch, "Social Mobilization and Political Development" *American Political Science Review* 55 (1961), 493–515.

3. Wayne A. Cornelius, "Urbanization and Political Demand-Making: Political Participation Among the Migrant Poor in Latin American Cities," *American Political Science Review* 68 (1974), 1125.

4. Milton J. Esman, "Perspectives on Ethnic Conflict in Industrialized Societies," in *The Mobilization of Collective Identity: Comparative Perspectives,* ed. Milton J. Esman (Washington, D.C.: University Press of America, 1979), p. 377.

5. Howard J. Wiarda, "Corporative Origins of the Iberian and Latin American Labor Relations Systems," *Studies in Comparative International Development* 13 (Spring 1978), 3.

6. Charles W. Anderson, "Political Design and the Representation of Interests," in *Trends Toward Corporatist Intermediation,* ed. Philippe C. Schmitter and Gerhard Lehmbruch (Beverly Hills, Calif.: Sage Publications, 1979), p. 274.

7. Giovanni Sartori, *Parties and Party Systems: A Framework for Analysis,* vol. 1 (Cambridge: Cambridge University Press, 1976).

8. Samuel P. Huntington, *Political Order in Changing Societies* (New Haven, Conn.: Yale University Press, 1968), p. 198.

9. Samuel P. Huntington and Joan M. Nelson, *No Easy Choice: Political Participation in Developing Countries* (Cambridge, Mass.: Harvard University Press, 1976), 28.

10. John Booth and Mitchell Seligson, "Images of Political Participation in Latin America," in *Political Participation in Latin America: Citizen and State,* vol. 1, ed. John Booth and Mitchell Seligson (New York: Holmes and Meier, 1978), p. 16.

11. Gary W. Wynia, *The Politics of Latin American Development* (Cambridge: Cambridge University Press, 1978), p. 51.

12. Jose Luis de Imaz, *Los Que Mandan* (Albany: State University of New York Press, 1970), p. 166.

13. Claudio Veliz, *The Centralist Tradition of Latin America* (Princeton, N.J.: Princeton University Press, 1980), pp. 273–74.

14. John W. Freels, "Industrialists and Politics in Argentina," *Journal of Interamerican Studies* 12 (July 1970), 442.

15. Stanley M. Davis, "The Politics of Organizational Underdevelopment: Chile," in *Workers and Managers in Latin America,* ed. Stanley M. Davis and Louis W. Goodman (Lexington, Mass: D.C. Heath, 1972), p. 289.

16. Wiarda, "Comparative Origins," pp. 12–13.

17. Ibid., p. 14.

18. Louis Wolf Goodman, "Legal Controls on Union Activity in Latin America," in *Workers and Managers in Latin America,* ed. Stanley M. Davis and Louis W. Goodman (Lexington, Mass: D. C. Heath, 1972), p. 232.

19. Ibid., pp. 232–33.

20. Henry A. Landsberger, "The Labor Elite: Is It Revolutionary?" in *Elites in Latin America,* ed. Seymour Martin Lipset and Aldo Solari (New York: Oxford University Press, 1967), 260.

21. R. D. Mallon and J. V. Sourrouille, *Economic Policymaking in a Conflict Society: The Argentine Case* (Cambridge, Mass: Harvard University Press, 1975), pp. 7–8.

22. Dale Story, "Sectoral Clash and Political Change: The Role of Industrial Entrepreneurs in Argentina, Venezuela, and Mexico," presented at the Southwest Social Science Convention, Dallas, Texas, April 1977, p. 8; Peter H. Smith, "Argentina: The Uncertain Warriors," *Current History* 78 (Feb. 1980), 85.

23. Wiarda, "Comparative Origins," p. 26.

24. James L. Payne, *Labor and Politics in Peru: The System of Political Bargaining* (New Haven, Conn.: Yale University Press, 1965), p. 53.

25. Edward C. Epstein, "Anti-Inflationary Policies in Argentina and Chile: Or Who Pays the Costs?" *Comparative Political Studies* 11 (July 1978), 223.

26. Wynia, *The Politics of Latin American Development,* p. 56.

27. Luigi R. Einaudi and Alfred C. Stepan, "Changing Perspectives in Peru and Brazil," in *Beyond Cuba,* ed. Luigi R. Einaudi (New York: Crane, Russak, 1974), p. 100.

28. Wynia, *The Politics of Latin American Development,* p. 58.

29. Howard Wiarda, "Corporatism and Development in the Iberic-Latin World: Persistent Strains and New Variations," in *The New Corporation: Social Political Structures in the Iberian World* (Notre Dame, Ind.: University of Notre Dame Press, 1974), p. 31.

30. Huntington, *Political Order,* pp. 30–31.

31. Enrique A. Baloyra, "Criticism, Cynicism, and Political Evaluation: A Venezuelan Example," *American Political Science Review* 73 (1979), 988.

32. Frank Bonilla, *The Failure of Elites* (Cambridge, Mass.: MIT Press, 1970) p. 180.

33. Hopkins, "Democracy and Elites in Latin America," p. 148.

34. Daniel H. Levine, "Issues in the Study of Culture and Politics: A View from Latin America," *Publius* 4 (Spring 1974), 93.

35. Huntington and Nelson, *No Easy Choice,* pp. 23–24.

36. Alfred Stepan, "Political Leaderships and Regime Breakdown: Brazil," in *The Breakdown of Democratic Regimes: Latin America* (Baltimore: Johns Hopkins University Press, 1978), p. 111.

37. Glen Dealy, "The Tradition of Monistic Democracy in Latin America," *Journal of the History of Ideas* (Oct.–Dec. 1974), 640.

38. John A. Booth, "Political Participation in Latin America: Levels, Structure, Context, Concentration and Rationality," *Latin American Research Review* 14 (1979), 43.

39. James M. Malloy, *The Politics of Social Security in Brazil* (Pittsburgh, Pa.: University of Pittsburgh Press, 1979), p. 16.

40. Albert Hirschman, "Policymaking and Policy Analysis in Latin America," *Policy Sciences* 6 (Dec. 1975), 390.

41. José Nun, "The Middle Class Military Revolution in Latin America," in *Latin America: Reform or Revolution?* ed. James Petras and Maurice Zeitlin (Greenwich, Conn.: Fawcett, 1968), p. 174.

42. Wynia, *The Politics of Latin American Development,* p. 165.

43. Riordan Roett, *Brazil: Politics in a Patrimonial Society,* rev. ed (New York: Praeger, 1978), p. 54.

44. Philippe C. Schmitter, *Interest Conflict and Political Change in Brazil* (Stanford, Calif.: Stanford University Press, 1971), p. 384.

45. Guillermo O'Donnell, "State and Alliances in Argentina, 1956–1976," *Journal of Development Studies* 15 (Nov. 1979), 25.

46. Gary W. Wynia, *Argentina in the Postwar Era* (Albuquerque: University of New Mexico Press, 1978), p. 255.

47. Emanuel Adler, "Argentina's Deep Cleft," Op-ed page, *New York Times,* 2 Feb. 1982. ·

48. Harvey F. Kline, "Colombia: Modified Two Party and Elitest Politics," in *Latin American Politics and Development,* ed. Howard J. Wiarda and Harvey F. Kline (Boston: Houghton Mifflin, 1979), p. 291.

49. Jorge I. Dominguez, *Cuba: Order and Revolution* (Cambridge, Mass.: Harvard University Press, 1978), p. 5.

50. Mark Rosenberg and James M. Malloy, "Indirect Participants Versus Social Equity in the Evolution of Latin American Social Security Policy," in *Political Participation in Latin America,* ed. John A. Booth and Mitchell A. Seligson (New York: Holmes and Meier, 1978), p. 162.

51. Mary Jeanne Reid Martz, "Studying Latin American Political Parties," *Journal of Latin American Studies* 12 (May 1980), 147.

52. Robert H. Dix, *Colombia: The Political Dimensions of Change* (New Haven, Conn.: Yale University Press, 1967), p. 191.

53. Robert H. Dix, "Consociational Democracy: The Case of Colombia," *Comparative Politics* 12 (April 1980), 312.

54. Wynia, *Argentina in the Postwar Era,* p. 198.

55. *New York Times,* 13 Sept. 1974. sec. 1, p. 13.

56. Wynia, *Argentina in the Postwar Era,* pp. 175–76.

57. Douglas A. Chalmers and Craig H. Robinson, "Why Power Contenders Choose Liberalization Perspectives from Latin America," presented at the annual meeting of the American Political Science Association, Washington, D.C., August 1980, p. 21.

58. Quoted in Alfred Stepan, *The State and Society; Peru in Comparative Perspective* (Princeton, N.J.: Princeton University Press, 1978), p. 194.

59. Sandra L. Woy, "Infrastructure of Participation in Peru: SINAMOS," in *Political Participation in Latin America,* ed. John A. Booth and Mitchell A. Seligson (New York: Holmes and Meier, 1978), p. 192.

60. Stepan, *The State and Society,* p. 121.

61. Kenneth Paul Erickson, *The Brazilian Corporative State and Working Class Politics* (Berkeley and Los Angeles: University of California Press, 1977), p. 1.

62. Stepan, *The State and Society,* p. 47.

63. Linn A. Hammergren, "Corporatism in Latin American Politics: A Re-examination of the 'Unique' Tradition," *Comparative Politics* 9 (July 1977), 448.

64. Philippe C. Schmitter, "Still the Century of Corporation?," in *The New Corporation,* ed. Frederich B. Pike and Thomas Stritch (Notre Dame, Ind.: University of Notre Dame Press, 1974), pp. 93–94.

65. Ruth Berins Collier and David Collier, "Inducements versus Constraints: Disaggregating Corporatism," *American Political Science Review* 73 (1979), 968.

66. Stepan, *The State and Society,* pp. 54, 78–79, 123, 176–77.

67. Ibid., p. 54.

68. Philippe C. Schmitter, "Paths to Political Development in Latin America," *Academy of Political Service Proceedings* 30 (Aug. 1972), 104–05.

69. Erickson, *The Brazilian Corporatist State,* p. 4.

70. Pablo Gonzalez Casanova, "The Economic Development of Mexico," *Scientific American* 243 (Sept. 1980), 196.

71. Salvatore Bizzarro, "Mexico's Poor," *Current History* 74 (Nov. 1981), 370.

72. Susan Kaufman Purcell and John F. H. Purcell, "State and Society in Mexico: Must Stable Polity Be Institutionalized?" *World Politics* 32 (Jan. 1980), 205.

73. Alan Riding, "Facing the Reality of Mexico," *New York Times Magazine,* 16 Sept. 1979, p. 128.

74. José Luis Reyna, "Redefining the Authoritarian Regime," in *Authoritarianism in Mexico,* ed. José Luis Reyna and Richard S. Weinart (Philadelphia: Institute for the Study of Human Issues, 1977), p. 161.

75. Peter H. Smith, *Labryinths of Power: Political Recruitment in Twentieth Century Mexico* (Princeton, N.J.: Princeton University Press, 1979), pp. 50–51.

76. Roger D. Hansen, *The Politics of Mexican Development* (Baltimore: Johns Hopkins Press, 1971), p. 205.
77. Peter H. Smith, "Does Mexico Have a Power Elite?" in *Authoritarianism in Mexico,* ed. José Luis Reyna and Richard S. Weinart (Philadelphia: Institute for the Study of Human Issues, 1977), p. 146.
78. Smith, *Labyrinths of Power,* p. 261.
79. Purcell and Purcell, "State and Society in Mexico," p. 201.
80. Ann L. Craig and Wayne A. Cornelius, "Political Culture in Mexico: Continuities and Revisionist Interpretations," in *The Civic Culture Revisited,* ed. Gabriel Almond and Sidney Verba (Boston: Little, Brown, 1980), p. 370.
81. Wynia, *The Politics of Latin American Development,* p. 310.

Chapter 6. Public Policy in Cuba and Brazil Compared

1. Carmelo Mesa-Lego, *Cuba in the 1970s: Pragmatism and Institutionalization,* rev. ed. (Albuquerque: University of New Mexico Press, 1978), Jorge I. Dominguez, *Cuba: Order and Revolution* (Cambridge, Mass.: Harvard University Press, 1978); Hugh Thomas, *The Cuban Revolution* (New York: Harper and Row, 1971); Edward Boorstein, *The Economic Transformation of Cuba* (New York: Monthly Review Press, 1968); and Archibald M. Ritter, *The Economic Development of Revolutionary Cuba: Strategy and Performance* (New York: Praeger, 1974).
2. K. S. Karol, *Guerrillas in Power: The Course of the Cuban Revolution* (New York: Hill and Wang, 1970), p. 458.
3. *Granma,* 11 Nov. 1979, p. 4.
4. Dominguez, *Cuba: Order and Revolution,* p. 384.
5. Irving Louis Horowitz, *Cuban Communism,* 3d ed. (New Brunswick, N.J.: Transaction Books, 1977), p. 85.
6. *New York Times,* 11 Mar. 1972, sec. 1, p. 3.
7. Mario Henrique Simonson, preface to M. Mello Filho, *O modelo brasilero,* 3d ed. (Rio de Janeiro: Block Editors, 1974), p. 2.
8. Eul-Soo Pang, "Brazil's New Democracy," *Current History* 70 (Feb. 1983), 56.
9. Rollie E. Poppino, "Brazil: Second Phase of the Revolution," *Current History* 56 (Jan. 1969), 11.
10. Carmelo Mesa-Lago, "Availability and Reliability of Statistics in Socialist Cuba," *Latin American Research Review* 4 (Summer 1969), 48–49.
11. Boorstein, *The Economic Transformation of Cuba,* p. 116.
12. Sergio Roca, "Cuba Confronts the 1980s," *Current History* 70 (Feb. 1983), 75; see also statement by Carlos Rafael Rodriguez, *Granma Weekly Review,* 20 June 1982, p. 9; Lawrence H. Theriot, "Cuba Faces the Economic Realities of the 1980s," a study prepared for the use of the Joint Economic Committee, Congress of the United States, March 22, 1982 (Washington, 1982: Government Printing Office), pp. 1–49.
13. Mesa-Lago, "Availability and Reliability," p. 51.
14. Mesa-Lago, *Cuba in the 1970s,* p. 308.

15. *New York Times,* 9 Aug. 1970, sec. 1, p. 2.

16. Sergio Roca, "Cuban Economic Policy," p. 55.

17. Wassily Leontief, "The Trouble with Cuban Socialism," *New York Review of Books,* 7 Jan. 1971, p. 21.

18. *Fidel in Chile, Selected Speeches of Major Fidel Castro During His Visit to Chile, November 1971* (New York: International Publishers, 1972), p. 156.

19. *Houston Chronicle,* 5 Jan. 1983, p. 12; Theriot, "Cuba Faces the Economic Realities," pp. 7–24.

20. Mesa-Lago, *Cuba in the 1970s,* p. 95.

21. Nelson P. Valdes, "The Cuban Revolution, Economic Organization, and Bureaucracy," presented at the annual meeting of the American Political Science Association Convention, Washington, D.C., September 1977, p. 24.

22. Dominguez, *Cuba: Order and Revolution,* p. 229.

23. *Granma,* 17 Dec. 1978, p. 7.

24. Leon Goure and Julian Wenkle, "Cuba's New Dependency," *Problems of Communism* 4 (Mar.–Apr. 1972), 69.

25. *New York Times,* 9 July 1974, sec. 1, p. 1.

26. José Serra, "Three Mistaken Theses Regarding the Connection Between Industrialization and Authoritarian Regimes," in *The New Authoritarianism in Latin America,* ed David Collier (Princeton, N.J.: Princeton University Press, 1979), p. 146.

27. Bruce Handler, "Flying High in Rio," *New York Times Magazine,* 8 June 1975, p. 87.

28. Stefan H. Robock, *Brazil: A Study in Development Progress* (Lexington, Mass.: D. C. Heath, 1975), p. 104.

29. W. L. Ness, Jr., "Financial Markets Innovation as a Developmental Strategy: Initial Results from the Brazilian Experience," *Economic Development and Cultural Change* 22 (Apr. 1974), 465.

30. Handler, "Flying High in Rio," p. 88.

31. Serra, "Three Mistaken Theses," p. 136.

32. Inter-American Development Bank, *Economic and Social Progress in Latin America, 1983 Report* (Washington, D.C., 1983), pp. 171–79.

33. Albert Fishlow, "The U.S. and Brazil: The Case of the Missing Relationship," *Foreign Affairs* 60 (Spring 1960), 916. See also Eul-Soo Pang, "Brazil's New Democracy," pp. 54–57.

34. Ritter, *The Economic Development,* p. 107.

35. Claes Brundenius, "Measuring Income Distribution in Pre- and Post-Revolutionary Cuba," *Cuban Studies* 9 (July 1979), 29; and Susan Eckstein, "Income Distribution and Consumption in Post Revolutionary Cuba: An Addendum to Brundenius," *Cuban Studies* 10 (Jan. 1980), 91. Dominguez, *Cuba: Order and Revolution,* p. 228.

36. Joseph A. Kahl, "Cuba Paradox: Stratified Equality," presented at the annual meeting of the Latin American Studies Association, Austin, Texas, 1971, p. 5.

37. Mesa-Lago, *Cuba in the 1970s,* p. 40.

38. Dominguez, *Cuba: Order and Revolution,* p. 179.

39. Werner Baer, "The Brazilian Growth and Development Experience,

1964–1975," in *Brazil in the Seventies,* ed. Riordan Roett (Washington, D.C.: American Enterprise Institute for Public Policy Research, 1976), p. 54.

40. José Serra, "The Brazilian Economic Miracle," *Latin America: From Dependence to Revolution* (New York, John Wiley, 1973), p. 119; World Bank, *Brazil: Human Resources Special Report* (Washington, D.C.: World Bank, 1979), pp. iii, iv.

41. Ibid., p. iv.

42. *Christian Science Monitor,* 26 Oct. 1978, p. 1.

43. *Brazil Today,* 21 Nov. 1977, p. 1.

44. James M. Malloy, *The Politics of Social Security in Brazil* (Pittsburgh, Pa.: University of Pittsburgh Press, 1979), pp. 138–39.

45. *Granma,* 21 Jan. 1979; 17 July 1983.

46. Riordan Roett, *Brazil: Politics in a Patrimonial Society,* rev. ed. (New York: Praeger, 1978), p. 16.

47. World Bank, *Brazil: Human Resources Special Report,* annex 3, p. 132.

48. Ibid., p. 31.

49. *Granma,* July 17, 1983.

50. World Bank, *Brazil: Human Resources Special Report,* p. vii.

51. Ibid., p. 14.

52. Irving Louis Horowitz and Eldon K. Trimberger, "State Power and Military Nationalism in Latin America," *Comparative Politics* 8 (Jan. 1976), 237.

Chapter 7. Conclusion

1. Raúl Prebisch, *Change and Development: Latin America's Great Task* (Washington, D.C.: Inter-American Development Bank, 1970), p. 12.

2. Richard N. Adams, *The Second Sowing: Power and Secondary Development in Latin America* (San Francisco: Chandler, 1967), p. 231.

3. ECLA, *Economic Survey of Latin America, 1967* (New York: United Nations, 1969), p. 46.

4. Manuel Gollas, "Temas de investigation sobre empleo y distribucion del ingreso," *El Trimestre Económico* 43 (Apr.–June 1967), 243, my translation.

Index

Accumulation: in Brazil, 31, 215, 226; in Cuba, 313; defined, 22–26, 51; versus distribution, 8–9, 126, 243; and income inequality, 59; in Mexico, 31–32
Adams, Richard, 245
Adler, Emanuel, 186
Agrarian policy. *See* Landowners; Land policy; Land reform; Rural conditions
Agriculture, 32–34, 73–76, 77, 95, 161, 220, 225
Alba, Victor, 34
Alberti, Juan Bautista (Argentina), 13
Albuquerque Lima, General (Brazil), 241
Alemán, Miguel (Mexico), 75, 147
Alfonsín, Raúl (Argentina), 190
Alliance for Progress, 69, 116
Almond, Gabriel, 7, 54
Ames, Barry, 17
Anderson, Charles W., 19, 156
Andrés Pérez, Carlos (Venezuela), 95
Argentina: agrarian policy of, 32–34; business groups in, 162, 163; corruption in, 146–47; economic policies of, 35, 131; income distribution in, 63–64; labor movement in, 168–69; military dictatorship in, 190, 193; political participation in, 186–87
Armed forces. *See* Military
Arnove, Robert, 89
Authoritarianism, 150–51, 184–85, 197
Autonomous agencies, 135–36

Balance of payments, negative, 38, 47, 50, 51, 57, 77, 82, 221–22
Balassa, Bela, 36
Baloyra, Enrique, 175
Barraclough, Solon, 129

Batlle y Ordoñez, José (Uruguay), 68
Belaunde Terry, Fernando (Peru), 79, 83, 194
Berry, Albert, 64, 66
Betancourt, Rómulo, 190
Birth control, 14. *See also* Population growth
Birth rate, 12–13, 14, 40
Bizzarro, Salvatore, 203
Boliva, 76–77
Booth, John, 160
Bourgeoisie, 8, 26, 29, 38, 64, 131, 162–63, 167, 227. *See also* Business elite
Bourque, Susan C., 82
Brazil: bureaucracy in, 134; Capital Markets Law (1965), 226; cities in, 15; coup of 1964 in, 108; distribution in, 223; economic growth of, 31–32, 216, 224–28, 231; education in, 233–36; foreign debt of, 49; FUNRURAL, 108–09; IAP, 107; IAPI, 107; INPS, 108–10; IPASE, 109; medical policy in, 236–39; National Steel Company of, 29; politics of, 179, 180, 185–86, 216, 224–28; poverty in, 231–32; SINPAS, 109; Social Insurance Organic Law (1960), 107; social security in, 105–10, 182; unemployment in, 14
Briggs, Asa, 55
Bureaucracy: in Brazil, 231; colonial origins of, 128–29, 149; complexity of, 134–35; corruption of, 113–14, 145–48; in Cuba, 213; and development, 128–31, 148–53; insecurity of, 139–40; in Mexico, 128, 138; versus mobilization, 128, 129; as power group, 170; problems of, 136–37, 139–40,

PITT LATIN AMERICAN SERIES

Cole Blasier, Editor

PLAS

PITT SERIES IN POLICY
AND INSTITUTIONAL STUDIES

Bert A. Rockman, Editor

The Aging: A Guide to Public Policy
Bennett M. Rich and Martha Baum

Clean Air: The Policies and Politics of Pollution Control
Charles O. Jones

Comparative Socialist Systems: Essays on Politics and Economics
Carmelo Mesa-Lago and Carl Beck, Editors

Congress Oversees the Bureaucracy: Studies in Legislative Supervision
Morris S. Ogul

Foreign Policy Motivation: A General Theory and a Case Study
Richard W. Cottam

The Politics of Public Utility Regulation
William T. Gormley, Jr.

Public Policy in Latin America: A Comparative Survey
John W. Sloan

Roads to Reason: Transportation, Administration, and Rationality in Colombia
Richard E. Hartwig

DATE DUE

DEMCO 38-297